An Illustrated History of the

NAVIES
OF WORLD WAR II

Antony Preston

An Illustrated History of the

NAVIES
OF WORLD WAR II

with special drawings by John Batchelor
Introduced and Edited by S. L. Mayer

HAMLYN
LONDON NEW YORK SYDNEY TORONTO

A BISON BOOK

This book was designed and
produced by
Bison Books Limited
21 Hartham Road
London N7 England

Designed by David Eldred

Published by
The Hamlyn Publishing Group Limited
Astronaut House, Hounslow Road
Feltham, Middlesex, England

Printed in Hong Kong

ISBN 0 600 36569 7

CONTENTS

INTRODUCTION 6

1 THE ROYAL NAVY 1939-41 16

2 THE ITALIAN AND FRENCH NAVIES 42

3 NAVAL OPERATIONS
SEPTEMBER 1939–DECEMBER 1941 61

4 THE GERMAN NAVY 94

5 THE US NAVY 130

6 THE IMPERIAL JAPANESE NAVY 148

7 THE BATTLE OF THE ATLANTIC 162

8 AMPHIBIOUS WARFARE 180

9 MIDWAY TO OKINAWA 200

CONCLUSION 216

INDEX 222

ACKNOWLEDGEMENTS 224

INTRODUCTION
BY S. L. MAYER

If the principal causes of World War II can be explained in any simple way, it would be summarised in two words: Versailles and Depression. The Treaty of Versailles was considered to be unfair by the Germans, and it was a harsh peace, handed to the Weimar government without prior negotiations, with an ultimatum to sign or face an armed, Allied occupation of the whole of Germany. Germany signed the treaty on June 28, 1919, five years to the day after the Archduke Franz Ferdinand was shot in Sarajevo, the incident which led to the outbreak of World War I. The protests, however, were loud and long, and the first was the scuttling of the

German High Seas Fleet, anchored at Scapa Flow, which was to be handed over to the Allies once the peace was signed. The Germans preferred to send their fleet to the bottom a few days before the Treaty was signed rather than to relinquish it to their enemies. Thus the interwar period began with Germany in possession of no naval forces, the British and American fleets intact dominating the seas, with the French, Italian and Japanese navies straggling far behind in the race for naval supremacy in the world.

With Germany prostrate and Russia in the throes of revolution and civil war, the Allies' chief concern was to rebuild their

wartorn economies. For their war-weary populations, demobilisation was met with a cry echoed by victors and vanquished alike: No More War. Wilsonian idealism struck a triumphant chord throughout the world. The League of Nations would make war an impossibility. Never Again was the hope of the postwar era.

Naval experts were not so naïvely optimistic. For Britain and America, armies might disappear to the four winds, but the ships remained, and with them the basis for their defence policy and a means of protecting their commerce around the world. The immediate and crucial issue in the immediate postwar period for Britain

ABOVE: USS *Somers*, DD-381, at New York in June 1939, one of the newer destroyers of the US Navy.

RIGHT: British cruiser *Glasgow* manoeuvring with a sister ship. This class was built to match Japanese designs in order to keep pace with naval expansion of the Axis in the 1930s.

BELOW: Hitler arrives to inspect naval personnel at the launching of the battleship *Tirpitz* in 1939. The *Tirpitz* and her sister ship *Bismarck* were intended to be the first instalment of the massive expansion of the Kriegsmarine. In fact she was destined to be the last capital ship built by the Third Reich.

was whether or not the old prewar two-power standard could or should be maintained. While it was generally considered that the exigencies of postwar civilian demands for more and better homes, schools and welfare facilities would rule out a two-power standard, Britain hoped to be as strong or stronger on the high seas than any single foreign power. Only the United States had that capability in 1919, and therefore she became Britain's principal naval rival in the 1920s. Although conflict between the Anglophone allies was never seriously mooted, both in London and Washington questions were raised, for the public mood which determined budgetary demands in the two parliamentary democracies would not put up with heavy military expenditures of any kind. And ships, as well as their maintenance, represent a high initial investment on the part of any nation which must be maintained over a period of years if not decades. Anglo-American distrust, combined with a recognition by both London and Washington that an imbalance of power now existed in the Western Pacific, led to the calling of the Washington Naval and Disarmament Conference of 1921–22. Japan had increased expenditure on naval armaments to almost 250 million dollars, about one-third of the total budget of the Imperial Government. This figure was increased to about 400 million by 1927 at a time when neither Britain nor America could afford this sort of expenditure. Thus the Anglophone powers sought to limit the increase in Japanese naval power

RIGHT: The massive hull of the *Tirpitz* towers over the Führer who inspects the guard of honour and the massed bands at the launching ceremony.

LEFT: Hitler seldom went on board ship. In his only cruise he sailed to Memel after it was annexed to the Reich in 1939. Here he inspects the officers of the *Tirpitz*, but this time he did not get seasick. A pocket battleship appears in the background.

BELOW: Destroyers of the British Home Fleet were the fast, hard-hitting spearhead of the Royal Navy when war broke out.

BELOW: USS *Goff*, DD-247, lying at anchor in the Hudson River in July 1939.

BOTTOM: The destroyer USS *Pope*, DD-225, was sunk by Japanese forces in the Battle of the Java Sea in February 1942.

while watching each other closely to see that neither got a decisive upper hand in the Atlantic.

The Washington Conference did several things. It ended the twenty-year Anglo-Japanese alliance, replacing it with the four-power pact with France and the US which carried none of the weight of its predecessor. It was a polite way for Britain to bury the now-obsolete relationship. In the nine-power pact lip service was paid to the sovereignty, territorial integrity of and economic 'open door' in China. But the five-power pact was the most important and far-reaching in terms of naval disarmament. Secretary of State Charles Evans Hughes called for the scrapping of 66 battleships displacing almost two million tons. He asked for a ten-year moratorium on the construction of capital ships (defined as those exceeding 10,000 tons). The US was called upon to scrap 30 of these, two of which had just been launched and six of which were under construction at the time. The British were asked to abandon the three *Hood* class battleships which had not yet been laid down and to scrap 19 older battleships. Japan was to abandon her plan to construct four battlecruisers and to scrap

three new capital ships, one just launched, and three which were under construction, as well as ten older ships – 17 in all. This scheme would establish a 5:5:3 ratio in capital ships among the three countries, with Japan getting the smaller share because her interests were concentrated in the Pacific, unlike the Anglo-Americans, whose interests were worldwide.

Japan was unhappy with this proposal. She wanted parity, but was willing to settle for a 10:10:7 ratio. After some hard bargaining Japan was forced to accept the 5:5:3 ratio, while Italy and France were obliged to accept a 1:7 ratio with respect to the others. Furthermore fortification of America's Pacific possessions was confined to Hawaii, while Britain and Japan would only be allowed to fortify Australia, New Zealand and, of course, the Japanese home islands. This allayed Japanese fears of surprise attack, an ironic suggestion in the light of previous and subsequent events. Since capital ship building was forbidden to Germany by the Treaty of Versailles, Britain and America felt confident that together they could rule the waves at least until the five-power pact expired in 1936. This hope remained a reality throughout the 1920s.

It is often cynically assumed that every law is made to be broken. The history of disarmament lends considerable credence to cynicism. Britain and America, at least, could not actively consider major naval construction as long as the tide of pacifism and, in the case of America, isolationism ran high. The Kellogg-Briand Pact of 1928, which outlawed war as an instrument of national policy, was probably the high-water mark of the naïve idealism which Woodrow Wilson had engendered. Labelled the 'international kiss' by its critics, the Paris Peace Pact assumed that nations, like gentlemen, kept their word as their bond. Gentlemen, if they ever existed, were getting more thin on the ground during the interwar period, and nations have never acted more coarsely than they did between the wars. Dictatorship, often thought to be a product of the 1930s, was already on the rise in the '20s, with Mussolini, Hungary's Admiral Horthy and Poland's Pilsudski being three prime examples. The naval powers who felt short-changed by Versailles and Washington sought ways to evade their stipulations. Germany built a new class of warship, the pocket battleship, which was supposed to displace not more than 10,000 tons. When the *Deutschland* was launched in 1929 in a paroxysm of national pride by the Weimar Republic, it was said to come within the limits imposed by Versailles, which forbade the building of capital ships by Germany. Actually it displaced 13,200 tons, as its armour was not allowed to be closely inspected by foreign observers. The Japanese too became adept at building warships just under the Washington limit, remaining within the letter of the five-power pact if not its spirit. So by 1930 the fabric of the balance of naval power and therefore of world peace was slowly unravelling.

Perhaps it would be useful to define the various major classes of ships which existed during the interwar period, for it was these warships which fought the Second World War. A battleship usually had an upper limit of 35,000 tons. It bore the maximum armour to withstand fire from other capital ships. Speed was not its principal asset, as its function was to sink other battleships. Cruisers, however, were built for speed as well as endurance. Their role as a lighter ship was to protect trade and commerce, act in a reconnaissance role, and support the main fleet. Their armour was less thick to increase their speed, and their principal function was to sink other cruisers. One reason why their numbers were not limited either by Versailles or Washington was that alone they could not play an aggressive role in naval war. But in conjunction with battleships they could be deadly. More warships of this class were built by the major naval powers than any other, for not only could they support the battle fleet; they were less expensive to construct and therefore, in the mood of the interwar years, at least within the democracies, less politically emotive. Destroyers were built for speed and attack, and as such had no armour. Their light guns enabled them to fight other destroyers attacking their own fleet, but in addition they carried torpedoes for attacking any and all surface ships, including battleships. In addition to these main classes were the aircraft carriers, which had seen little action in World War I and whose capabilities had never been fully tested and therefore could only be surmised; landing vessels of varying types; and the submarine, which had almost defeated the British Grand Fleet in 1916–17.

The larger the surface ship the more expensive it was to produce – and the most politically volatile. Further, until the mid-1930s no country was prepared to openly violate the immediate postwar status quo. One could build cruisers, destroyers and submarines at leisure and at relatively low cost without raising hackles at home or abroad. The aggressor nations opted for this policy as they sought to revise the terms of Washington and Versailles. The London Naval Conference of 1930 pointed up Japan's dissatisfaction with the Washington terms and the Anglo-Americans' unwillingness to alter them substantially despite the onset of the economic crash and reluctance of democratic governments to spend vast sums on ships, with the notable exception of the perennial paranoid, France, which spent vast amounts on construction of the Maginot Line and which was prepared to spend a bit more on naval construction. A 10:10:7 ratio for light cruisers was established at London, and the same ratio was agreed for destroyers. But parity with Britain and the US in submarines was agreed with Japan. The United States retained the principle of overall naval parity with Great Britain.

Thus, as the Thirties and the Depression began Japan was in a position to greatly expand her already modern navy without interference from the West and with a considerable measure of cost-effectiveness. Once Manchuria and Jehol were invaded and absorbed into the Japanese sphere of influence, Japan withdrew from the League of Nations and announced the abrogation of the Washington

LEFT: The pocket battleship *Admiral Graf Spee* in the Baltic surrounded by pancake ice. She went to the South Atlantic before the declaration of war in September 1939 to avoid British patrols.

BELOW: The old battleship *Schlesien* was one of six obsolescent capital ships that were permitted to the German Navy by the Treaty of Versailles. She and her sister, *Schleswig-Holstein*, took part in the attack on Poland in September 1939.

treaties in 1934, two years in advance in accordance with the 1921–22 agreements. But Japan did not wait to fortify her island possessions in the Pacific until 1936. Nor did she refrain from instituting an extensive expansion of her fleet. America retreated further into isolation in the first years of the Roosevelt Administration, as US public opinion supported the public works projects and socialist experiments of the New Deal. Not until the first New Deal ran out of momentum when FDR suffered setbacks in the Supreme Court as two pet projects, the NRA (National Recovery Administration) and AAA (Agricultural Adjustment Act), were deemed unconstitutional did Roosevelt turn his attentions to his first love, the Navy. In 1936 he authorised the construction of a big merchant navy, which, incidentally, could easily be refitted with artillery, but still under the guise of a public works project whose main purpose was to reduce unemployment. Despite war and rumours of war in the Far East, the American public was more determined than ever to stay out of any foreign war in 1936.

British public opinion was hardly in a more advanced state of realism. The 1933 by-election in Fulham convinced the National Government of Ramsay MacDonald and his political masters in the Conservative Party, which held a majority of seats in Parliament, that rearmament was still unpopular. In the same year the Oxford Union resolved that under no circumstances would it fight for King and Country. Hitler took power in Germany in 1933. Never a great naval advocate and indeed quite ignorant of the importance of sea power, Hitler nevertheless stepped up the Weimar programme of pocket battleship and submarine construction to the point when, in 1935, Britain felt obliged to revise the Treaty of Versailles in a bilateral pact with Germany. Nazi Germany was permitted to build a fleet not greater than 35 per cent of the size of the British. The Anglo-German naval pact was hailed in Labour and even some Tory circles as a victory for disarmament. When the London Naval Conference of 1935 ended in total failure to stop the naval arms race, both British and American naval experts pressed their governments, as they had done throughout the interwar period, to build battleships, cruisers, submarines, destroyers and aircraft carriers. Contrary to the spirit of isolationism in America and appeasement in Britain, their governments began to take notice of their warnings and quietly began preparations for the un-

thinkable, but apparently inevitable war. France, which had heretofore held its own, came under the influence of the Popular Front government of Leon Blum, which proceeded to introduce a series of long-delayed and long-needed social reforms – at the expense of the navy and to a lesser extent, the army. Its final demise in 1938 left little time, but in any event, the French were depending on British support if war came. The outbreak of hostilities still left Britain and America supreme on and below the seas, but the gap between them and the Axis powers had dangerously narrowed. Fortunately for the Allies Italian naval building was more hot air than hardware, so supremacy in the Mediterranean was also virtually assured when Italy joined the war in 1940. Although the Russian Fleet was surprisingly well developed, it played little part in the

naval war after 1941, although on land the Red Army did more than its share.

The course of World War II indicated that politicians and naval hegemonists were equally wrong in their prewar assumptions. Although procrastination and lack of public support for naval construction were dangerous, they were not fatal. The Germans and Italians never were more than a nuisance to the British Navy in the Mediterranean, although those who fought with the Royal Navy would think otherwise. As the German High Seas Fleet and its campaign of unrestricted submarine warfare hampered British and Allied shipping in World War I, the Germans taxed the Anglo-Americans sorely in the Battle of the Atlantic by 1943 as submarines took a heavy toll. Although Pearl Harbor wiped out much of the American Pacific Fleet, the

blow was not decisive, despite two close-run things in the Coral Sea and at Midway. The battleships over which there was so much controversy in the interwar period were obsolete by the end of World War Two. The 20-mile range of naval ordnance could not be compared with the 300-mile range of planes on aircraft carriers. Cruisers and destroyers were obsolescent by 1945 because of the advances made in radar. In the European Theatre of Operations, at least, there was no Jutland or Trafalgar. As in the Pacific, aircraft carriers and submarines were the vital weapons of modern naval warfare.

But in war, as in life, illusions persisted in the face of new realities. Their interplay, the lessons learned from the war, the ships, the men and the battles they fought are dramatically portrayed in this epic analysis of the Navies of World War II.

Capital Ships in 1939						
	Royal Navy	US Navy	German Navy	Italian Navy	French Navy	Japanese Navy
In service	15	15	2	4	7	10
Building	9	8	8*	4	4	4†

*Only two of these were completed. †Rumours of these ships had leaked out, but no official news; two were completed as battleships and a third became an aircraft carrier.

RIGHT: The battlecruiser HMS *Renown* was a veteran of World War I, but her prewar modernisation made her one of the best-equipped capital ships in the British Fleet.

When the British and French governments declared war on Germany on September 3, 1939, they had little cause for complacency as their armies and air forces were still in the process of hurried rearmament and reorganisation. But they had one trump card, naval power, for both Great Britain and France had powerful navies which separately outnumbered the German Navy. Not even the likelihood of Italy's honouring her commitment to the Berlin-Rome Axis could match the combined fleets of Britain and France, and the British were fully confident that their allies were a match for Mussolini's ships.

The fundamental strategy of the Royal Navy differed little from that which it had pursued so relentlessly in World War I – to prevent the Germans from breaking out of the Baltic and North Sea and to use their own command of the Atlantic and Mediterranean to bring supplies of war matériel from the United States and Canada to the British Isles and manpower from the British Empire, and then deploy its strength against whatever weak spot exposed itself. In this way it was hoped to wear down the German land forces to the point when Anglo-French land forces could take the offensive against them.

To achieve these broad aims the British had organised their navy into striking forces and trade protection forces. The striking forces took the form of the main battle fleet, naval air power and submarines, all capable of sinking or neutralising German surface ships. But the British Empire was an island empire relying on ocean trade to survive, and so the forces allocated to the protection of trade, in the form of light anti-submarine and surface escort forces,

RIGHT: The battleship *Nelson* fires her 16-inch guns in a practice shoot. Note how the massive muzzle blast churns up the water to starboard.

were far more numerous than the strike forces. In the event the British Admiralty turned out to have foreseen the requirements of the main striking forces fairly well. Although they had underestimated the strain which would fall on the escort forces, timely countermeasures were in hand in September 1939. But numbers were not adequate until near the end of hostilities.

Having expressed the main characteris-

LEFT: HMS *Rodney* buries her forecastle in a heavy swell. The small guns on the roof of 'B' 16-inch gun turret are 20 mm. Oerlikon weapons for close range defence against aircraft. She was the sister ship to *Nelson*.

tics of the British Fleet in over-simple terms it is now necessary to describe the makeup of the Royal Navy in detail. The core of the Royal Navy's striking forces was its fleet of battleships and battle-cruisers, which was limited to 15 units by international agreement, giving it parity with the United States Navy but considerable superiority over all other fleets.

Despite limitations imposed by the financial burdens of World War I and by international treaties (in themselves only formal expressions of what was already fact) the Royal Navy was the largest in the world. Furthermore it had been, until shortly before the outbreak of war, an all-volunteer force of remarkable calibre. Not only were the officers and seamen imbued with the glorious traditions of the 17th and 18th centuries, but the older men had served in World War I. Shortcomings in tactics, training and communications had been revealed in 1914–18, and much effort had been devoted in peacetime to eliminating these problems.

But numbers are misleading, for the British total of ships built, like that for all navies except the German, contained a large number of old ships dating from World War I. The five old *Royal Sov-*

ereign Class, for example, were un-modernised, and the three battlecruisers, *Hood*, *Renown* and *Repulse*, although quite capable of dealing with the German 'pocket-battleships' and cruisers, were too lightly armoured to face the latest foreign ships in a prolonged gunnery duel. Because of financial stringency, and less obviously because of the British peace-time policy of keeping its battle fleet in full commission as an instrument of for-eign policy, only four capital ships had been taken in hand for full modernisation. These four, the battleships *Warspite*, *Queen Elizabeth* and *Valiant* and the battlecruiser *Renown*, proved the worth of modernisation by their lengthy war careers and ability to take heavy damage, whereas the unmodernised ships suffered heavily.

Battleships

The two modern British battleships, *Nelson* and *Rodney*, were controversial ships with their armament grouped forward to save weight. Although peculiar in ap-pearance, they were the only battleships in the world whose design had the full benefit of battle experience learned in World War I, and they proved to be very well-protected and well-designed ships. Only the British and the Germans had suffered action damage to their capital ships, but the defeat of Germany in 1918 had meant that her design-team had been dispersed, so that the continuity which is so vital to good design was lost. Further-more, the British experience in World

LEFT: *Renown, Ark Royal,* and *Sheffield* were always linked through their long association with Force 'H'. This striking force was based on Gibraltar and was commanded through most of its existence by Admiral Somerville.

LEFT: The battlecruiser *Repulse* was an unmodernised sister of the *Renown*. Apart from the addition of a few small anti-aircraft guns and radar control for her main armament, she was unaltered when she was sent out to the Far East late in 1941 to face the Japanese Imperial Navy.

BELOW LEFT: *Repulse*'s hangar and crane for handling her reconnaissance float planes can be seen at the base of the second funnel.

OPPOSITE LEFT: The 15-inch guns of *Repulse* fired a 1920-lb. shell a distance up to 23 miles.

British and Empire Naval Strength In September 1939

Figures in parentheses indicate ships under construction.

15 Battleships (+9)
2 *Nelson* Class completed 1927
1 *Hood* completed 1920
2 *Renown* Class completed 1916[1]
5 *Queen Elizabeth* Class[2]

[1] *Renown* modernised 1936-39 [2] *Warspite* modernised 1933-36 and *Queen Elizabeth* and *Valiant* in hand from 1938.

6 Aircraft Carriers (+6)
1 *Ark Royal* completed 1938
2 *Courageous* Class completed 1917 but conversion completed 1930
1 *Furious* completed 1917 but conversion completed 1925
1 *Eagle* completed conversion 1924
1 *Hermes* completed 1924.

15 Heavy Cruisers
2 *Exeter* Class completed 1930-31
13 "County" Group completed 1928-30[1].
[1] 2 Australian.

ABOVE HMS *Nelson* at Scapa Flow in 1941. On her turrets she carries the notorious 'UP' anti-aircraft rocket launchers, which may have contributed to the loss of HMS *Hood* in the same year.

40 Light Cruisers (+8)
2 *Edinburgh* Class completed 1939
8 *Southampton* Class completed 1937-39
4 *Arethusa* Class completed 1935-37
3 "Modified" *Leander* Class[1] completed 1935-36
5 *Leander* Class[2] completed 1933-36
2 *Emerald* Class completed 1926
3 *Effingham* Class completed 1919-25[3]
8 *Despatch* Class completed 1918-22
2 *Capetown* Class completed 1917-18[4]
3 *Caledon* Class completed 1917.

[1] All with Australian Navy by 1939. [2] 2 with New Zealand Navy. [3] 1 modernised 1938. [4] With the *Caledon* Class scheduled for conversion to AA cruisers (see below) but not yet in hand.

6 Anti-Aircraft Cruisers (+16)
6 "C" Class completed 1917-19 but converted 1936-39.

1 Cruiser-Minelayer (+4)
1 *Adventure* completed 1927.

113 Modern Destroyers (+24)
All completed 1927-39.

68 Old Destroyers
All completed 1916-24[1].
[1] A further 11 were in hand for conversion to escort vessels.

47 Modern Submarines (+12)
All completed 1927-39.

12 Old Submarines
All completed 1918-19.

54 Escorts (+80)
All completed or converted 1929-39[1].
[1] 4 Australian, 2 Indian.

42 Fleet Minesweepers (+10)
All completed 1917-39.[1]
[1] Planned to be supplemented by requisitioned trawlers.

2 Monitors
2 Netlayers

ABOVE: The destroyer *Jackal* was one of the newest destroyers in the Royal Navy in 1939. Her armament was six 4.7-inch guns, one 4-barrelled pom-pom, two quadruple machine guns and ten 21-inch torpedo tubes. Maximum speed: 36 knots.

RIGHT: The 16-inch guns of *Rodney*. The turrets allowed 40 degrees elevation, and on occasion the *Rodney* and *Nelson* fired long-range barrages against aircraft.

War I had been much more valuable than the German, since their ships had seen far more action and had suffered more varied damage. This, combined with the opportunity to study German designs after 1918 and the use of German ships as targets for shells, mines and torpedoes, made the British ship-designers the most experienced in the world.

The results of this experience were incorporated in two new classes of battleship under construction in 1939. The first was a group of five known as the *King George V* Class, but a very similar second group, the four *Lion* Class, did not last long, as they were suspended to release much-needed armour plate and armament production capacity for other purposes. The *King George V* Class was unusual in a number of ways: they had the heaviest armour belt and deck of any ships apart from the Japanese giants, they were the first to have a dual-purpose secondary armament which could fire at surface and aircraft targets, and they were the first to include aircraft as an integral part of their design.

Because of the intricacies of the international disarmament treaties the British had chosen to arm their ships with 14-inch guns rather than delay construction until other navies declared their intentions. This feature did not handicap them in battle to any extent, as things turned out, for long-range gunnery duels

were relatively few, and the differences in range between the various heavy guns in different navies were not decisive.

Only one other battleship was begun by the British during World War II, as it was obvious after 1941 that the Royal Navy had an ample margin in battleships over Germany and Italy. This extra ship was the *Vanguard*, planned before the war as an additional fast unit to reinforce the British and Empire navies in the Far East.

BELOW: The battleship *Queen Elizabeth* completed a three-year modernisation late in 1940. After suffering heavy damage from an Italian 'human torpedo', she was repaired in the US and returned to the Mediterranean in 1943.

The third and fourth *Lion* Class battleships, *Conqueror* and *Thunderer*, would not be ready until late 1944, so it was proposed to build a similar ship and arm her with the well-tried and efficient 15-inch gun mounting, four of which were in store from ships converted to aircraft carriers in the 1920s. As the time taken to build these giant gun-mountings (each one weighed over 1000 tons) was the factor delaying the two *Lions*, this proposal

FAR LEFT: The two-pounder (40-mm.) pom-pom first appeared in 1927 as an eight-barrelled weapon to be used against air attacks. Just before World War II a lighter four-barrelled version (left) was produced for destroyers and other smaller warships.

was taken up immediately, and work started in 1941. Unfortunately too much attention was paid to making her the best-equipped battleship ever to leave a British shipyard, and despite being intended to complete in 1943, she finally missed the war completely and joined the Fleet in 1946, a magnificent white elephant, the last of her kind.

British battleships were used from the outbreak of war to guard the exits from the North Sea. The Home Fleet was based on Scapa Flow, the bleak anchorage in the Orkneys which had been the home of the Grand Fleet from 1914 to 1918. From here it was able to intercept German heavy units moving out into the Atlantic, but the first moves and countermoves in the autumn and winter of 1939 proved, not surprisingly, abortive.

The old battleship Royal Oak, a veteran of the Battle of Jutland 23 years before, took part in a Home Fleet sortie on October 8, 1939, to intercept the German battlecruiser Gneisenau, a cruiser and nine destroyers, but she and the rest of the Fleet returned to Scapa Flow three days later. In the early hours of October 14 the German submarine U.47 under her daring commander, Gunther Prien, penetrated the base defences and sank the Royal Oak with the loss of 833 men. Much has been made of the fact that the old ship blew up, but the facts seem to be that U.47's first torpedo detonated only partially on striking the forward part of the ship, and the reload salvo of three exploded underneath the Royal Oak's hull, her most vulnerable spot. Like all unmodernised ships she lacked up-to-date magazine protection and this probably contributed to the detonation of live ammunition.

Although hardly a front-line unit the Royal Oak's loss was a blow to British morale, as their main fleet base had been thought secure. In the months that followed urgent work was done to strengthen Scapa Flow's defences, but during that time the Home Fleet had to use extemporised bases on the west coast of Scotland. U-Boats were quick to take advantage, and it was not long before the Nelson was badly damaged by a magnetic mine and the Barham was torpedoed. The Home Fleet under Sir Charles Forbes came close to intercepting the German battlecruisers Scharnhorst and Gneisenau after they had sunk the armed merchant cruiser Rawalpindi on November 23, 1939, as a result of a successful sighting by a cruiser, but the German ships shook her off in bad weather.

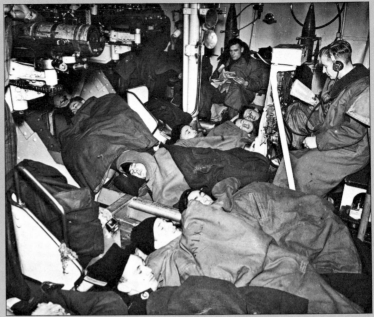

Although the big ships on both sides did not engage during these early months of 'phoney war' (which was far from phoney at sea), the British battleships played a vital part in safeguarding communications. Three large convoys of troopships brought Canadian troops across the Atlantic. They could have been slaughtered by even one German capital ship, but each group of liners had its patient grey shepherd, and Hitler had given Admiral Raeder strict orders not to expose his ships to battle damage. Even without these disastrous fetters on their freedom of action, the German admirals did not prove very enterprising in the early months of the war, when matching two new and powerful capital ships against such elderly units as the *Malaya* and *Revenge*, with the added tactical advantage of surprise.

Aircraft Carriers

The British naval air force, known as the Fleet Air Arm, was a shadow of the once proud force which had owned 5000 aircraft in 1918, and had pioneered all the most advanced techniques in the art of getting aircraft off a ship's deck and back again in one piece. On the appropriate April Fool's Day 1918, the Royal Air Force had been formed out of the old Royal Naval Air Service and the Royal Flying Corps, and for twenty years the RAF and the RN had starved the naval air arm of funds. There were faults on both sides; the Navy did not stress the importance of air power soon enough and the Air Force felt that its limited funds could be better spent elsewhere. However, what was bitterly resented by the Navy was the totally unjustified and barely concealed RAF sponsorship for a press campaign to

replace the battleship (and by implication any other large warship-type) with the bomber. The public and the politicians were encouraged to believe that a thousand bombers could be bought for the price of one battleship and that no ship could survive near a shore-based air squadron. The truth was that the ratio was about 37 bombers to a battleship and that RAF bombing techniques were not good enough to hit a battleship. Nor did the RAF succeed in giving the Navy any help in tactical exercises to show how a potential enemy air force would behave; what was learned off Norway was how unrealistic prewar training had been, since the Luftwaffe obstinately refused to attack on the broadside and thereby give the ship's guns maximum advantage.

Only just before the war did the RAF finally let naval aviation go, and then only

FAR LEFT: Loading a 4·7-inch gun aboard the destroyer HMS *Hesperus*. The rope netting normally hangs down at the rear of the gun to catch the ejected brass cartridge case and to break its fall.

LEFT: Royal Marines in a cruiser's 6-inch gun turret take a nap or read during a 'stand easy'.

TOP RIGHT: Gun crew of the *Orion* ram a cordite charge into the gun breech. The man in the foreground is picking up a second charge from the ammunition hoist at his feet.

CENTRE RIGHT: A 6-inch casemate gun in the old battleship *Malaya*. The two men on the left are carrying cordite charges.

BELOW RIGHT: The massive breech of one of the *Malaya*'s 15-inch guns with part of the gun crew standing by, dressed in anti-flash gear.

ABOVE: The cruiser *Orion* fires her 6-inch guns.

BELOW: For much of the war the British Home Fleet patrolled in the stormy waters of the North Atlantic and the Arctic. The *Renown* leads the new battleship *Duke of York* in mountainous seas.

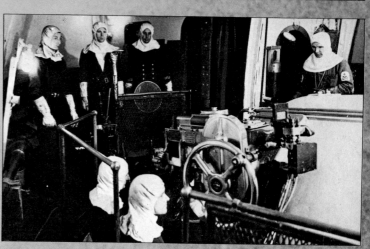

RIGHT: The old destroyer leader *Malcolm* was converted to an anti-submarine escort, with three 4·7-inch guns replaced by depth charges and light anti-aircraft weapons.

because it had no intention of spending money on re-equipment. But there is more to running an air force than possession of pilots and aircraft; what was lacking was any forward planning for modern aircraft. The Fleet Air Arm had to start pilot-training and at the same time draw up specifications for all types of aircraft to replace a thoroughly obsolete range of types. Typical of the state to which naval aviation had declined was the fact that its principal strike aircraft was the biplane Fairey Swordfish, capable of a speed of 138 mph at a time when monoplane fighters in service with other air forces had speeds of 300 mph and upwards. A replacement, the Albacore, was simply a 'cleaned up' version with the luxury of an enclosed cockpit. The current models of dive bomber and fighter, the Skua and Fulmar, were inferior to contemporary land-based aircraft, although not as badly outclassed as the Swordfish and Albacore.

Only one modern aircraft carrier existed, the new *Ark Royal*. She was fast, well-protected and had a heavy defensive armament of sixteen 4·5-inch dual-purpose guns and six eight-barrelled pom-poms. She had been designed for a maximum aircraft capacity of 72, but never carried more than 54 in her lifetime. Backing her up were a trio of carriers of similar size, but all converted from light battlecruisers between 1922 and 1930, and therefore suffering from a low capacity of 33–48 aircraft. The *Furious* had been armed with 18-inch guns in 1917, but underwent a series of piecemeal alterations which were still in progress in 1939, when she finally received a small island superstructure, and had her obsolescent low-angle defensive guns replaced by twin 4-inch AA guns. The *Glorious* and *Courageous* had originally been near-sisters but they benefited from experience with *Furious*, and had proper island superstructures as well as a high-angle armament of sixteen 4·7-inch guns. The other two carriers were of less value because they were slow (the *Ark Royal*, *Glorious*, *Courageous* and *Furious* were all good for 29–30 knots) and carried only a small number of aircraft. The *Eagle* was the better of the two, carrying 21 aircraft at a speed of 24 knots, but the *Hermes* could only carry the miserable total of twelve aircraft at 25 knots.

It was fully appreciated that aircraft had an important role to play in countering submarines, but the Admiralty's first essay in this direction was disastrous. The

Home Fleet's carriers were deployed on anti-submarine patrols, *Ark Royal* in the North-Western approaches to the British Isles, and *Courageous* and *Hermes* in the South-Western approaches. As the convoy organisation was not yet in full force the air patrols were aimless, and achieved virtually nothing in return for risking a major fleet unit. On September 14 *U.39* narrowly missed the *Ark Royal* but three days later *U.29* put three torpedoes into the *Courageous* and sank her with heavy loss of life. The idea was sound in principle and later the carrier and its aircraft would play a vital role in winning the Battle of the Atlantic, but the big fleet carrier was not the ship to do it and naval aircraft in 1939 lacked the weapons to be effective. *Furious*, on the other hand, was used to good effect on escort duties in the North Atlantic, particularly helping the battlecruiser *Repulse* to escort troop convoys from Halifax to the United Kingdom. *Hermes* was sent to the West Indies and then to Dakar to work with the French battlecruiser *Strasbourg* early in 1940. HMS *Eagle* went down to Aden, while *Ark Royal* joined the *Renown* in the South Atlantic looking for the *Graf Spee*; the two ships remained almost inseparable partners for the next two years.

The *Furious* was the only carrier in Home Waters when the Germans began their invasion of Norway on April 9, 1940. Although refitting on the Clyde she cut this short and sailed on April 10 without her fighters, a saving of time which proved disastrous to the Anglo-French ground troops who needed air cover badly in the first two weeks of the campaign. The *Ark Royal* was absent on training duties off Gibraltar, but fifteen of her Skuas and their experienced pilots had been left at Hatston in the Orkneys. On April 10 these aircraft made history by sinking the German *Königsberg* at Bergen, the first warship sunk by dive bombing.

The *Ark Royal* and *Glorious* relieved the *Furious* and rendered valuable support to the troops ashore, but the campaign was doomed, and by early June they were covering the withdrawal. The surviving RAF Gladiators and Hurricane aircraft from Bardufoss made a heroic effort to avoid destruction by flying out to the *Glorious* and landing on her deck safely, despite the fact that they were not equipped to land on carriers. The sequel was tragic, for most of the RAF personnel were lost next day when the carrier was intercepted by the German battlecruisers *Scharnhorst* and *Gneisenau*. Her two es-

corting destroyers *Acasta* and *Ardent* went down fighting, and the only crumb of comfort was *Acasta*'s parting torpedo shot which put *Scharnhorst* out of action for some months.

The loss of two of the more effective British carriers in the first eight months of the war was a bad blow to the Royal Navy, but two new carriers joined late in 1940 to redress the balance more than handsomely. For these two ships were very different to the previous ships, being the first of the new armoured deck carriers of the *Illustrious* Class, heavily armoured against bombs and so capable of taking heavy punishment. The *Illustrious* was sent to the Mediterranean to bolster its strength against the Italian Fleet. Italy had a strong shore-based air force and a strong surface fleet, and the British Mediterranean Fleet under Admiral Cunningham needed greater reconnaissance and strike power. Such a situation was exactly what the new carriers were designed for, and they soon proved their worth.

The armoured deck carrier was a totally new departure and was a British conception which evolved because of the lack of good naval aircraft and the likelihood of the Royal Navy having to fight within easy reach of land-based enemy aircraft. Whereas the US Navy and the Japanese developed the idea of a soft-skinned carrier which was protected by her aircraft, the British felt that their inferior aircraft might not always be able to prevent the ship from being attacked. Thus they built in as much protection for the aircraft as possible. This meant in effect that the hangar under the flight deck was encased in an armoured box, while the carrier was given a very heavy battery of AA guns (twice that of a contemporary USN carrier). The idea certainly worked in action, when the *Illustrious* was bombed, but it was not without its drawbacks. It restricted capacity to 43 aircraft in the original design and it necessitated special precautions in dealing with hangar fires. Had better aircraft been available the ship might have had an even higher degree of immunity, but in the light of conditions at the time it was an excellent

LEFT: The destroyers of the 'V and W' Class were officially over-age under the disarmament treaties, but all gave sterling service, like HMS *Velox*, seen here in 1940.

BELOW LEFT: Some of the 'V and W' Class, such as HMS *Wolsey*, were rearmed with modern anti-aircraft guns and fire control.

RIGHT: The cruiser *Argonaut* was a unit of the Dido Class, the first cruisers designed specifically for the anti-aircraft role, with a combined high-angle/low-angle armament of ten 5·25-inch guns.

idea. Furthermore the stringent fire-precautions developed by the RN proved to be literally a lifesaver even in carriers without armoured decks.

Strenuous efforts were made to increase the aircraft capacity in the later ships of the *Illustrious* Class, even to the extent of redesigning the last pair, *Implacable* and *Indefatigable*. HMS *Indomitable* was given an extra half-hangar to increase her capacity to 54 aircraft, and later deck stowage increased this figure, but in the first year of the war the supply of naval aircraft was so bad that the carriers never carried even their maximum complement. At the time of the attack on Taranto in 1940 the *Illustrious* only carried 15 Fulmars and 18 Swordfish, while *Formidable* carried a maximum of 18 Fulmars and 21 Albacores.

Cruisers

The Royal Navy's cruisers lightened the burden on the battle fleet, for although not designed to fight capital ships they were capably handled against surface raiders. The newest of them, HMS *Belfast*, gave devastating proof of the power of the new German mine in November 1939, when an underwater explosion broke her back, ie almost broke her in two, in the Firth of Forth. She and her sister were the first examples of a new type of cruiser which combined the qualities of the old 'heavy' or 8-inch gunned cruiser and the 'light' or 6-inch gunned type. Just as the Washington Treaty kept battleship size at 35,000 tons, so the cruiser was defined as a 10,000-ton ship armed with either 8-inch or 6-inch guns, and the numbers of the heavy type were limited in the same ratio as battleships. Later treaties tackled the subject of the light cruiser, and tried to limit numbers by allocating totals of tonnage.

The British position was badly affected by these restrictions, since the Royal Navy had a large proportion of older ships built during World War I. To avoid having to scrap too many useful ships (it must be remembered that the naval treaties stipulated age-limits for ships as well) it was

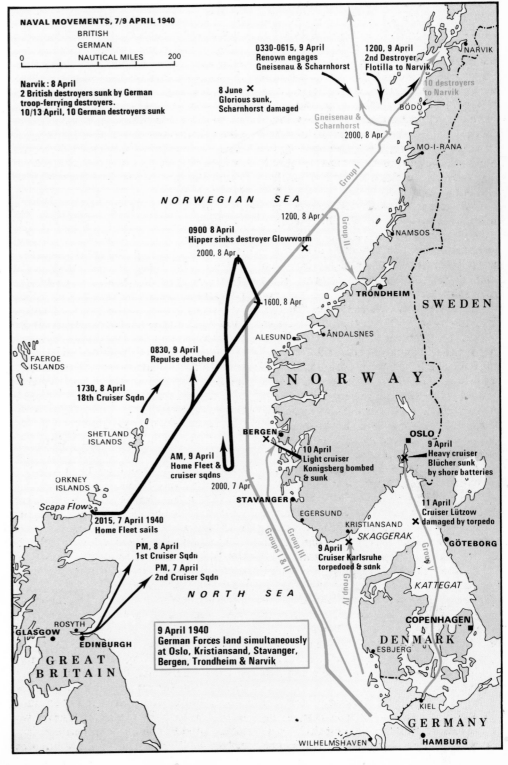

NAVAL MOVEMENTS, 7/9 APRIL 1940

BRITISH
GERMAN

0   NAUTICAL MILES   200

Narvik : 8 April
2 British destroyers sunk by German troop-ferrying destroyers.
10/13 April, 10 German destroyers sunk

0330-0615, 9 April
Renown engages
Gneisenau & Scharnhorst

1200, 9 April
2nd Destroyer
Flotilla to Narvik

NARVIK

10 destroyers
to Narvik

BÖDÖ

8 June ✕
Glorious sunk,
Scharnhorst damaged

Gneisenau &
Scharnhorst

2000, 8 Apr

MO-I-RANA

Group I

NORWEGIAN SEA

1200, 8 Apr

Group II

NAMSOS

0900 8 April
Hipper sinks destroyer Glowworm

2000, 8 Apr

✕

TRONDHEIM

SWEDEN

1600, 8 Apr

ALESUND

ÅNDALSNES

0830, 9 April
Repulse detached

NORWAY

1730, 8 April
18th Cruiser Sqdn

FAEROE
ISLANDS

BERGEN

✕

10 April
Light cruiser
Konigsberg bombed
& sunk

OSLO

9 April
Heavy cruiser
Blücher sunk
by shore batteries

✕

SHETLAND
ISLANDS

AM, 9 April
Home Fleet &
cruiser sqdns

2000, 7 Apr

STAVANGER

EGERSUND

11 April
Cruiser Lützow
✕ damaged by torpedo

ORKNEY
ISLANDS

KRISTIANSAND

SKAGGERAK

GÖTEBORG

Scapa Flow

2015, 7 April 1940
Home Fleet sails

Groups I & II

Group III

✕

9 April
Cruiser Karlsruhe
torpedoed & sunk

Group IV

Group V

KATTEGAT

PM, 8 April
1st Cruiser Sqdn

PM, 7 April
2nd Cruiser Sqdn

NORTH SEA

COPENHAGEN

ROSYTH

9 April 1940
German Forces land simultaneously
at Oslo, Kristiansand, Stavanger,
Bergen, Trondheim & Narvik

DENMARK

ESBJERG

GLASGOW

EDINBURGH

GREAT
BRITAIN

KIEL

GERMANY

WILHELMSHAVEN

HAMBURG

necessary to rearm them to allow them to be reclassified. At the time of the Abyssinian Crisis in 1936 this device was used to retain the old 'C' Class cruisers, and they were re-rated as anti-aircraft ships. In the light of the sterling work done by these ships the Royal Navy showed foresight, but there can be no doubt that properly-designed new ships would have been a better investment. In fact a new class of anti-aircraft cruiser was designed at the same time, the *Dido* Class, with a dual-purpose armament of 5·25-inch guns, and they proved a worthwhile addition to the Fleet.

To comply with the 1935 London Naval Treaty the displacement of the new fleet cruisers was reduced to 8000 tons, and this led to the *Fiji* or 'Colony' Class, which had the armament of the previous *Southampton* group and only slightly less speed. The *Southampton* Class had their origin in an attempt to reply to the Japanese cruisers of the *Mogami* Class. The Director of Naval Construction announced that he could not produce a design with fifteen 6-inch guns on a displacement of only 10,000 tons, and so amid widespread criticism the British ships had only twelve guns. Only after World War II did the US Navy Technical Mission discover what many had suspected, that the Japanese designers had been unable to keep within the limits, and the displacement of the *Mogami* Class, as a result of additional strengthening, replacement of welded seams by riveting etc., had risen to 13,000 tons. The British ships proved more than adequate for all the tasks set them during the war, and they were able to take heavy damage.

One good effect of the international treaties was to speed up technical progress. Because new equipment had to be incorporated within a fixed set of dimensions and weights the designers had to look to lighter boilers and turbines, new structural steels, and economical methods of construction to offset the weight of new armament. Before World War I the answer had usually been to increase size, and cruiser displacements rose to battleship-size, but in the 1930s ship-armament rose faster than tonnage. Thus the *Fiji* in 1940 could mount twelve 6-inch guns and eight 4-inch AA guns on the same displacement as the *York* of 1928, with six 8-inch and four 4-inch AA. Nor did the *Fiji* design lack protection, and the economies of design included a more efficient arrangement of armour than in the larger *Southampton* and a new hull form.

Apart from the old cruisers converted to anti-aircraft ships, the newer cruisers were all modernised to varying extents. The principal improvement was to replace the old single AA guns with the twin 4-inch mounting, but after 1936 the original heavy cruisers of the *Kent* Class were modernised to include better protection. In the days before radar it was necessary to use aircraft to spot shell-splashes at long-range, and most of the battleships had been fitted with catapults for launching floatplanes. But the cruiser was designed to operate in distant oceans, and if she was to locate an enemy raider or even merchant ships to capture, she had to extend her range of vision. Only aircraft could do this, and so great ingenuity was devoted throughout the 1920s and 1930s to the problem of installing aircraft in cruisers. The British, along with the Americans, came to the conclusion that it was vital to protect the aircraft from weathering, and so hangars began to appear. The *Southampton* Class was the first British design with an integral hangar for two floatplanes, but the *Kent* Class were given a hangar in their 1936–38 reconstruction. It was ironic, therefore, when war experience showed that the aircraft was something of a liability in action as its fuel was a fire hazard, and the problems of launching from the catapult under fire, let alone recovering the aircraft, a diversion that any captain could do without. The only recorded launching in action was when HMS *Ajax* launched a Seafox at the start of the Battle of the River Plate. By 1942 there were sufficient aircraft carriers to provide aerial reconnaissance for cruisers, and in any case the demand for light AA guns and radar sets took precedence, so catapults were removed and hangars

BELOW: A prewar view of the British cruiser *Ajax*, one of the three ships which brought the pocket battleship *Admiral Graf Spee* to action at the River Plate. These 7000-ton cruisers were regarded as the most economical size to build, but Japanese competition forced the European navies to build larger cruisers.

BELOW: By 1942 HMS *Ajax* showed the extra equipment added as a result of war experience. Tripod masts were needed to carry the weight of air-warning radar aerials; twin 4-inch anti-aircraft guns replaced the singles; most of the searchlights gave way to 20-mm. guns; around her hull she carried a cable for 'degaussing' against magnetic mines.

LEFT: The *Punjabi* comes alongside the cruiser *Kent*.

RIGHT: Destroyers of the 'Tribal' Class such as HMS *Bedouin* were the largest in the Royal Navy with six 4.7-inch guns, two 4-inch anti-aircraft guns and four torpedo tubes.

were either dismantled or converted to other uses.

The British favoured the 6-inch gun for their cruisers, partly because the shell could be manhandled if power-loading failed in action, but partly because of the extended teething troubles of the 8-inch. The 'County' Class had taken a long time before their 8-inch mountings could be regarded as reliable, principally because of the advanced nature of the mounting. In a misguided attempt to meet the threat from air attack the twin 8-inch mounting was designed with 70° elevation, a requirement which put a great strain on the mechanism. Another requirement was rapid fire, and this put a great strain on the design. Despite these problems the 8-inch gun was a formidable weapon, and in 1926 HMS *Kent* achieved the astonishing feat of firing an 8-inch shell every 11·6 seconds, or a broadside of more than 104,000 lbs per minute. With the knowledge of this in mind, it is not hard to see why the Admiralty were content to ignore paper comparisons with Japanese cruisers.

One good feature of modern British cruiser design was the provision of an adequate ammunition supply to the anti-aircraft guns. Other cruisers might have more guns or even a better disposition but in the dark days in the Mediterranean British cruisers showed that they could fight sustained battles against aircraft. The two modern cruisers sunk during the evacuation of Crete in May 1941, HMS *Fiji* and HMS *Gloucester*, were only sunk by Stukas when they had fired away all their 4-inch ammunition and nearly all pom-pom shell; in the closing moments of the action both ships were reduced to firing practice shell.

BELOW: The destroyer HMS *Javelin* and a sister manoeuvre at speed. Up to the 'Tribal' Class, British destroyers had two funnels, but from the 'J' Class the single funnel became standard.

The Battle of the River Plate in December 1939 was not only a great tonic to British morale at a period when the war at sea was not going well, but it was a classic illustration of how cruisers were designed to function. Every year cruisers on foreign stations carried out a 'raider exercise' with one cruiser playing the role of a German pocket battleship. The solution to a powerful enemy ship on the trade-routes was not, as so many commentators claimed, another pocket battleship, but a concentration of cruisers; this is the reason why numbers of cruisers was always more important than individual quality. The anti-raider tactics relied on the speed of the cruisers, 30 knots or more, to keep them out of trouble, for their 4-inch armour belts and thin deck armour would not keep out heavy shell. In the case of the pocket-battleships

another factor overlooked by the naval pundits of the 1930s was that the German *Panzerschiff* was really only a large cruiser armed with two battleship-type gun-mountings. She was not heavily armoured, nor was she fast, and her heavy armament was actually too cumbersome to cope with fast targets. In fact one could say that the *Graf Spee* and her sisters were too heavily armed for their role, as the 11-inch guns were no better at sinking merchant ships or even cruisers than 8-inch or only 6-inch, and the enormous weight of armament made a higher speed impossible.

The Battle of the River Plate also demonstrated how tough cruisers were. Although the *Exeter* was badly hit and eventually had all guns out of action she could still steam, while *Ajax* had both her after turrets put out of action by an 11-inch shell. The German fire was accurate, and the battle was in fact the first time that radar-control was used in action, but still the British cruisers were not in danger of sinking. Another lesson learned from the battle was the wisdom of retaining torpedo tubes in British cruisers, for the *Graf Spee*'s captain said later that he had not dared close the *Exeter* to finish her off because of her six 21-inch torpedo-tubes. However, he omitted to mention that his ship had eight torpedo-tubes, and could theoretically have kept the British cruisers away. What helped the British ships to survive was the poor quality of 11-inch shells, as the Admiralty report on the damage reported a number of non-bursting shells. This is a strange reversal of roles, for it was the poor quality of British shells in 1916 which prevented the Grand Fleet from gaining a conclusive victory at Jutland.

It is easy to be wise after the event, but what happened off Montevideo on December 13, 1939 was inevitable provided that the British commodore and his cruiser-captains kept their heads and followed the tactics which had been developed. The German ship concentrated on the 8-inch gunned *Exeter* as her most dangerous opponent and the British ship was severely punished, but just as the *Graf Spee* looked likely to put her completely out of action, the two 6-inch gun ships, the *Ajax* and *Achilles*, pushed their attack home and forced the *Graf Spee* to switch target. They dared not face the 11-inch broadsides for too long, and had to withdraw. The diversion forced the *Graf Spee* to leave the *Exeter* alone, and the slow-firing 11-inch turrets could not change elevation and bearing fast enough to land a crippling hit. As soon as the German ship tried to find the *Exeter*'s range once more the small cruisers came in again, and as they kept apart the *Graf Spee* could not cope with them both. Nor was the British fire ineffective against the *Graf Spee*'s armour, and soon a number of hits were scored. Like a tormented bull the pocket battleship turned for neutral waters and the Uruguayan port of Montevideo. There her captain received orders from Hitler to scuttle rather than attempt a breakout and the long haul back to Germany in damaged condition, which might lead to her interception in northern waters. The *Exeter* had been put out of action, and had to go to the Falkland Islands, but the *Cumberland* replaced her, and even if *Graf Spee* had broken out she would have faced the same situation.

Many British cruisers served on the Northern Patrol to prevent neutral merchant ships from running contraband goods through the blockade to Germany, and to intercept or shadow any German warships trying to break out into the Atlantic. This was a heavy commitment in men and ships, in waters notorious for bad weather and bitter cold in winter. To relieve cruisers for more urgent duties with the Fleet or on distant stations the Admiralty fell back on a device which they had used in World War I. They requisitioned fifty large liners on the outbreak of war and armed them with 6-inch guns to serve as Armed Merchant Cruisers (AMCs). The AMC was hardly ideal for the job as her towering sides made her a good target; her capacious passenger decks made an excellent fire-trap, and her lightly plated hull offered only enough resistance to a shell to trigger off its fuse. Yet two armed merchant cruisers, the *Jervis Bay* and the *Rawalpindi*, fought actions against German capital ships which equalled the deeds of any regular cruiser. As the war progressed the Admiralty paid off the AMCs and converted them to troopships or amphibious transports, but the type re-emerged in another form, the Auxiliary Anti-Aircraft Ship. These were cargo-vessels stripped of their derricks and cargo-handling gear to make way for a battery of four twin 4-inch AA guns and pom-poms. With proper naval-type fire-control they now had the defensive armament of a cruiser, and although they might steam at only 11 or 12 knots, in the middle of a slow-moving convoy one AA-ship offered the same protection as a cruiser. Nothing underlines the value of the cruiser in World War II more than these examples of attempts to provide the qualities of a cruiser if one was not available.

Destroyers

The destroyer-flotillas of the Royal Navy were organised into tactical units of eight each, with a ninth slightly enlarged type accommodating the senior officer of the Flotilla, known as Captain (D), short for Captain (Destroyers). As the policy had been to build one flotilla each year and to allocate each flotilla an initial letter the standard fleet types built between 1926 and 1935 were known as the 'A to I' Classes, sturdy two-funnelled boats armed with four 4·7-inch guns and two quadruple sets of 21-inch torpedo tubes. They were actually little different from the older 'V&W' Class dating from 1917, but two experimental prototypes built in 1926, the

Amazon and *Ambuscade*, had introduced some improvements in detail. By 1936 the big French, Japanese and Italian ships were so obviously superior to the standard British destroyer that there was increasing pressure inside and outside the Royal Navy to build a larger and better-armed destroyer. The result was the 'Tribal' Class, with double the armament of the previous 'I' Class, but only four torpedo-tubes. The opportunity was also taken to abolish the rather clumsy idea of having a ninth vessel as leader, because recent tactical exercises indicated that the normal flotilla was too unwieldy, and that divisions of four destroyers each were ideal in action. The solution was quite simple: to alter the internal accommodation of the standard destroyer (as the 'Tribals' were bigger there was more space in any case) to make room for Captain (D) and his clerical and communications staff. If the leader became overcrowded extra personnel were transferred to other destroyers in the flotilla.

The next class of destroyers was a more positive step forward. By introducing a new stronger form of longitudinal construction the Admiralty was able to reduce the size, increase torpedo armament to ten tubes, and sacrifice only one twin gun-mounting. This more balanced design was known as the 'J' or *Javelin* Class, and a further innovation made them the first single-funnelled destroyers, as two improved boilers gave the same power as three of the old type in the 'Tribals'. Both these classes rectified a serious omission in previous destroyers by having a four-barrelled 2-pounder (40-mm) pom-pom for close-range defence against aircraft. At last small ships had some defence against divebombers, and the weapon remained standard throughout World War II. The drawback to the new destroyers was the Admiralty's failure to produce a workable high-angle gun-mounting for the main armament. The new expensive and weighty twin 4·7-inch mount in the 'Tribals' and *Javelins* could elevate only to 40°, which allow it to fire only at distant aircraft formations. The reason was partly financial, in that the Naval Estimates did not allocate enough money to R & D on small ship fire control and AA gun-design, and to discouraging experience with the high-angle 8-inch gun of the 1920s.

Destroyers saw much patrol work in the early months of the war, but their first taste of real action was in the Norwegian campaign in the spring of 1940, when the Home Fleet covered first the Anglo-

BELOW: A modified 'W' Class British destroyer, HMS *Worcester*. Launched in 1919, it displaced 1090 tons; Armament: four 4.7-inch guns, two single pom-poms and six 21-inch torpedo tubes. She was badly damaged in February 1942 during an unsuccessful daylight attack on the German battlecruisers *Scharnhorst* and *Gneisenau* in the English Channel.

BOTTOM: A British *Bangor* Class mine sweeper, of the type built in large numbers in British and Canadian yards. Despite the enormous quantity of fleet sweepers built during the war, fishing trawlers had to be converted to cope with the German mine-laying offensive in the North Sea.

BOTTOM: The British submarine *Torbay* had an active career in the Mediterranean, scoring many successes against Axis shipping.

French force's landing, and then its withdrawal. Norway gave the Royal Navy its first rude lesson in the potency of bombing, and an immediate result was that destroyers with two banks of torpedo-tubes lost the after one in favour of a 3-inch or 4-inch AA gun, while the 'Tribals' received a twin 4-inch mount in place of an after 4.7-inch mount.

The next class of destroyers was a repeat of the 'J' Class, the eight 'K' Class, of which the *Kelly* would in due course become the most famous. Following the alphabetical system, the 'L' Class were enlarged versions in which the main fault was rectified by providing a dual-purpose main armament. The destroyers which resulted were among the most handsome ever built, with large gunhouses, but the gun-mounting and its fire-control were not entirely successful. Also, the cost of each unit rose alarmingly, and the Admiralty wisely decided to return to the 'J' design after only 16 of the bigger ships had been ordered. At the outbreak of war only a few of the 'Js' had been finished, and it was to be 1942 before the last of the 1939 programme, the 'N' Class, were completed. In the meantime the decision had been made to adopt the 'J' design as the basis for a standard wartime design, to be known as the 'Emergency' design.

The other innovation in the destroyer field occurred as a result of the acute shortage of destroyers. In 1938 a specification was drawn up for a smaller and slower destroyer, with dimensions approximating to the 'S' Class of 1917. This resulted in the 'Hunt' Class, originally known as fast escort vessels to get around Treasury reluctance to vote more money for destroyers, but re-rated as escort destroyers in 1940. The first twenty 'Hunts', so-called because they commemorated well-known hunts, were intended to have three twin 4-inch AA gun-mountings, a pom-pom and three torpedo-tubes, an exceptionally heavy armament on a hull displacing less than 1000 tons. But the lead ship, HMS *Atherstone*, showed that the limits had been exceeded and the torpedo-tubes and one twin 4-inch mounting had to go. They were basically a small edition of the 'J' Class, but to compensate for the heavy armament they were fitted with fin-stabilisers, the first warships in the world to have this device. The second group of 'Hunts' had their hulls widened during construction to improve stability, and so they were able to mount the third 4-inch AA mounting.

The old 'V&W' classes were over twenty years old in 1939, and the handful of 'R' and 'S' boats were even older. The international treaties stipulated that destroyers be replaced after 15 years (one year of war service counting as two), but the Abyssinian Crisis had reprieved them. The Admiralty did not regard them as fit for front-line service with the Fleet on account of their age, but a plan to refurbish the 'V&W' boats for service as escorts had been started in 1938. This provided for an armament of twin 4-inch high-angle guns and an outfit of anti-submarine gear. The older 'S' Class were converting to minelayers for service in the Far East, but in both cases the outbreak of war cut back the programme, and many served initially without alterations.

Submarines

The British had tried at the Washington Disarmament Conference in 1921–22 and later to have the submarine outlawed, having suffered so much at the hands of German U-Boats in 1914–18, but this move was vetoed by France and the United States. With their enormous mercantile marine the British had everything to lose from Submarine warfare, and conversely their opponents offered no similar temptation. Therefore the Royal Navy's submarine force before 1939 was trained and equipped for surveillance and attack in enemy warships. Experience in World War I had led to a series of experimental submarines in the 1920s but by the outbreak of war only three types were in production, the ocean-going 'T' Class of 1000-tonners, the 700-ton 'S' Class for more restricted waters such as the North Sea, and the smaller coastal 'U' Class originally intended for training.

British submarines were the first to adopt the heavy bow salvo of six or even eight torpedoes, in recognition of the fact

LEFT: The 'T' Class submarines came into service in 1939, and were built in large numbers throughout the war. HMS *Tuna* returns to harbour after a patrol.

BELOW: A German photograph of the British submarine *Shark*, forced to surrender after she had sustained heavy damage from German escorts. A German U-Jäger appears in the background.

BELOW RIGHT: The submarine *Tribune* takes on fuel from a depot ship, while her sister ship *Trident* lies alongside.

RIGHT: HM Submarine *Seadog*, a unit of the 'S' Class, medium-sized subs built for the Royal Navy from the early 1930s through 1945. Their chief asset was their diving time of 25 seconds. They operated successfully from the Arctic to the Pacific.

RIGHT: A rating watches the hydroplane indicator in a British sub. Hydroplanes control the angle of ascent and descent of a submarine underwater.

that attacks on warships would have to be made at greater range than before; a bigger spread would increase the chances of a hit. Deck guns were carried for use against small targets but these were only light, and the concept of the cruiser-submarine with heavy guns had been abandoned. Design of hulls and machinery proved sound, and it was not necessary to introduce any radical changes throughout the war. As had been foretold by British submariners, they did not find many targets, and their biggest contribution in the early part of the war was intelligence on ship movements. During the Norwegian campaign in 1940 the *Clyde* succeeded in torpedoing the battle battlecruiser *Gneisenau*, but this was the only outstanding success in return for ceaseless patrolling and some losses from enemy counteraction.

Escorts

As a result of the bitter experience of World War I, when the Admiralty had reluctantly been forced into accepting convoy as an antidote to submarines, the Royal Navy paid a lot of attention to anti-submarine vessels. Throughout the 1920s and 1930s old escort vessels, known as sloops, were replaced by new con-

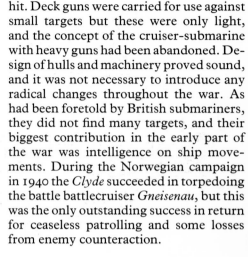

CENTRE LEFT: HM Submarine *Sceptre* takes on a fresh torpedo from the depot ship. When subs operated from their main base, depot ships accompanied them and supplied spare torpedoes, fuel and provisions.

LEFT: The destroyer *Wolverine* and the *Renown* return to Plymouth after hunting the *Graf Spee*.

BELOW: The armed merchant cruiser *Jervis Bay* was taken over at the outbreak of war for service with the Royal Navy. She was stripped of her passenger accommodation and her peacetime luxury fittings to make way for seven 6-inch guns. She was sunk in action by the pocket battleship *Admiral Scheer* in November 1941.

LEFT: The *Egret*, an anti-aircraft sloop, typical of the small but powerful escorts designed before the war.

BELOW LEFT: Motor torpedo boats were built in large numbers to counter similar German craft. In the background is the destroyer *Wivern*.

struction. A steady growth in size and offensive power was achieved, until a powerful class of anti-aircraft sloop was in service shortly before World War II, armed with four twin 4-inch AA guns and capable of steaming at 19 knots. Sloops were intended to be fast enough to escort all but the fastest merchant ships and to concentrate on endurance and specialised weaponry such as minesweeping or anti-submarine gear and anti-aircraft guns.

As in all other categories the British were desperately short of ships and in 1938 work began on choosing a design for a mass-produced escort. Using the experience gained in World War I it was decided to use mercantile expertise rather than traditional naval builders' know-how. After looking at trawler designs the Royal Navy decided to build an enlarged whalecatcher, and the design was worked out by one of the leading British yards specialising in this field. As soon as war broke out large numbers of the new escort vessel were ordered from the smaller yards, and when they came into service in the spring of 1940 they were christened 'corvettes', a term which had lapsed sixty years before. They were named after flowers and herbs, just like the escorts of World War I, and as a result reports of convoy actions sounded like seed catalogues, with *Hibiscus* and *Geranium* competing with *Hydrangea* and *Buttercup*. The 'Flower' Class proved rugged and well-designed, and by the summer of 1940 they achieved their purpose in mastering the U-Boats in the coastal waters around the British Isles. But in forcing the U-Boats out of coastal waters they revealed their own fundamental weakness; further out in the Atlantic the corvettes were exposed to worse weather conditions and their crews suffered from the spartan accommodation and lack of size. Another drawback was their lack of speed, only 16 knots, and when U-Boats took to attacking on the surface by night they could outrun a corvette. Nevertheless the corvette was a good seaboat, however uncomfortable she might be, and somewhat over 300 were built.

Weapons and Equipment

The standard British heavy gun was the 15-inch 42-calibre of 1912 design, mounted in a twin turret. This mounting was outstanding for its simplicity and ruggedness, and although the gun was theoretically outclassed by later weapons it proved more than satisfactory under World War II conditions. All the modernised ships had the elevation of the mounting increased to 30°, but older ships had a special supercharge for their guns to boost range. The *Nelson* and *Rodney*'s 16-inch 45-cal. guns proved rather disappointing as the mounting had so many safety devices built in that it was almost impossible to fire! After modification it was improved, but the gun was nowhere near as successful as the 15-inch. The 14-inch 45-cal. used in the *King George V* was modelled on the older type, although the quadruple turret was a completely new conception. The designers tried to pack in too many novel features, including all-round all-angle loading, and here again the mounting failed to achieve that blend of ruggedness and simplicity which had made the twin 15-inch so successful. Small wonder that the Admiralty had no hesitation in arming the new battleship *Vanguard* with spare 15-inch turrets left over from World War I.

The 8-inch gun was used in a twin mounting designed in the 1920s, but it was no longer in production. The twin 6-inch used in light cruisers was similar in basic design but was a more modest mounting and so it avoided the snags of the 8-inch. Pressure to match the American and Japanese cruisers had led to the introduction of a triple 6-inch mounting in the *Southampton* Class, and this became standard for wartime cruisers. The need for a dual-purpose gun led to the 5·25-inch twin-mounting, and this was used as the secondary gun for battleships and as the main armament of the new anti-aircraft cruisers. It was not a complete success, for apart from technical problems with the mounting its shell was rather too heavy for the anti-aircraft role. After a brief reign it gave way to more sophisticated versions of the 6-inch gun.

Going down the scale the next calibre was the 4·7-inch, which had been the standard destroyer gun since 1918. There was also an anti-aircraft gun of this calibre, used in the aircraft carriers *Courageous* and *Glorious* and the battleships *Nelson*

ABOVE: A quadruple 14-inch gun turret as mounted in the *King George V* Class battleship. Hoists lifted separate shells and cordite charges from shell rooms and magazines deep in the bowels of the ship. Passing through a series of flashtight scuttles (or hatches), the ammunition was brought level with the open breech of the gun and then rammed into place mechanically. Over 200 men were involved in the various and complex stages of this operation.

RIGHT: Motor gunboats (MGBs) were developed to operate with MTBs by subduing enemy defences with gunfire before the final torpedo attack.

BELOW: MTB-238 was a $72\frac{1}{2}$-footer built by the noted Vosper firm, typical of the later, more heavily-armed MTBs.

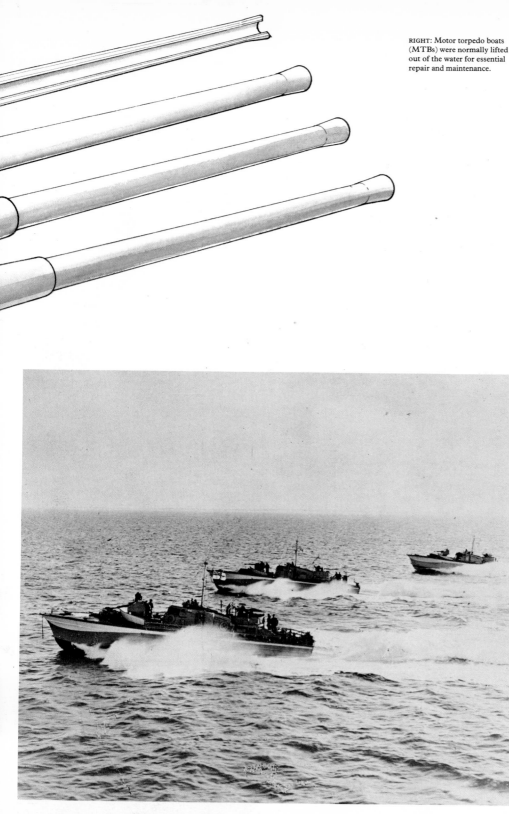

most successful against aircraft, and during the war was even thought good enough as a main armament for destroyers. But in 1939 the air menace was not sufficient for it to displace the low-angle guns still being put in destroyers, a mistake which was to have dire repercussions. Older ships had single 4-inch anti-aircraft guns, which were not as effective, mainly because the mounting did not allow fast training.

The worst shortage in 1939 was in close-range weapons, and in this the Royal Navy was no worse than other navies. The eight-barrelled pom-pom had been introduced in 1927 as a defence against divebombers, and with its eight belt-fed guns pumping out ammunition at a prodigious rate it was the most effective weapon of its kind. A four-barrelled version had recently been introduced for small ships, but the main disadvantage was the low velocity of the 2-pounder 40-mm shell. The Swedish Bofors company had offered its 40-mm gun to the Royal Navy, but this had been turned down in the prewar period on what proved to be flimsy grounds. The British Army had adopted the 40-mm Bofors gun, and in 1940 the Navy was only too glad to receive a number on loan. Similarly the Swiss 20-mm Oerlikon heavy machine gun was first ignored and then put into quantity production with frantic haste in 1940. The only light anti-aircraft weapon available was a quadruple 0·5-inch machine gun, a useless weapon which was subject to frequent jamming.

In torpedoes the Royal Navy narrowly missed a great development. In the 1920s it had introduced torpedoes running on liquid oxygen with greatly improved performance, but a series of incidents led to the abandonment of the idea. Later the Japanese were to prove just how good the idea could be. So in 1939 the Royal Navy was still using the well-tried steam-driven torpedo which had proved its worth for twenty years. One improvement, however, had just been successfully tested, a magnetic exploder which would set off a torpedo underneath a target and do far greater damage. As it increased the lethalness of the torpedo and its chance of scoring a hit, the magnetic pistol was very important, but it had its drawbacks as it could be influenced by the earth's magnetism if it ran too deep. The countermeasure was discovered to be degaussing, or electric neutralisation of a target ship's magnetism, and in order to counter this the magnetic pistol had to be set to even more sensitive levels.

and *Rodney*. Extensive ballistic tests led to a big increase in the weight of the 4·7-inch shell, but before the war it had been decided to change to a new calibre, 4·5-inch, in order to standardise calibres with the army. The ballistics of the 4·5-inch dual-purpose gun were even more favourable. The first version was a twin high-angle mounting for aircraft carriers and depot ships, but during the war a single barrelled version was produced for destroyers, and this is still in service.

From 1937 the standard light anti-aircraft mounting for small ships was the twin 4-inch, a highly successful weapon which remained in production for thirty years. With nearly 90° elevation it proved

THE ITALIAN AND FRENCH NAVIES

THE ITALIAN NAVY

The Italian Navy had many advantages, notably a long-established shipbuilding industry and talented designers. In World War I its fleet had contained the Austrian Navy, and although it had not acted with great enterprise its officers and men had served with devotion. What was revealed under war experience, however, was that individual acts of heroism were better suited to the Italian temperament than the concerted, disciplined pursuit of a distant objective. On the debit side the Italian economy suffered from periodic reverses, and it proved difficult to carry through any long-term programme to its conclusion, despite a government under the dictator Benito Mussolini which spent money on armaments to maintain full employment. Another problem was the steady erosion of loyalty by political interference, the principal evil being the promotion of juniors over the heads of senior officers, provided that their political beliefs were suitable.

The Italians had acquired a North African empire and territories bordering on the Red Sea before World War I. To protect these possessions it was necessary to run convoys, and so after World War I the Italian Navy built a series of heavy cruisers, subject like all others to the provisions of international treaty limitations. Because of financial limitations no replacement of the surviving World War I battleships was attempted until 1934, when four powerful units were laid down, but simultaneously a comprehensive reconstruction of the four old units was begun. Thus by 1939 Italy was the major

BELOW: The battleship *Vittorio Veneto*, in her 1943 camouflage scheme. The class was armed with nine 15-inch guns and could steam at 30 knots. The *Littorio* was sunk at Taranto in 1940 but was salvaged; the *Vittorio Veneto* was torpedoed before Matapan; the *Roma* was sunk by German aircraft after Italy changed sides in 1943.

FAR LEFT: The *Turbine* Class destroyers reached 39 knots on trials. Each Italian destroyer carried initial recognition letters on the bow (TB equals *Turbine*).

LEFT: The torpedo boat *Calatafimi* was completed in 1924 as a destroyer, but she was downgraded in 1938. As the German TA.19 she was torpedoed by a Greek submarine in August 1944.

BELOW LEFT: The *Antonio Pigafetta* was one of the large 1900-ton 'Navigatori' Class destroyers.

BELOW: The *Antonio Pigafetta* was scuttled in September 1943 but was refloated by the Germans and renamed TA.44. She was sunk by British aircraft at Trieste in 1945.

naval power in the Mediterranean, and looked likely to challenge French supremacy. With ample shore-based air power available no attempt was made to develop aircraft carriers, apart from an elderly seaplane carrier.

The purpose of the battle fleet was mainly defensive, and the cruisers were intended to safeguard communications with the North African colonies. The strike element of the fleet took the form of submarines and destroyers, and in both categories the Italians had built impressive numbers. Over 100 submarines and 60 large destroyers were in service when Italy declared war on France and Great Britain in June 1940. Despite the recognition of the need to safeguard communications with the colonies very little attention was devoted to convoy escorts, presumably as it was assumed that air cover would suffice. France was the main rival, but as Mussolini's ambitions waxed the British became a second opponent, and the Abyssinian Crisis of 1936 confirmed this. Unfortunately the quality of Italian naval equipment was not all that it seemed, and in retrospect it can be seen that the Italian Navy would have been hard put to challenge two strong navies in the Mediterranean, particularly navies with bases stretching from Gibraltar to Syria. Even the unexpected collapse of France in June 1940 did not lighten the navy's burden, and it never gained the initiative from the Royal Navy.

The Germans hoped to make use of Italy's efficient shipyards to make good their own shortages, and many captured

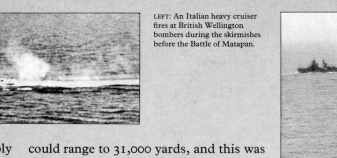

LEFT: An Italian heavy cruiser fires at British Wellington bombers during the skirmishes before the Battle of Matapan.

warships were taken in hand, notably French warships taken at Toulon and Yugoslavian ships captured in 1941. But shortages of steel and other raw materials held up production, and the performance of Italian yards was disappointing. Allied air raids inflicted heavy damage, and by 1943 very little of the war programme construction had been completed.

Battleships

The core of the Italian battle fleet in June 1940 comprised four ships completed in 1914/15. The two *Conte di Cavour* Class and the two *Andrea Doria*s were very similar dreadnoughts originally armed with thirteen 12-inch guns, and capable of 21 knots. In what must be the most ingenious ship-reconstruction in modern times, General Francesco Rotundi redesigned them to be faster and better armed. The midships triple turret was removed and the vacant space was used to expand the engine power to give another five knots. Deck armour was increased and a unique Pugliese system of underwater defence was incorporated, and cylindrical sections were built into the anti-torpedo protection.

The chief difference between the two classes was that the *Conte di Cavour* Class, being slightly earlier, had 4·7-inch secondary guns in six twin turrets and eight single 3·9-inch anti-aircraft guns, whereas the *Andrea Doria*s had a heavier armament of four triple 5·3-inch mountings, all grouped forward, and ten single 3·5-inch anti-aircraft guns. The main armament in both groups was changed to ten 12·6-inch in the original disposition, a triple and twin turret forward, and a twin and triple aft. The new gun had 30° elevation and

could range to 31,000 yards, and this was the reason that the older British battleships were given supercharges for their 15-inch guns. *Caio Duilio* was the last to enter service in July 1940.

All four of the older battleships saw action. *Conte di Cavour* was an early casualty when British carrier-borne Swordfish torpedo-bombers struck at Taranto on November 12, 1940. She sustained one hit from an 18-inch torpedo and sank in shallow water, and although salved in July 1941 she had not completed repairs when the Allies invaded Italy in 1943. She was scuttled in September 1943, salvaged a second time by the Germans, and finally sunk by US aircraft during a bombing raid on Trieste in February 1945. The *Caio Duilio* was hit during the Taranto raid, but she managed to stay afloat and was repaired. As rebuilt they were handsome ships, and they foreshadowed the new *Littorio* Class. Despite their ingenuity they were not comparable to foreign battleships, partly because of their light belt armour, only ten inches, and partly because the Pugliese shock-absorbing cylinder could not be made fully watertight. Like all Italian warships, they emphasised speed at the expense of armour, despite convincing proof in World War I of the fallacy of this doctrine.

The new battleships of the *Littorio* Class (only two completed by August 1940) were altogether more powerful units, but they resembled the older ships in appearance and layout. In place of the four 12·6-inch mountings they had three triple 15-inch 45-cal. turrets; the secondary armament comprising four triple 6-inch mountings at the corners of the superstructure, and twelve 3·5-inch anti-

aircraft guns were carried. A catapult and crane for three aircraft were carried on the quarterdeck. Armour was nearly 14 inches in thickness, and speed was increased to a nominal 30 knots. The gun was a development of a World War I weapon, itself deriving from British designs, and with 35° elevation it could range to 46,800 yards (27½ miles). Despite these impressive statistics the *Littorio* Class did not achieve any results in battle. Their speed in service did not exceed 28 knots, and in battle the phenomenal range of their guns did not give them any great advantage. Nevertheless the British did investigate the possibility in 1944 of using the two survivors as fast carrier escorts in the Pacific.

The *Littorio*s were good ships in many ways, but when considering their good points it should be borne in mind that they exceeded the international limit on tonnage by 6500 tons, a discrepancy of nearly 20 per cent. And yet, this flagrant dis-

LEFT: The surrender of the Italian Fleet spelled an ignominious end to Mussolini's dreams of creating an Italian lake out of the Mediterranean Sea.

BELOW: The *maiale* (pigs) were small torpedo-like submarines with two operators riding astride. These human torpedoes crippled two British battleships and were copied by the British.

BOTTOM: The light cruiser *Bartolomeo Colleoni* sacrificed armour to reach the incredible speed of 42 knots. But this did not stop her from being caught and sunk by the Australian cruiser *Sydney* in July 1940.

Strength Of The Italian Navy, June 1940

Figures in parentheses indicate ships under construction.

6 Battleships (+2)
2 *Cavour* Class 2 *Littorio* Class[2]
2 *Doria* Class[1]

[1] 1 to complete in July. [2] Both to complete in August, with 2 more building.

7 Heavy Cruisers
3 *Trento* Class
4 *Zara* Class (all built 1925-33)

12 Light Cruisers (+12)
4 *Da Barbiano* Class 2 *Montecuccoli* Class
2 *Cadorna* Class 2 *Aosta* Class
2 *Garibaldi* Class (all built 1928-37)

3 Old Cruisers
San Giorgio, *Taranto* and *Bari* (built 1905-14)

54 Modern Destroyers (+5)
2 *Sella* Class 4 *Dardo* Class
4 *Sauro* Class 4 *Folgore* Class
8 *Turbine* Class 4 *Grecale* Class
12 "Navigatori" Class
4 *Oriani* Class
12 *Alpino* Class[1] (all built 1921-39)

[1] A further 5 of improved type ordered 1940.

5 Old Destroyers (ex-Scouts)
2 *Mirabello* Class
3 *Leone* Class (all built 1914-24)

63 Torpedo Boats/Light Destroyers
1 *Audace* 7 *La Masa* Class
7 *Pilo* Class 4 *Palestro* Class
4 *Sirtori* Class 6 "Generali" Class
4 *Curtatone* Class (all built 1913-24)
30 *Spica* Class (built 1934-39)

112 Submarines (+17)
4 *Balilla* Class 6 *Marconi* Class[1]
1 *Fieramosca* 4 *Mameli* Class
2 *Archimede* Class 4 *Pisani* Class
2 *Glauco* Class 4 *Bandiera* Class
1 *Pietro Micca* 4 *Squalo* Class
3 *Calvi* Class 2 *Bragadin* Class
3 *Foca* Class 7 *Argonauta* Class
9 *Marcello* Class 2 *Settembrini* Class
2 *Cappellini* Class 12 *Sirena* Class
5 *Brin* Class 10 *Perla* Class
4 *Liuzzi* Class 17 *Adua* Class
2 *Argo* Class (built 1925-40)

7 Old Submarines
5 "H" Class
2 *X.2* Class[2]

[1] 1 nearly completed. [2] Both laid up in September 1940.

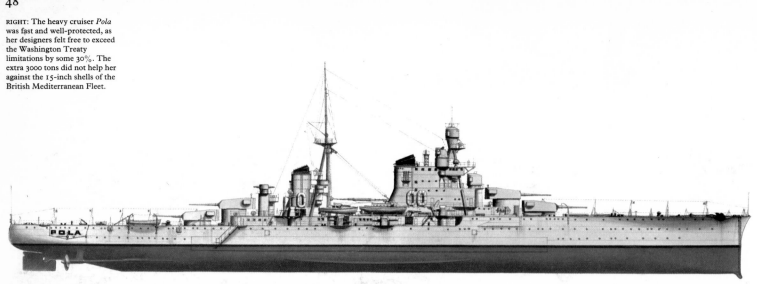

regard of tonnage restrictions did not produce any qualities which made them superior to possible opponents. The Pugliese system of underwater protection was a disappointment as we have seen, and the effective speed was no greater than that of the British, American or French contemporaries. In battle they proved equally disappointing, with *Littorio* put out of action by three torpedoes at Taranto in November 1940 and *Roma* sunk by glider bombs in September 1943.

The *Vittorio Veneto* was the most active of the class, and survived damage from carrier aircraft at the Battle of Matapan in March 1941. The *Littorio* (*Lictor*, the Roman bearer of the Fascist emblem), was renamed *Italia* on July 30, 1943 after Mussolini was unseated, and both she and *Vittorio Veneto* were surrendered to the British at Malta. The last two were not so lucky; *Impero* fell into German hands incomplete and was sunk by bombs in 1945, while *Roma* was attacked with glider bombs while fleeing southwards to join the Allies.

ABOVE: When the Italians overran Yugoslavia in 1941 they captured the destroyer *Beograd*. As the *Sebenico* she was then seized by the Germans in 1943 and renamed *TA 43*.

RIGHT: The torpedo boat *Audace* had been built in World War I as a Japanese destroyer but was taken over by the Italian Navy. As the German *TA 20* she was sunk by British destroyers in November 1944.

Aircraft Carriers

The prewar assumption by the Italian Navy that it did not need aircraft carriers was soon shown to be wrong when British carriers proved so troublesome in 1940–41, and in any case poor liaison with the Regia Aeronautica robbed the Navy of many chances. Therefore in July 1941 work began on converting the liner *Roma* into a carrier at Genoa. Under her new name *Aquila* work proceeded slowly and at the time of the Armistice in 1943 she was still incomplete and lacked aircraft. She fell into German hands, and became a target for attack by bombers and human torpedoes, and was finally scuttled in 1945. Another liner, the *Augustus*, was taken in hand for a less ambitious conversion. As the *Sparviero* she made even less progress than the *Aquila*, and in September 1943 had only been stripped of her superstructure. She fell into German hands and was scuttled in 1944.

Cruisers

The oldest cruiser was the old armoured cruiser *San Giorgio*, built in 1910, which had been converted to a coast defence ship in 1937–38. She was set on fire and scuttled in the harbour of Tobruk in Libya in January 1941. Two other cruisers survived from World War I, the ex-German prizes *Taranto* (ex-SMS *Strassburg*) and *Bari* (ex-SMS *Pillau*, ex-Russian *Muraviev Amurski*). Both were used mainly on colonial service before the

LEFT: The *Ardito* was one of the numerous *Animoso* Class torpedo boats built during the war. As the German *TA.26* she was torpedoed by British MTBs.

LEFT: Only one of the *Ariete* Class torpedo boats was completed in the war, and the *Eridano* and 14 others were completed for the Germans in northern Italian shipyards.

BELOW: The British-built Yugoslavian destroyer *Dubrovnik* became the Italian *Premuda*, but after her capture by the Germans she was totally rebuilt and rearmed as the *TA.32*.

BOTTOM: The German destroyer *TA.32* ex-*Premuda*, ex-*Dubrovnik*, was rearmed with four 5.3-inch guns, and three 7-mm and 20-mm anti-aircraft guns.

LEFT: A torpedo boat of the *Ariete* Class, all but one of which were taken over by the Germans in 1943.

RIGHT: The torpedo boat *Impavido* of the *Animoso* Class was captured by the Germans in 1943 and renamed *TA.23*. She was armed with three 3.9-inch guns and four 17.7-inch torpedo-tubes.

war, and were sunk in harbour at the time of the Armistice.

Like the other signatories of the Washington Disarmament Treaty the Italians built heavy cruisers to the limits allowed, 10,000 tons with 8-inch guns. The *Trento* Class were good looking ships with eight guns in four twin mountings, and widely spaced funnels. They were designed for 35 knots and had 150,000 shaft horsepower, as against 80,000 shp in their British equivalents, and although this speed was reached on trials the ships were only good for about 31 knots in service – the same as the British 'County' Class.

BELOW: As the German *TA.29* the ex-Italian torpedo boat *Eridano* was sunk by two British destroyers in March 1945.

Their side armour was thin, 3-inch thick, and they had little internal protection against torpedoes. The *Trento* sank after being torpedoed by a British submarine, as a result of her ammunition exploding. The *Bolzano* was built about five years later than the first pair.

The next class, the four *Zara*s were an expansion of the same basic design, and incorporated much heavier armour, a 6-inch belt, at the expense of three knots' speed. But this was achieved by allowing the standard displacement to rise to 11,500 tons, a 15 per cent increase over the treaty limit. Their most remarkable fea-

ture was the amount of power, 95,000 shp developed with only two propeller-shafts, a credit to Italian engineering. Three out of the four were sunk in the disastrous night action off Cape Matapan, when the 1st Cruiser Division (*Zara*, *Pola* and *Fiume*) was ordered to screen the damaged battleship *Vittorio Veneto*. The *Pola* was hit at dusk on March 27, 1941 by a torpedo launched by an Albacore from HMS *Formidable*, and was forced to drop back.

The rest of the 1st Cruiser Division was ordered back to find the *Pola* that evening, and ran into the British Mediterranean Fleet under Admiral Sir Andrew Cun-

LEFT: *Barbarigo* was a submarine of the *Marcello* Class, successful boat which served in the Atlantic with German U-Boats. With the decline in the Regio Navale's fortunes by early 1943 the *Barbarigo* was converted to a transport submarine and she was sunk by Allied aircraft in September.

ningham, its Commander-in-Chief. With the aid of radar plotting the British found the *Pola* at almost the same time as Admiral Cattaneo in the *Zara*. The Italian cruisers were destroyed in a hail of 15-inch shells from the battleships *Barham*, *Valiant* and *Warspite* at less than 4000 yards. Apart from lacking radar the Italian Navy had not devoted much attention to night-fighting drill and flashless cordite for night action was not available. Some idea of how far British night-fighting had advanced since World War I can be guessed from the fact that *Fiume* was hit by five out of six shells from *Warspite*'s first salvo, and also by *Valiant*'s complete salvo of four shells. The *Pola* was not fired on, but her captain realised how hopeless his situation was and gave the order to scuttle as the British destroyers closed in.

The light cruisers of the Italian Navy followed the general lines of their heavy cruisers, big handsome ships with eight 6-inch guns known as the 'Condottieri' Class because they were named after the most famous Renaissance mercenaries. In these ships the Italian fetish of speed was even more evident; one of the first group reached the incredible speed of 42 knots on trials, but in service none of them came near their designed speeds. The *Bartolomeo Colleoni* came to grief at the hands of the Australian cruiser HMAS *Sydney* in July 1940, although the British-built ship had a designed speed five knots lower. The final group, the *Garibaldi* Class, were a more balanced design with 5-inch side armour and ten 6-inch guns.

In 1939 a new class of small cruisers was begun, known as the 'Capitani Romani' Class. These 'sports model' cruisers were more like enlarged destroyers than cruisers, with eight 5·3-inch guns, no armour whatsoever, and a speed of 41 knots. Only three were completed by mid-1943, and

BELOW: The torpedo boat
Dragone was captured by the
Germans while under
construction at Genoa. As the
TA.30 she was torpedoed by
British MTBs in June 1944.

THE FRENCH NAVY

The French Navy in 1939 was emerging from a comprehensive overhaul of equipment and ship-design initiated after World War I. A succession of energetic Ministers of Marine, notably Georges Leygues, ensured a continuity of policy which had been sadly lacking before, and when Admiral Darlan became Chief of the Naval Staff in 1937 he brought the whole navy to a new peak of efficiency. From being an obsolescent force in World War I the Marine Nationale became a byword for fast and powerful ships of novel design, despite the inevitable dominance of the Army in defence planning.

The Mediterranean was vital to France for it gave her access to her North African empire, but she also had a flourishing mercantile marine operating in the Atlantic and the Pacific. Light forces were maintained in the Far East to protect Indo-China, but part of her heavy forces were stationed on the Atlantic coast. Her main bases were Brest on the coast of Brittany, and Toulon in the Mediterranean. Although France had thought a war against Great Britain was not impossible, the two countries came together after the Abyssinian Crisis of 1936, when it became evident that Italy was the likeliest enemy, and that Germany was rearming. By 1939 both navies had achieved a degree of co-operation, to the extent that the French had adopted the design of the British 4-inch anti-aircraft gun and were building 'Flower' Class corvettes in their own shipyards. It was agreed that the French fleet would hold the Mediterranean, but until the Italian intentions became clearer units would be made available to help the British in the Atlantic.

The biggest problem faced by the French Navy was the political instability of the country, which caused interference with the naval programme as well as financial stringency. The introduction of a five-day week under Leon Blum's Popular Front in 1936 hamstrung the shipyards. After the Munich Crisis of 1938 a six-day week was made compulsory once more, but the programmes dropped behind, and much precious time was lost. The problem was so acute that the French Government had to order escorts from British yards in 1939, and aircraft from the United States.

Battleships

The three oldest units of the battle fleet, the *Courbet* Class, dated from 1914 and were not suited for front-line duty as they were slow and weakly protected. They

the rest were sunk before completion or stopped on the stocks. The only other cruisers undertaken during the war were two begun for the Thai Navy in 1939. They were taken over in 1941 and altered to anti-aircraft cruisers, but like so many other Italian ships they fell into German hands and were finally scuttled at Trieste.

Destroyers

The Italians were the first to build extra-large destroyers when they produced the *Carlo Mirabello* and *Augusto Riboty* in 1916. These ships were originally rated as 'esploratori' or scouts, and they led to a steady growth in destroyer-size, first in the Japanese Navy and then in others. In theory the super-destroyer had a lot to recommend it, for it combined some of the robustness and armament of a cruiser with the speed of a destroyer, but in World War II this notion was finally discredited. The big destroyer proved too well-armed to carry out destroyer-duties efficiently and nowhere near large enough or well-armed to perform cruiser tasks. The latest destroyers in 1940 were handsome single-funnelled ships of 1700 tons, capable of impressive speeds on trials but armed with only two twin 4·7-inch guns and six 21-inch torpedo-tubes.

Many older destroyers of World War I vintage had been downgraded to torpedo boats, and these functioned as escorts and minesweepers. The thirty *Spica* Class were similar to the British 'Hunt' Class escort destroyers, both in size and function. They augmented numbers of destroyers without making the same demands on building capacity and materials,

and rate as one of the most successful Italian warship designs of the period.

Strenuous attempts were made to put captured French and other foreign warships into service, but with little success. The ex-Yugoslavian destroyer *Dubrovnik* was only finished by the Germans, but the *Beograd* and *Ljubljana* were completed, as were some French vessels.

Submarines

The Italian Navy built a comparatively large number of submarines with a view to providing a less costly alternative to a big battle fleet. With France and Great Britain as the probable enemies it was felt that submarines would be well suited to cut communications through the Mediterranean, but many of the submarines were too big and clumsy. After the fall of France in mid-1940 the Italian Navy sent submarines through the Straits of Gibraltar to join the German U-Boats in the Bay of Biscay ports, but the submarines needed many modifications to make them fit for Atlantic operations.

The area in which the Italians shone most was in the development of human torpedoes. Known as *maiale* or 'pigs', these two-man craft could enter a defended anchorage and place a heavy charge under an enemy ship. In December 1941 the battleships *Queen Elizabeth* and *Valiant* were severely damaged in what could have been the turning point of the war had the Germans and Italians been able to exploit it, and later ships in Italian harbours were attacked. Bigger midget submarines were built but they achieved very little.

BELOW: After suffering damage at Dakar in 1940 the French battleship *Richelieu* went to the USA for a complete overhaul.

had received only partial modernisation in the 1920s, and the *Ocean* (ex-*Jean Bart*) had been relegated to harbour training duty in 1936. She was used as a target by the Germans in 1942, and although her two sisters escaped to England the Royal Navy only used them as hulks. The three *Bretagne* Class were slightly more modern but two of them had not been modernised. The *Lorraine* had been modernised in 1932–35, with a catapult in place of her midships gun-turret and a modern anti-aircraft armament. But here again her light armour ($7\frac{1}{4}$-inch) on the belt and lack of speed made her a liability in battle.

The French answer to the threat of the three German 'pocket battleships' had been to build up two fast *batiments de ligne* or capital ships of 26,500 tons, capable of nearly 30 knots. The two ships which resulted, *Dunkerque* and *Strasbourg*, were

The Strength Of The French Navy In September 1939

Figures in parentheses indicate ships under construction.

8 Battleships (+4)
3 *Courbet* Class	2 *Dunkerque* Class
3 *Bretagne* Class	4 *Richelieu* Class[1]

[1] *Richelieu* was afloat, *Jean Bart* was to be launched in the Spring of 1940, and 2 more were building.

1 Aircraft Carrier (+2)
1 *Béarn*[1]

[1] Ex-battleship, completed conversion 1927.

7 Heavy Cruisers (+1)
2 *Duquesne* Class	1 *Algérie*
4 *Suffren* Class	

12 Light Cruisers (+3)
3 *Duguay Trouin* Class
1 *La Tour d'Auvergne*[1]
1 *Jeanne d'Arc*[2]
1 *Emile Bertin*
6 *La Galissonière* Class

[1] Minelayer. [2] Designed as a training ship.

78 Destroyers (+27)
6 *Chacal* Class	26 *Bourrasque* Class
18 *Bison* Class	8 *Le Hardi* Class
6 *Fantasque* Class	12 *La Flore* Class
2 *Mogador* Class	

75 Submarines (+38)
9 *Requin* Class	6 *Saphir* Class
8 *Ariane* Class	1 *Surcouf* Class
29 *Acheron* Class	22 *Amazone* Class

63 Sloops And Escorts (+30)
33 old sloops (all built World War I)
11 *Bougainville* Class
13 *Elan* Class
12 *Chamois* Class[1]
4 "Flower" Class covettes[2]

[1] A further 12 building. [2] A further 8 building in England, and 6 more building in France.

handsome ships with two quadruple turrets grouped forward, much like the British *Nelson* Class. As an answer to the *Deutschland* they were superb but costly, but their light protection ($9\frac{3}{4}$-inch) armour was not enough to allow them to face a modern battleship.

Four well-protected battleships were ordered in 1935, the *Richelieu* Class. They were fast and well-armed, with a heavy $13\frac{3}{4}$-inch belt and eight 15-inch guns disposed in the same manner as the *Dunkerque*. The vicissitudes of the class are a microcosm of the subsequent history of the French Navy. The *Richelieu* fled to Dakar to escape the invading German armies in June 1940, and the *Jean Bart*, with guns in only one turret, sailed for Casablanca, but the hull of the third fell into German hands and the fourth was never begun. The *Richelieu* was damaged at Dakar by the British in 1940 but she subsequently joined the Free French and the Allies in 1942. The Americans undertook the job of refitting her, and late in 1943 she returned to service, and went to the East Indies.

Aircraft Carriers

The French neglected the carrier in the prewar period, but more for financial reasons than any scepticism about its value. Just after World War I when co-operation

BELOW: The battleship *Lorraine* was modernised in the prewar period, with a catapult in place of her midships 13.4-inch gun turret and additional anti-aircraft guns.

RIGHT: A Loire-130 spotter floatplane on the after 6-inch gun turret of the French cruiser *Gloire*.

BELOW: The bridge and funnel of the battleship *Richelieu*.

with the British was still flourishing, the incomplete battleship *Béarn* was re-designed as a carrier, and all the latest developments in British carriers, notably salt-water sprays in the hangar and the fire-resistant closed hangar, were incorporated. But the *Béarn* could only steam at 20–21 knots, which was too slow, and as she could only steam 6000 miles at her most economical speed she lacked the essential flexibility of a fleet carrier. After much discussion two new carriers, the *Joffre* and *Painlevé*, were authorised in 1938, but when the collapse occurred in June 1940 only one had been started. Had they been built they would have been the most unusual carriers afloat, with a flight deck offset to port.

Cruisers

The oldest heavy cruisers were the two *Duquesne* Class, built largely for speed, and lacking all but the lightest armour. They were so poorly thought of that in 1935 the Navy considered a detailed proposal to convert them to aircraft carriers, and the idea was raised once more in 1944–45. In the next class, the four *Suffren*s, speed took second place to protection, but like their predecessors they lacked the endurance for work on the trade routes. They were the only cruisers designed after World War I with coal-bunkers; *Suffren* and *Colbert* had two small coal-fired boilers as well, while the *Foch* and *Dupleix* retained the coal as protection but had additional oil fuel.

LORRAINE

The last heavy cruiser built was the *Al-gérie*, launched in 1932, and considered by many to be the best of all heavy cruisers built under the Washington Treaty limitations. She was fast, weatherly and well protected, and had about twice the endurance of previous French cruisers. She was refitted in 1940–41 with extra anti-aircraft guns but suffered the ignominy of being scuttled at Toulon in November 1942. Three vessels of similar but enlarged design were sanctioned in 1940 but did not get beyond the planning stage.

Light Cruisers

The first cruisers built after World War I were the three *Duguay Trouin* Class, very lightly protected but reliable 7000-tonners armed with eight 6·1-inch (155-mm) guns in twin turrets. They were far better investment than their 8-inch gunned counterparts, but no more true light cruisers were authorised for another ten years. Instead three unusual hybrids were built, each one unique among cruisers.

First came the minelayer *Pluton*, later renamed *La Tour d'Auvergne*, of light cruiser proportions but carrying only a light armament of four 5·5-inch guns and 290 mines. Next came the training cruiser *Jeanne d'Arc*, basically a cruiser with the same armament and protection as the *Duguay Trouin* Class but enlarged accommodation for midshipmen. As she was intended to provide tuition and training she had a complete outfit of guns, torpedo-tubes, and a catapult and two floatplanes. Despite her modest speed of 25 knots she was used as a cruiser from the outbreak of

RIGHT: By 1945 the *Georges Leygues* had been altered in similar fashion to other Allied cruisers. During her 1943–44 refit in the USA she was given a tripod foremast to carry radar aerials, lost her mainmast and hanger, and had numerous light guns added.

war, and fully justified her designers' intentions. The third ship was intended to be a much faster version of the *Pluton*, and embodied even more features of contemporary French destroyers, rather than cruisers. With minimum armour but an armament of nine 6-inch guns the *Emile Bertin* averaged 36·73 knots on trials, two knots more than her designed speed.

The *La Tour d'Auvergne* had no chance to lay mines as she blew up at Casablanca only ten days after the outbreak of war, following an accidental explosion on her mine-deck. The *Jeanne d'Arc* and *Emile Bertin* were both refitted in the United States late in the War after they had joined the Allies. The *Emile Bertin* never served as a minelayer, but instead she was used as a flagship for the big destroyers of the *Fantasque* and *Maille Breze* Class.

Destroyers

The French destroyers were outstanding as the largest and fastest in the world. Starting with the '2100-tonne' or *Chacal* type of the early 1920s, a series of big and fast destroyers was produced, culminating in the '2610-tonne' *Fantasque* Class, which had a designed speed of 37 knots but averaged more than 40 knots on trials. With their widely spaced funnels and their low silhouettes they presented an unmistakably handsome profile. The six ships formed the fastest light surface divisions (French destroyers operated in divisions of three) in the world. These vessels were known as *contre-torpilleurs* and were intended to catch and destroy enemy cruisers by torpedo-attack, and to brush aside

BELOW: The 7000-ton cruiser *Georges Leygues* was one of the most successful cruisers of her day, with an armament of nine 6-inch guns and a speed of 31 knots

BELOW RIGHT: The aircraft hangar of the *Georges Leygues*.

other destroyers by gunpower. With the high reported speeds of Italian cruisers these requirements seemed reasonable enough, but a heavy penalty was paid in building cost, running cost and, more important, reliability, in achieving them.

The final *contre-torpilleur* design, the two *Mogador* Class in 1936–37 proved that the idea had been taken too far as they were less successful than the smaller *Fantasque*s. An improved version, the *Hoche* Class, would have had stronger hulls, better machinery and more fuel, but they were stopped in the spring of 1940. In retrospect the building of super-destroyers was almost certainly carried too far, as it reduced the number of ordinary destroyers and light cruisers which the French Navy could build on its annual budgets, but the policy did produce the most remarkable warships of their day.

RIGHT: A twin anti-aircraft machine gun aboard the cruiser *Marseillaise*.

FAR RIGHT: A twin 90-mm anti-aircraft gun aboard the *Marseillaise*. The ship was operating off Halifax in December 1939 when these photographs were taken.

Building of smaller destroyers did continue, and the *Bourrasque* and *Adroit* Classes were authorised in the 1920s. They were neither fast nor particularly weatherly, and when the fast capital ships of the *Dunkerque* and *Richelieu* Classes were planned it was clear that their 28–29-knot sea speed was insufficient to escort 30-knot ships. The new *Hardi* Class, authorised in 1932, attempted to remedy this with a designed speed of 37 knots, and what resulted was a handsome two-funnelled design with the twin 5·1-inch low-angle mounting forward and two aft. Building was slow, and only six were ready by 1941, by which time it was realised that a low-angle armament was not suited to the Mediterranean; the later ships were to be armed with the new 3·9-inch (100-mm) AA gun copied from the British 4-inch.

To make up numbers a so-called '600-tonne' light destroyer was designed, similar to the Italian torpedo boats of the period. Known as the *Agile* Class, they proved useful and a number saw service under the British and Free French flags.

Submarines

Having invented the first practicable submarine in 1888 the French never lost their interest in the type. In March 1920 it had even been proposed to abolish the surface fleet entirely and replace it by 250–300 submarines. This startling idea was not pursued, but France nevertheless built a large number of submarines. They fell into three main types, a '1500-tonne' oceangoing class, a '600-tonne' class for coastal defence, and minelayers. With typical French hyperbole there was also a gigantic cruiser-submarine, the *Surcouf*, built up to the limits of the Washington Treaty, 2880 tons surfaced, and two 8-inch guns.

French submarines were not an unqualified success. Although handy and fast-diving they proved too unreliable, and their torpedoes were not wholly successful. The best proved to be the *Saphir* Class minelayers, of which the *Rubis* had an outstanding war career. Yet the Normand-Fenaux minelaying device was only an updated version of a system tried in British submarines in 1915, and the bulk of her mines laid were actually of British origin. The new submarines under construction were fourteen of the *Roland Morillot* Class, fifteen of the *Aurore* Class, four additional *Saphir* Class minelayers and thirteen *Phénix* Class, were all caught in the 1940 débâcle, but five of the *Aurore* Class were towed to England, and *L'Aurore* herself survived only to be scuttled at Toulon in 1942.

Escorts

The French Navy had not paid a great deal of attention to the problems of anti-submarine escorts, but they had a number of useful ships: The 1st Class sloops of the

ABOVE: The destroyer *Mistral*, seen at Halifax late in 1940, was rearmed after she fell into British hands, and had 4.7-inch guns from an old British destroyer. Shortage of spares and ammunition forced the British to rearm many French warships in this way.

LEFT: In 1943 the cruiser *Gloire* sported a 'zebra' camouflage scheme unique among Allied navies.

Bougainville Class were intended for colonial service but proved very handy escorts, while the 2nd Class *Elan* and *Chamois* Class were a welcome reinforcement to the Royal Navy and the Free French Navy in mid-1940.

Weapons and Equipment

The French Navy followed a separate line of development in all its weapons. Its most valuable contribution was the invention of colour-indicators in shells, so that two ships firing at the same target could distinguish their fall of shot more easily. As one story had it, in the spring of 1940 a French warship signalled to her British opposite number, 'what colour do you want to fire?'. When the British ship replied that she did not understand, the Frenchman said, 'You fire white, then'.

Some of the more modern French gun-mountings were complex and fragile, particularly the new 5·5-inch twin mounting, and the remorseless quest for novelty sometimes resulted in progress backwards. The torpedoes suffered from difficulties with gyro-angling, but the special 15·7-inch (400-mm) torpedoes intended for use against merchant shipping proved a dismal failure. When the *Beveziers* torpedoed the British battleship *Resolution* off Dakar in 1940 the report on the damage stated that the Admiralty could only hope that German torpedoes were as ineffective as the French variety had been.

NAVAL OPERATIONS
SEPTEMBER 1939-DECEMBER 1941

BELOW: A British battleship of the *King George V* Class with her destroyer escort.

THE ATLANTIC 1940-41

BOTTOM: The British and Canadian navies built some 300 corvettes of the 'Flower' Class for escort duties in the Atlantic. HMCS *Cobalt*, seen in an Icelandic harbour, had one 4-inch gun and a speed of 16 knots.

BELOW RIGHT: The submarine *Snapper* sank four German ships in the Norwegian campaign and is seen here landing prisoners.

BOTTOM RIGHT: HM Submarine *Severn* was one of three fast ocean-going submarines built in the 1930s. She torpedoed the German battlecruiser *Gneisenau* in the Norwegian campaign, putting her out of action for months.

The naval war began in earnest on the morning of September 3, 1939, only hours after the expiry of the Anglo-French ultimatum. The liner *Athenia* was torpedoed by *U.30*, one of the 21 U-Boats already at sea and stationed between Gibraltar and the Irish Sea. The sinking was contrary to Hitler's orders, for he was anxious at this early stage not to alarm neutral opinion, but it proved to the British that the hopes about avoiding a repetition of the World War I holocaust of shipping were futile.

The lessons of 1917 had been learned well, and the Trade Division of the Admiralty had drawn up detailed plans for a convoy system and arming of merchant ships, but as we have already seen there was a serious shortage of escorts.

The first step was to set up a patrol line of cruisers between the Orkneys and Greenland, to prevent German warships from slipping out into the Atlantic and to intercept any merchant ships, German or neutral, carrying material to Germany. Just as in World War I liners were hurriedly armed as Armed Merchant Cruisers to relieve warships maintaining the Northern Patrol. But another important responsibility of the Royal Navy was to cover the crossing of the Army, the British Expeditionary Force, to France. By Oc-

tober 7, just over a month after the outbreak of war, 161,000 men, 24,000 vehicles and 140,000 tons of stores were transported across the Channel without loss. Apart from a few mines laid off Dover and Weymouth, neither of them ports of embarkation, the German Navy made no attempt to hinder this great movement of its enemy's main land forces. By June 1940 the total grew to 500,000 men, but not until the evacuation did the Germans try to disrupt this traffic with light surface units.

Units of the German Navy were attacked by RAF bombers, the *Scharnhorst* and *Gneisenau* at Brunsbüttel and the *Emden* off Wilhelmshaven, but the techniques were still too crude to achieve any results. Other attacks showed that neither the RAF nor the Luftwaffe had given sufficient thought to sinking warships, part of the problem being the lack of suitable armour-piercing bombs. The submarine patrols were more effective, for as we have seen, a U-Boat sank the aircraft carrier *Courageous* on September 17, and *U.47* penetrated Scapa Flow to sink the battleship *Royal Oak* a month later. Although this was hardly a severe dent in the overall strength of the British Navy as the *Royal Oak* was an obsolescent unit, it had

the important strategic effect of forcing the Home Fleet to desert its main base at Scapa Flow, until the defences could be brought up to date.

This was a marvellous opportunity for the German Navy had it been able to seize it, for the British were not well placed to intercept German sorties from extemporised bases on the west coast of Scotland. Furthermore the menace of the new German magnetic mine threatened these bases, and the new cruiser *Belfast* was badly damaged off Rosyth in the Firth of Forth and the *Nelson*, flagship of Admiral Forbes, the Home Fleet C-in-C, was put out of action in Loch Ewe.

The German High Command was aware of the British problems, and dispatched the battlecruisers *Scharnhorst* and *Gneisenau* on a raid into the Atlantic on the morning of November 21. In the circumstances it is not surprising that the British failed to intercept them. The first intimation was a sighting report from the armed merchant cruiser *Rawalpindi*, which stated erroneously that she was under attack from a pocket battleship, believed to be the *Deutschland*. The mistake was understandable as German capital ships bore a remarkable resemblance to one another, but as the Admiralty already

Allied Hunting Groups (Force F to N)

Force F British heavy cruisers *Berwick* and *York*.
Force G British cruisers *Exeter*, *Cumberland*, *Ajax* and *Achilles*.
Force H British cruisers *Sussex* and *Shropshire*.
Force I British carrier *Eagle* and cruisers *Cornwall* and *Dorsetshire*.
Force K British battlecruiser *Renown* and carrier *Ark Royal*.

Force L French battlecruiser *Dunkerque*, carrier *Béarn* and three French 6-inch gun cruisers.
Force M Two French heavy cruisers.
Force N French battlecruiser *Strasbourg* and British carrier *Hermes*.

knew that two pocket battleships were in the Atlantic, it was assumed that the attacker was trying to get home. The gallant *Rawalpindi*, with her obsolescent 6-inch guns from World War I, and her vast unprotected bulk, fought for fourteen minutes, but obtained a hit on the *Scharnhorst* at 8000 yards before sinking. The moves of the Home Fleet to intercept the German ships were rapidly deciphered by the 'B-Dienst', and they returned to their bases safely. Against such a gloomy background the British were already heartened by the news that three cruisers had brought the pocket battleship *Graf Spee* to action off Montevideo.

The Battle of the River Plate on December 13, 1939 has been discussed earlier, but its broad strategic effect was more important than the mere scuttling of one German ship might suggest. The *Deutschland* and *Graf Spee* between them had tied down a large number of Allied ships. In October there had been eight Hunting Groups (Force F to N) (above).

These hunting groups ranged from the West Indies down to the Cape of Good Hope and as far as Ceylon in an attempt to locate the German raiders.

As soon as the news of the Battle of the River Plate came through the strain on the

RIGHT: The slim funnels betray the American origin of a 'four-stacker' destroyer of the Royal Navy in the Atlantic in the autumn of 1940.

British and French squadrons was reduced. In any case the *Deutschland* had been recalled on November 1, after she had sunk only one ship. Even the *Graf Spee* had taken two-and-a-half months to sink only nine ships totalling 50,000 tons. This was hardly a princely return, and the two pocket battleships had caused great concern but they had never come near to disrupting Allied shipping. Although the Germans had paid lip service to the value of commerce raiding in their planning, they cannot be said to have prosecuted the idea with much vigour, and by December 1939 the distant oceans were firmly under British control.

In home waters the beginning of 1940 saw greater activity on both sides. The British were anxious to disrupt the flow of iron ore from Norwegian ports to Germany, but as Norway was a friendly neutral nothing could be done until such time as the Germans showed that they were violating Norwegian neutrality. German destroyers laid mines off the east coast of England in January, and as these night raids were undetected the minefields soon caused casualties and disruption of coastal shipping. German propaganda boasted a new secret weapon, the magnetic mine, but the Germans would not have been happy to know the truth. The British had been developing magnetic mines since 1918, and were only holding back their own version to avoid giving away its secrets prematurely. When the first German magnetic mine was recovered intact the Royal Navy's mine warfare experts were delighted to find that its firing mechanism was far more primitive than the latest British device.

German inhibitions about using their U-Boats vanished rapidly and by the beginning of 1940 a virtual sink on sight policy was in force around the British Isles. To meet the urgent need for escorts a large number of trawlers were taken up and converted to anti-submarine vessels, and in April 1940 the first of the 56 'Flower' Class corvettes came into service. But an apparent lull in the submarine campaign in the spring of 1940 was not

LEFT: The lookout of an escort destroyer reports a sighting from his masthead position.

BELOW: HMCS *Clayoquot* was a Canadian fleet minesweeper of the *Bangor* Class. These handy little ships were also used as anti-submarine escorts.

Force L
Dunkerque (B/c)
Béarn (A/c)
3 French cruisers

Force F
Berwick (C)
York (C)

Forces M and N
Hermes (A/c)
2 French cruisers

Force K
Renown (B/c)
Ark Royal (A/c)

Force Y
Strasbourg (B)
Neptune (C)

Record of the Graf Spee's activities

30 Sept	Clement sunk
5 Oct	Newton Beech boarded
7 Oct	„ sunk
7 Oct	Ashlea sunk
10 Oct	Huntsman boarded
17 „	„ sunk
22 Oct	Trevanion sunk
14 Nov	Holland sighted
15 Nov	Africa Shell sunk
16 Nov	Mapia stopped
2 Dec	Doric Star sunk
3 Dec	Tairoa sunk
7 Dec	Streonshalh sunk

WILHELMSHAVEN
21 August 1939
Graf Spee sails

**13 December
'Battle of the River Plate'**

Force G
Cumberland (C)
Exeter (C)
Ajax (C)
Achilles (C)

Force H
Sussex (C)
Shropshire (C)

23 Dec 1939/21 Jan 1940
Waiting area 'Altmark'

Force H   CRUISE OF THE GRAF SPEE
          BRITISH HUNTING GROUP
          A/c = Aircraft carrier
          B/c = Battle cruiser
          C = Cruiser

Mercator's projection

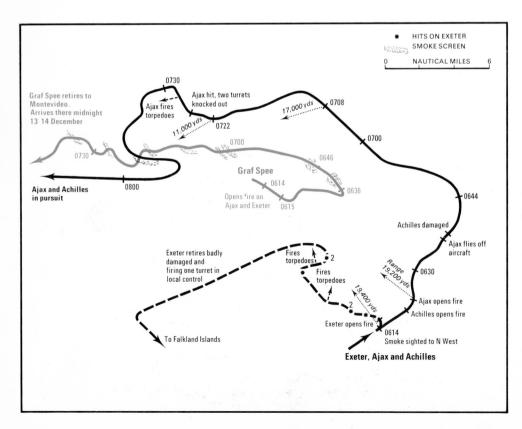

HITS ON EXETER
SMOKE SCREEN
0   NAUTICAL MILES   6

Graf Spee retires to
Montevideo.
Arrives there midnight
13/14 December

Ajax hit, two turrets
knocked out

Ajax fires torpedoes

17,000 yds   0708

11,000 yds   0722

0700

0730

0646

0800

Graf Spee

0700

0614   0636

Opens fire on
Ajax and Exeter   0615

**Ajax and Achilles
in pursuit**

Achilles damaged

Ajax flies off
aircraft

Exeter retires badly
damaged and
firing one turret in
local control

Fires
torpedoes   2

Fires
torpedoes

Range
19,200 yds

0630

19,400 yds

2

To Falkland Islands

Ajax opens fire
Achilles opens fire

Exeter opens fire   0614
                     Smoke sighted to N West

Exeter, Ajax and Achilles

BELOW: Destroyer gunners
stand by to load a 4-inch shell
into the breech.

caused by British and French counter-measures but by the withdrawal of the U-Boats for regrouping prior to the attack on Norway.

British attention had been focused on Norway for some time, particularly after the *Altmark* incident had shown how difficult it was for the Norwegians to police their own territorial waters. This German fleet oiler had been refuelling the *Graf Spee* in the South Atlantic the previous year, but she had parted company with the pocket battleship before the Battle of the River Plate, taking nearly 300 British prisoners with her. She was lucky to make her bid to return to Germany during the bad winter weather of January 1940, and passed between the Faeröes and Iceland undetected to reach Trondheim on February 14. She was sighted by two RAF Hudson aircraft. Captain Philip Vian RN, Captain (D) of the 4th Destroyer Flotilla in HMS *Cossack* picked her up four miles off the Egerö Light. After some diplomatic haggling the Admiralty ordered the *Cossack* to pursue the *Altmark* into Jössing Fjord and to release the prisoners. The destroyer boarded the oiler in traditional style, but after the prisoners were released the *Altmark* was released to proceed on her way to Germany, despite the proof of her breach of neutrality.

With the Home Fleet moving back to Scapa Flow in March the Admiralty felt more confident, and the *Altmark* incident provided a fresh incentive to tackle the

BELOW: An air lookout scans the sky from his position. The ship is an ex-American 'four-stacker' destroyer and the weapon in the foreground is an anti-aircraft machine gun.

BELOW: Ratings carry out maintenance work on torpedoes. These complicated weapons needed constant attention to keep them in running order.

problem of the Norwegian iron ore traffic. During the winter months, when the Baltic was frozen, an estimated nine million tons of Swedish ore, about 70 per cent of Germany's imports, passed from the Norwegian port of Narvik through the 'Inner Leads' to the Skagerrak. Winston Churchill, then the First Lord of the Admiralty, repeatedly demanded that the Navy be allowed to cut off this vital supply-line and so, finally, Operation Wilfred, a plan to lay mines in the Inner Leads, was sanctioned at the end of March. Unfortunately for the British the Germans also had plans for Norway, and they were moving to forestall any British move.

The invasion of Norway was carried out with great precision, and when the risks of the operation are considered, the German Navy can be considered lucky in that the British were taken as badly by surprise as the luckless Norwegians. Despite the fact that a Polish submarine, *Orzel*, one of two which fled to England on the outbreak of war, torpedoed a troop transport on the way to Bergen, no attention was paid to the news in London and Oslo. The German forces landed successfully at Trondheim, Bergen and Narvik, but at Kristiansand a stout-hearted crew of elderly reservists stood by their coastal guns and riddled the heavy cruiser *Blücher* at point-blank range. At Bergen the shore batteries damaged the light cruiser *Königsberg*, and in a brilliant opportunist attack the next day, a group of Fleet Air Arm Skuas sank her with bombs. This was the first war-

BELOW: To improve the anti-aircraft capability of destroyers the Royal Navy introduced a new 55° elevation 4.7-inch gun in 1941. With radar control and power operation it proved a sturdy and reliable weapon which remained in service for many years.

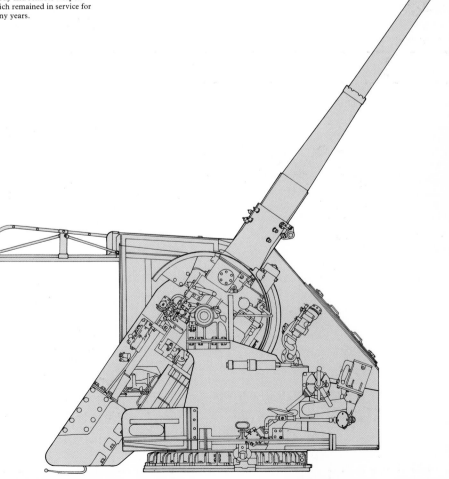

BELOW: The British submarine *Sturgeon* returns to base after a successful operation off Denmark in September 1940.

German Losses In The Norwegian Campaign

1 Heavy Cruiser *Blücher*
2 Light Cruisers *Königsberg* and *Karlsruhe*
10 Destroyers

ship to be sunk by dive bombing, and it is all the more remarkable as the Skuas were operating from the Orkneys, at the extreme limit of their endurance.

Although caught flat-footed by the German attacks, the Royal Navy was quick to react. Early on the morning of April 9 the battlecruiser *Renown* and nine destroyers sighted the *Scharnhorst* and *Gneisenau* through intermittent snow squalls. The *Renown* opened fire with her 15-inch guns at a range of nine miles, taking the Germans completely by surprise. Although both turned to engage the British ship it was the *Renown* which scored first by knocking out the *Gneisenau's* main fire control. Mindful of Hitler's strict injunction against sustaining damage in action, Admiral Lütjens tried to break off the action, but the 26-year old *Renown* pursued her and landed another hit on *Gneisenau's* forward turret, and a third hit aft. Although the *Renown* was hit twice by 11-inch shells her damage was negligible, and the vigour of Admiral Whitworth's pursuit kept the initiative firmly in his hands, and the two German ships were robbed of what could

have been a comparatively easy victory.

The C-in-C Home Fleet, once his forces were concentrated, ordered the 2nd Destroyer Flotilla under Captain Warburton-Lee to 'send some destroyers up to Narvik, to make certain that no troops land'. This was the prelude to the First Battle of Narvik, in which five destroyers steamed all the way up the winding Ofot Fjord to attack what they thought were six large German destroyers. In fact the odds were greater, as there were ten German ships, and in the ensuing action the British destroyers sank the Commodore's ship *Wilhelm Heidkamp* and the *Anton Schmidt*, and damaged five more, as well as a number of transports. It was a fierce action with gun-fire and torpedo-explosions echoing around the Fjord, and the British lost the *Hardy* and the *Hunter*, while the *Hotspur* was damaged. But the Germans had been badly mauled. As the British sank their ammunition ship on the way out, the survivors were in a desperate situation, low on ammunition and certain that the British were still outside.

Three days later, on April 13, Admiral

Whitworth, now flying his flag in the battleship *Warspite*, took nine destroyers into Ofot Fjord once more to finish the work started by the 2nd Flotilla. In the Second Battle of Narvik the German destroyers were harried to destruction, with the *Warspite's* 15-inch salvoes booming out in support. Although there was a risk in taking so large a ship up a badly charted fjord, the *Warspite's* aircraft did valuable reconnaissance for the destroyers and even sank a U-Boat. But the success was of little use to the British and French, whose hurriedly organised expeditionary force was shortly to be evacuated in the face of German air superiority. Also, it was now May, and the news that German forces had attacked in the Lowlands made any further adventures in Norway not only foolhardy but positively dangerous to the Allied strategic plans.

Submarines played an important part in the Allied naval effort in Norway, in giving warning of enemy ship movements and in attacking ships. One of the last blows of the campaign was struck by the submarine *Clyde* on June 20, when she hit the *Gneisenau* with a torpedo. Aircraft car-

State Of Readiness In August 1940

Gneisenau	Torpedoed, under repair, not ready before November.
Scharnhorst	Torpedoed, under repair, not ready before October
Admiral Scheer	Refitting, to be ready by September.
Lützow ex-Deutschland	Refitting, to be ready April 1941.
Prinz Eugen	In commission.
Admiral Hipper	Refitting, to be ready September.
Nürnberg	In commission.
Leipzig	Under repair since December 1939, to be ready November.
Köln	In commission.
Emden	In commission for training duties.
1 von Roeder Class	In commission.
8 Leberecht Maass Class destroyers	3 refitting.
20 Torpedo Boats	1 completing, to be ready October.
35 MTBs	12 refitting.

riers provided invaluable air support to the troops ashore and it was all the more tragic that the *Glorious* was trapped by the *Scharnhorst* and *Gneisenau* while evacuating the aircraft and RAF personnel from northern Norway. The carrier was quickly sunk and the loss of life was heavy, but one of her two escorting destroyers managed to torpedo the *Scharnhorst* before going down.

The Norwegian campaign was muddled, and it seemed at the time that British and French warships had been needlessly risked in an ill-conceived operation which had little to do with winning the war. The heavy losses suffered by the German Navy were a crucial factor in the following months when ships were needed to support the invasion of England. The following table (above left) shows how badly the German Navy fared in the Norwegian campaign.

Up to this point the Anglo-French naval strategy seemed to be working well, for despite some losses to U-Boat and aircraft attack the Allies' total strength was growing each month. The campaign in Norway had been disappointing, but the

Allies' control of the sea had enabled them to extricate their ground forces. Italy was still neutral, and so the Mediterranean Fleet was able to provide reinforcements for the Home Fleet. As soon as the new battleships, aircraft carriers and escorts were ready the British would be in a much stronger position. But this optimism was not justified, and the situation was shortly to change disastrously.

The opening of the German Army's offensive in the West in the early hours of May 10, 1940 was followed by the swift dissolution of the Anglo-French ground forces, which fell back under the hammer-blows of German armoured columns. Even before the full-scale of the disaster became apparent the British War Cabinet ordered the Royal Navy to evacuate the remainder of the troops from Norway, and at the same time the Admiralty reinforced its light squadrons in the south.

The Nore Command, covering the southern part of the North Sea and the eastern part of the English Channel, had contingency plans for the evacuation of personnel from Holland and Belgium, and so its reaction was swift and effective. The

Dutch Army surrendered on May 15, 1940, but eight days earlier British destroyers had taken demolition parties to the principal Dutch ports. In the days following the Dutch Royal Family was evacuated, the bullion reserves were carried to England, and the demolition of oil tanks, lock-gates and other vital installations were accomplished. The French Navy's *Amiral Nord*, Vice-Admiral Abrial, took responsibility for the blocking of Antwerp and operations off the Belgian coast. The cost was heavy, for the ships were operating in heavily mined waters and under constant air attack from the Luftwaffe.

On May 19 the Admiralty had the first request from the War Cabinet for its advice on the possibility of withdrawing the entire British Expeditionary Force from France, and next day an emergency meeting was held with Admiral Ramsay, the Flag Officer Dover. The word 'miracle' has been used of the Dunkirk evacuation, but it was a miracle of planning rather than luck, and it is no coincidence that Ramsay also planned the naval side of the Normandy landings four years later. Under the code-name 'Operation Dynamo' Ramsay gathered all the ships that could be spared – destroyers, minesweepers, cross-channel transports, coasters etc – and meticulously planned the mechanics of lifting an army of some 400,000 men. At the same time he ran in ammunition and supplies at the rate of 2000 tons each day to the British Army's new base on the French coast, Dunkirk. This small Channel port was not suitable for the job, but other ports were now far away, and in any case the German advance had cut the original supply route.

There is insufficient space to tell the whole story of 'Dynamo' but the figures give some impression of the achievement. On Monday, May 27, the second day of the evacuation, over 7000 men had been taken off, and the next day the flow speeded up, especially after fifty Dutch 'Schuyts' or fishing craft were sent in. By Wednesday, May 29, the total rose to 47,300 men. Naval officers were ashore supervising the evacuation, and this helped to reduce the chaos. It must be remembered that Dunkirk was still functioning as a bridgehead, with a fierce battle raging around the perimeter and a constant bombardment from artillery and aircraft. When the destroyer *Shikari* left Dunkirk at 0340 on June 4, 'Dynamo' had accomplished the rescue of 338,226 men of the British and French armies. Six British and three French destroyers were sunk, with eight personnel ships. Out of 848 known craft 72 were sunk by enemy action, 163 were sunk in collision or other accidents and 45 were damaged.

Why did the Germans fail at Dunkirk? They had an army trapped, they had air superiority, and they had an overwhelming preponderance of tanks and artillery. Yet they failed to pinch off the bridgehead and failed to interrupt the evacuation to any extent. The answers are not obvious, but they are important. In the first place, the British and French troops of the rearguard fought an heroic battle to hold the perimeter, and while both sides were fatigued the British and French fought with desperation, whereas the Germans felt that a short delay would not alter the outcome. Second, the German armoured formations were out of fuel and showed signs of wear and tear after two weeks constantly on the move. Had they pushed around the flanks of their perimeter they would have come under fire from the large number of destroyers stationed there for just that purpose. Third, and most important of all, the Luftwaffe had done little training in attacks on shipping. The ships at Dunkirk were in the worst position, crowded in a small harbour or picking their way through a tortuous channel to avoid sandbanks and minefields with their decks crowded with soldiers, yet only a small number were sunk. In passing it is important to correct the impression that Dunkirk was a matter of 'little ships'. The hundreds of small craft which went over

BELOW: MGB-502 and a sister in line ahead.

to Dunkirk played a very important part in ferrying troops out to the high-capacity ships like destroyers and cross-channel steamers, but they did not ferry thousands of soldiers across the Channel. Destroyers took off the most men, followed by the personnel ships.

The evacuation from Dunkirk did not end the Royal Navy's involvement with France. 'Operation Aerial' and 'Operation Cycle' evacuated another 191,000 men from the ports of the Bay of Biscay and north-west France between June 16 and June 26. As many French warships as possible were brought out of the naval dockyards, and the new battleships *Richelieu* and *Jean Bart* went to Dakar and Casablanca. Two old battleships, four destroyers, seven submarines and a number of small warships reached England. But the majority of French warships were at Toulon or in North Africa when the French Government sued for an armistice, and this was construed in London as an even bigger threat to Britain than the occupation of the Channel ports. As seen by the Admiralty and the War Cabinet the assurances from Marshal Pétain and Admiral Darlan that no French warship would fall into German hands were in contradiction of the armistice provisions that the French Fleet would be demobilised and disarmed under German or Italian control. Moreover, there was good reason to think that the French might be unable to prevent the Germans from seiz-

ing their ships. In Toulon there were only four heavy cruisers, but at Algiers there were six *Galissonière* Class cruisers, and four capital ships, a seaplane carrier and six large destroyers at Mers-el-Kebir. If these ships fell into German or Italian hands the British would be unable to hold the Mediterranean, and their whole maritime strategy would be jeopardised.

The attitude of the Italian Government had been threatening throughout May, and so the Admiralty had sent timely reinforcements to the Mediterranean. The Italians finally showed their hand by declaring war on France and Great Britain on June 10, and so any misgivings on the British side about the 'ownership' of the

French warships in North Africa are easy to understand. The campaigns in the Mediterranean will be covered later, but the elimination of the French Fleet completely altered the situation in the Atlantic as well. Warships and merchant ships which could not easily be spared had to be diverted to the Mediterranean, but what was even worse was that the German U-Boats now had bases opposite the British Isles, from the North Sea down to the Bay of Biscay. Within days of the fall of France road convoys were on their way from Kiel with all the spare torpedoes and gear necessary to set up forward bases in France, and before the end of August the Italians had set up their BETASOM command at Bordeaux to support an eventual total of 27 submarines. At a stroke, the U-Boats had outflanked the Royal Navy by eliminating the need to make a long voyage to their patrol areas, and had virtually doubled their effectiveness against the convoys in the Western Approaches to Britain.

The Battle of the Atlantic began at this point, and it was to last until the very moment of surrender in May 1945, but for the moment the Royal Navy was more concerned with the outcome of the Battle of Britain, or to be more precise, the German invasion threat. Dunkirk may have rescued the British Army, but it was an army stripped of tanks, artillery and even rifles, and so the German Army inevitably jumped at the idea of invading the British Isles. 'Operation Sealion' had its origins in a tentative proposal by Admiral Raeder to Hitler on May 21, but this was turned down as impossible. The directive from Hitler did not appear until July 16, with its well-known preamble, 'since England, in spite of her militarily hopeless position shows no signs of coming to terms, I have decided to prepare a landing operation . . . and, if necessary, to carry it out'.

Much has been made of the invasion plans of 1940, with some commentators even claiming that the British only escaped because Hitler did not genuinely believe in 'Sealion'. This is an absurd over-simplification of the facts, which are

that the Germans spent a great deal of energy to accomplish their project, and that there were a number of factors adding up to disaster for them if they had launched it. The most obvious factor was the Luftwaffe's failure to subdue the RAF, but even more important was the failure by the German air and land commanders to take account of the facts of sea power. For a start the German Navy was in a badly weakened condition after the Norwegian campaign, and could not neutralise the Royal Navy by any means. Second, the Royal Navy, although it had suffered losses at Dunkirk, had an overwhelming preponderance of ships available in its own home waters, and could be counted on to attack any invasion force which appeared. Those who accept Marshal Göring's view that the Luftwaffe could win alone must remember that the Luftwaffe was fully committed to an unsuccessful attempt to destroy the RAF, and in any case had shown little or no aptitude for sinking warships at sea.

Another drawback to 'Sealion' was that the German Army had no experience of an amphibious operation, and allowed far too little time, a month, for the planning. In the words of Germany's most eminent naval historian, the Army thought of the English Channel as nothing more than a river which was too wide for a pontoon bridge. But the Channel is not a river, and it is, moreover, one of the most treacherous areas of water on the north-west coast of Europe, liable to sudden squalls and storms. As the Germans had to rely largely on river barges converted to landing craft, they faced a possibility of disas-

ter in mid-Channel even without the help of the Royal Navy. The strongest opposition to 'Sealion' came from the German Navy, whose planners showed more awareness of the problems and the weaknesses of the plan. The initial plan was for a broad front landing between Ramsgate and the Isle of Wight. When the Kriegsmarine pointed out that a simultaneous landing was not possible at both ends of the bridgehead because of differences in tides, they were airily told to choose places where the tides *were* simultaneous! After much futile wrangling of this order, with the naval side patiently explaining the fundamental differences between land and sea, it was agreed that there would be four separate landings between Folkestone and Selsey Bill, but at the end of August both sides were still arguing over the details.

The British were not unaware of these preparations, and every night bombers raided the invasion ports from Delfzijl to Boulogne. British warships of the Nore Command, including the battleship *Revenge* and the 15-inch gunned monitor

BELOW: Ratings carry 3-inch shells aboard a British submarine. In a gun-action the shells would be passed up through the same hatch to the gun-crew.

BELOW: The British submarine *Sterlet* heads out to sea. Pre-war submarines had little or no provision for anti-aircraft defence, but during the war most British boats were given a platform at the after end of the conning tower to carry a 20-mm Oerlikon gun.

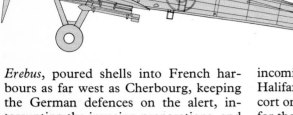

LEFT: The Fairey Swordfish torpedo-bomber dated from 1936, despite its antique look. Although slow it had outstanding ruggedness and manoeuvrability and could fly and operate from carriers in conditions which defeated more modern aircraft. It established a record by remaining in production longer than any other Allied plane in World War II, and proved ideal as an anti-submarine and anti-shipping aircraft when armed with 60-lb rockets.

Erebus, poured shells into French harbours as far west as Cherbourg, keeping the German defences on the alert, interrupting the invasion preparations, and also giving an unmistakable reminder of the perils awaiting the invasion force if it ever dared to put to sea.

In 1803 Lord St Vincent said to the British Parliament, 'I do not say the French cannot come, only that they cannot come by sea', and in October 1940 the Commander-in-Chief of the Home Fleet, Admiral Forbes, spoke in a similar vein to Winston Churchill, the Prime Minister: 'While we are predominant at sea and until Germany has defeated our fighter force, invasion by sea is not a practical operation of war'. Forbes reminded Churchill that it was possible to work out the likeliest invasion targets:

1. they must be within range of shore-based fighters, which limited the choice;
2. an invasion could not be sustained through the winter months without the capture of a port, all of which were strongly defended;
3. a sudden raid under cover of fog would not only be impossible to plan for, with only five foggy days a month on average, but would also be highly dangerous for the invaders.

Forbes was not believed at the time, but it is interesting to see that 'Sealion' had been postponed on September 17, and on October 12 it was deferred for 'reconsideration' in the spring of 1941. As the battle for air supremacy went against the Luftwaffe, it became clearer to the British that they could return to their previous naval dispositions to guarantee the import of raw materials, food and munitions. Incredible as it may seem the British were planning for a return to Europe as early as July 1940, when Churchill gave orders to raid the coast of Occupied Europe. The first designs for tank landing craft were in hand the same month, a small portent of things to come.

The war in the Atlantic was of paramount importance from the summer of 1940 onwards. To cope with the new conditions the organisation of escorts was radically changed. Up to the end of May convoys were only escorted to a point 200 miles west of Ireland, but between July and October the limit was extended to 19° west. From the dispersal point the convoy sailed in company for another 24 hours and then dispersed, while its escort moved to a new rendezvous to meet an incoming convoy. The Canadian Navy's Halifax Escort Force provided a local escort on the other side of the Atlantic, but for the major part of the voyage a convoy relied on a single escort, usually an armed merchant cruiser. Increasing the escorts was very necessary, but it put an immense strain on the hard-pressed British and Canadian Navies.

The most pressing problem was simply numbers of escorts. Until the new corvettes built in Britain and Canada were available in greater numbers the destroyers would have to bear the brunt, but in September 1940, a year after war broke out, the total of British destroyers had dropped from 184 to 171, as only 21 new ships had replaced the 34 sunk. Nearly half of the strength was under repair as a result of damage of one sort or another. It was at this moment that President Roosevelt committed the United States to a remarkable gesture of friendship. In exchange for a 99-year lease on base rights in Newfoundland and the West Indies, the US Navy lent 50 elderly destroyers and other war equipment such as rifles to re-equip the British Army.

These destroyers, known as 'flush-deckers' to the USN and 'four-pipers' to the RN on account of their unusual appearance, had appeared at the end of World War I, but despite their age they were just what the British needed. With some guns and torpedo-tubes replaced by depth-charges they were quickly turned into escorts, and provided a useful stop-gap until new construction was ready. Six joined the RCN, and the rest went to the RN. To commemorate their American origin they were named after towns common to the British Commonwealth and the USA. The British 'V&W' destroyers of the same vintage underwent similar alterations to suit them for Atlantic escort, but in all destroyers the problem was shortage of fuel. They were intended for high-speed dashes at the enemy battle fleet, and in the course of a normal convoy operation soon ran short of fuel. A dash to investigate a sighting or underwater contact was a constant requirement which drained fuel. Even depth-charges ran out if a convoy action continued, and it became necessary to send replenishment tankers with the convoys to provide fuel and depth-charges for the escorts.

The U-Boats were also perfecting their tactics. Once the bases in France were set up Admiral Dönitz was able to reintroduce his 'wolf pack' or *rudeltaktik* concept, a deadly answer to the British convoy. This was an extension of an idea first tried in 1918, whereby a U-Boat which sighted a convoy did not attack. Instead she signalled the convoy's position, numbers and course to U-Boat HQ. From Lorient U-Boat HQ messages went out to all U-Boats within reach, ordering them to rendezvous with the original U-Boat which was still shadowing the convoy, and only when the whole pack was together did the attack begin. These tactics were first introduced in October 1940, and they were ruthlessly effective.

A night attack on a convoy was a terrifying experience, with ships exploding in the darkness as the U-Boats came in from all points of the compass. Often the escorts were reduced to chasing from one sinking ship to another. Only daylight brought a respite as the U-Boats withdrew to reload their torpedo-tubes and report to Lorient on the night's work. As the U-Boats could now cruise beyond the range of the existing escorts and aircraft, they were able to sink 2,186,000 tons of shipping by December 1940. Long-range Focke-Wulf Kondor (FW-200) aircraft appeared in August and began to attack shipping as well as providing reconnaissance for the U-Boats.

The only effective answer to this grave situation was to strengthen the convoy escorts as fast as possible. Unfortunately the RAF treated Coastal Command as something of a Cinderella, and its average daily strength had only risen from 170 to 226 aircraft after a year at war. Nor was co-operation with the Navy all that it might be. It was a long time before the right degree of intregrated sea-and-air command was set up. The escorts had their Asdic detection sets and depth-charges, but Coastal Command started in 1939 with an anti-submarine bomb which was more likely to bounce back at the aircraft than sink a U-Boat. A hurriedly adapted Mark VII naval depth-charge remedied this defect, but aircraft had nothing but the eyesight of the aircrew to help them. Aircraft had one great advantage against submarines. They could force them to submerge, and so the presence of aircraft of any sort was always helpful to a convoy.

The U-Boats went a stage further in their night attacks. By attacking on the surface they found immunity from the escorts' Asdic sets, and as the conning tower of a trimmed down U-Boat is very small most lookouts failed to spot them. The high surface speed of a U-Boat gave it freedom to race ahead of the convoy to position itself for an attack or to take evas-

Atlantic Shipping Losses, 1940-41

	Month	Shipping Sunk Tons	Number of Ships	German U-Boats Operational	German U-Boats Sunk
1940	July	195,800	38	28	None
	August	267,600	56		None
	September	295,300	59		None
	October	352,400	63	27	1
	November	146,600	32		
	December	212,500	37		None
1941	January	126,700	21	22	None
	February	196,700	39		None
	March	243,000	41		6
	April	249,375	43	32	2
	May	325,400	58		1
	June	310,000	61		4
	July	94,200	22	65	1
	August	80,300	23		3
	September	202,800	53		2
	October	156,500	32	80	2
	November	62,100	13		5
	December	124,000	26		10

Causes Of Shipping Losses In 1941

	Tons	Number of ships		Tons	Number of ships
U-Boats	2,171,700	432	Raiders	226,500	44
Aircraft	1,017,400	371	E-Boats	58,800	29
Mines	230,800	111	Unknown	421,300	272
Warships	201,800	40	Total	4,328,300	1,299

ive action. Travelling at 17 knots a surfaced Type VII U-Boat could outrun the slower escorts, even if spotted. What was even more worrying to the Admiralty was that this ascendancy had been achieved by an operational force of only 30 U-Boats. What would happen when the new spate of U-Boats came into service?

The first answer to the night attacks on the surface was to equip escorts and merchantmen with powerful illuminant rocket-flares, known as 'Snowflakes', but what was really needed was an efficient radar set. A new type of radar set, Type 271, was rapidly produced, and went to sea in a corvette in May 1941. As it gave high definition of even the smallest target, it rapidly stopped the surface tactics of the U-Boats. Another important countermeasure was to fit high-frequency direction-finding radio sets in escorts. This enabled escorts to exploit the inherent weakness of the wolf-pack system, the need for signalling between Lorient and the shadowers, between a shadower and the gathering pack, and finally the largely unnecessary signalling back to Lorient of situation reports and estimates of tonnage sunk. Two ships fitted with 'Huff-Duff', as it was known (from its abbreviation HF/DF), could get a fix on a U-Boat which was accurate to within a quarter of a mile, and HF/DF rapidly became as vital a part of an escort's armament as radar or asdic. The first set was ready in July 1941, and the device was quickly put into quantity production.

One of the problems affecting all navies in World War II was training. U-Boat crews trained in the Baltic principally, and a number of U-Boats were always non-operational for this reason. On the British side, a number of anti-submarine training schools were set up. The prewar ASW training school had been at Portland, but after the fall of France it was moved to Scotland and a second school was started at Campbeltown. But the most important establishment was a new sea training centre, HMS *Western Isles*, started at Tobermory in July 1940. Here each newly commissioned escort vessel underwent one month's intensive training before being sent to join her group. At Liverpool, the main escort base, a tactical school was set up to train officers in the latest U-Boat tactics. The groups tended to operate together, although rarely at their average full strength of eight ships. Breaking up a group was not an intelligent use of the training and tactical cohesion achieved by ships which worked together.

In February 1941 the importance of Liverpool was recognised, and the Western Approaches Command HQ was moved from Plymouth to Liverpool. A duplicate of the Admiralty's Trade Plot was set up, and a joint RN/RAF organisation was started to co-ordinate the work of No. 15 Group, Coastal Command. The British can be criticised for taking a year and a half to discover that a joint-service organisation was more efficient, but the Germans never came near to such co-operation, and their naval effort was always hampered by the spirit of Reich Marschal Göring's dictum: 'Everything that flies belongs to me!'

One problem remained intractable: how to get aircraft to sea in order to go the whole way with a convoy. A desperate solution at the time was to fit a few merchant ships with a catapult on the forecastle to allow them to catapult a Hurricane fighter off when a FW-200 Kondor was sighted. The rate of attrition was quite simply one Kondor for one Hurricane, as the fighter pilot could do nothing but ditch and hope that he was picked up by one of the escorts. In June 1941 the small aircraft carrier *Audacity* appeared. She was a former German banana boat, the *Hannover*, captured in 1940 and put into service under the British flag as SS *Empire Audacity*. She was turned into a flush-deck carrier by stripping her superstructure and adding a small wooden flight deck. Six fighter aircraft were parked at the after end, and smoke was led out through side ducts. The *Audacity* was ready in August, and although she lasted only three months before being sunk, she was completely successful in defending the Gibraltar convoys against Kondor aircraft. The Admiralty now had the answer to the 'Black Gap', the area in mid-Atlantic without air cover, and before the *Audacity* was sunk the US Navy had begun further conversions for the RN and itself. The idea was not new, and had been around since before the war, but the chronic shortage of aircraft in the Fleet Air Arm had prevented anything from being done sooner. *Audacity*'s aircraft were Grumman Martlets (later known to the British by its American name, the Wildcat), but for mid-Atlantic operations against submarines the veteran Swordfish biplane proved the best aircraft on account of its ruggedness and its ability to take off and land in all weather.

In some ways 1941 was a much more critical year for the British than 1940 particularly on the naval side. The Battle of the Atlantic was going in favour of the German Navy, despite all efforts, as the above table of losses shows.

Nor were U-Boats the only threat to shipping, for surface warships were at sea. As we have seen in the previous chapter raiders were active in the first half of 1941, but the sinking of the *Bismarck* in May brought that threat under control. Aircraft, mines and other causes combined to push the 1941 shipping losses to the staggering total of 4,000,000 tons.

Clearly the Germans were within sight of victory at sea, for if they could cut the British off from America, they could literally starve them into submission.

THE MEDITERRANEAN 1940-41

Although the numerical strength of the Italian Navy was impressive, up to the moment of France's surrender in June 1940 the Anglo-French position in the Mediterranean was strong. Reinforcements had been sent from other stations in May, and a French squadron comprising the battleship *Lorraine* and the cruisers *Duquesne*, *Tourville* and *Duguay Trouin* under Vice-Admiral Godfroy was sent to Alexandria to co-operate with Admiral Cunningham's Mediterranean Fleet, But, of course, the fall of France meant that these ships had to be interned and immobilised just at the time they could be of most use.

Alexandria is too far to the east to dominate the whole Mediterranean, and as Malta was too close to Italian air bases to allow a main fleet to use it, the Admiralty decided to reinforce Gibraltar. Late in June 1940 a powerful force under Vice-Admiral Sir James Somerville was formed, with the carrier *Ark Royal*, the battlecruiser *Hood*, battleships *Valiant* and *Resolution*, two cruisers and four destroyers. Known as Force 'H', its purpose was to guard the western Mediterranean and the convoy routes from Sierra Leone and Gibraltar. Even if no French warships fell into German hands, a sudden vacuum had been created by the removal of the French Navy.

The first task which fell to Force 'H' was the sad one of turning on the French warships which had lately been allies. The British Cabinet, faced with disaster on land, was determined not to be weak in the use of its last offensive weapon, the Royal Navy. Somerville was ordered to carry out 'Operation Catapult' on July 3, to ensure that the French warships were put beyond the control of Germany, peacefully if possible, but by force if necessary. Accordingly Force 'H' arrived off the main anchorage at Mers-el-Kebir and negotiations began between Somerville and Admiral Gensoul. The points put by the British were:

1. Put to sea and continue to fight against Germany.
2. Sail with reduced crews to a British port.
3. Sail with reduced crews to a port in the French West Indies, where they could be immobilised.
4. Scuttle all ships within six hours.

The first condition might well appeal to the fighting spirit of the French Navy, but it would be a violation of the armistice which could lead to reprisals against French civilians. The second condition might seem fair to the British, but the French can be forgiven for thinking that it carried as little weight as Hitler and Mussolini's promises not to lay hands on the French Fleet. The third condition was the most lenient, but even that was a violation of the armistice, and what was to prevent the British sending an expedition to the West Indies if the temptation proved too strong? The last condition was one which no naval officer could accept with honour, and nobody in London can have expected the French to act on it.

Somerville put another suggestion to Gensoul, that the ships be immobilised at Mers-el-Kebir. Unfortunately Somerville was not the soul of tact, and as the Admiralty's conditions were almost impossible to fulfil, i.e. that within six hours the ships be so immobilised that a year in a fully equipped dockyard would be needed to repair them, the French admiral announced that he would fight. The action that followed was brutally efficient as Force 'H' poured 15-inch shells into the congested anchorage. The battleship *Bretagne* blew up and the *Dunkerque* and *Provence* were seriously damaged, but the *Strasbourg* skilfully extricated herself under cover of a smoke screen and broke out of the trap. Although attacked three times by *Ark Royal*'s torpedo-bombers she and her destroyers reached Toulon safely.

BELOW: The British destroyer *Verity* takes on soldiers during the evacuation from Greece in 1941. Almost as soon as the British arrived they were forced back to Crete and eventually Egypt after the Wehrmacht saved Mussolini from defeat.

The British had achieved their purpose, to remind Germany and all influential neutrals, particularly the United States, that she was not on the point of defeat and did not lack the will to remove a threat to her sea power. But the price was heavy in French lives and alienated a large section of the French Navy. It is significant that Cunningham at Alexandria was able to persuade Godfroy to immobilise his ships, and no bloodshed occurred. In Cunningham the Royal Navy was to find a second Nelson, a flag officer with that inspiration and extra fire which goes far beyond mere ability. Like Nelson, too, Cunningham was to win his laurels in the Mediterranean in a series of classic battles. Cunningham was an aggressive leader who used his numerically inferior ships to the maximum effect, and his greatest achievements were with obsolescent ships and aircraft.

The Battle of Calabria on July 9, 1940 was the first rude shock administered to the Italian Navy, when the *Warspite* hit the battleship *Giulio Cesare* at the impressive range of 26,400 yards (15 miles). The *Royal Sovereign* and *Malaya* had supercharges for their 15-inch guns, as they lacked the added elevation given to *Warspite*'s guns, but being slower they never got within range. The chase was pushed to within 25 miles of the Italian coast, and although the Italians escaped without further damage, the British had established a moral ascendancy over their opponents which would stand them in good stead. Eleven days later came the news that the Australian cruiser HMAS *Sydney* had intercepted two Italian cruisers north of Crete. The *Bartolomeo Colleoni* was sunk in a running fight but the *Giovanni Delle Bande Nere* escaped with damage. This action showed how little advantage could be gained from the sort of speeds claimed for Italian cruisers. In theory the *Colleoni* had a five-knot advantage over the *Sydney*, but her sea speed was one knot *slower*, while the Australian ship had another three inches of side protection and more than an inch on the deck.

78

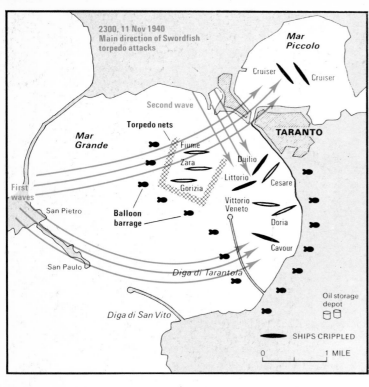

2300, 11 Nov 1940
Main direction of Swordfish
torpedo attacks

*Mar
Piccolo*

Cruiser   Cruiser

Second wave

Torpedo nets

*Mar
Grande*

Fiume

Zara   Duilio

Littorio   Cesare

Gorizia

First
waves

Vittorio
Veneto

San Pietro

Balloon
barrage

Doria

San Paulo

Cavour

Diga di Tarantola

Diga di San Vito

Oil storage
depot

SHIPS CRIPPLED

0   1 MILE

TARANTO

In August 1940 the arrival of the
carrier *Illustrious*, the newly modernised
battleship *Valiant* and two anti-aircraft
cruisers enabled the British to plan an
ambitious blow against the Italian Fleet.
By this time British and Commonwealth
troops had taken the offensive against the
Italians in the Desert, and it was essential
to keep them supplied with fuel and weapons, particularly tanks and artillery. The
safe route around the Cape of Good Hope
took months, and Churchill repeatedly
pressed the Admiralty to accept the risk of
passing a convoy through the Mediterranean to save time. But the stationing of
the Italian battle fleet at Taranto made
such a proposition too dangerous, and
Cunningham had to neutralise this fleet.
This was the strategic reasoning behind
the attack on Taranto.

On the night of November 11, 21 torpedo bombers flew off the *Illustrious* to
attack Taranto, and within a space of two
hours damaged the new battleship *Littorio*
and the *Caio Duilio*, and sank the *Conte di
Cavour*, all for the loss of two aircraft and
two aircrew. This was history in the
making, the first carrier strike against an
enemy fleet in its defended base, and it
showed how much could be achieved,
even with such slow aircraft as the
Swordfish. The lesson of Taranto was
learned diligently by the Japanese naval
air arm.

With two carriers under his command
Cunningham reasserted British control
over the Central Mediterranean very
quickly. Swordfish and Fulmar aircraft
attacked at random, dive-bombing, min-
ing and disrupting communications along
the North African coast. The Taranto raid
achieved one important but unspectacular
success when bombs wrecked the seaplane
base, thus eliminating a number of the

RIGHT: The inner harbour at
Taranto was attacked by British
torpedo bombers on November
11, 1940. Two damaged
cruisers of the *Trento* Class leak
oil over the harbour after the
strike.

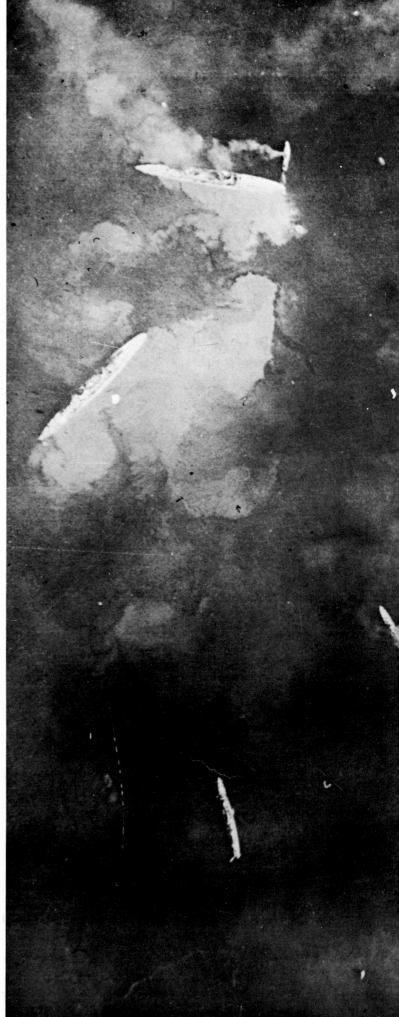

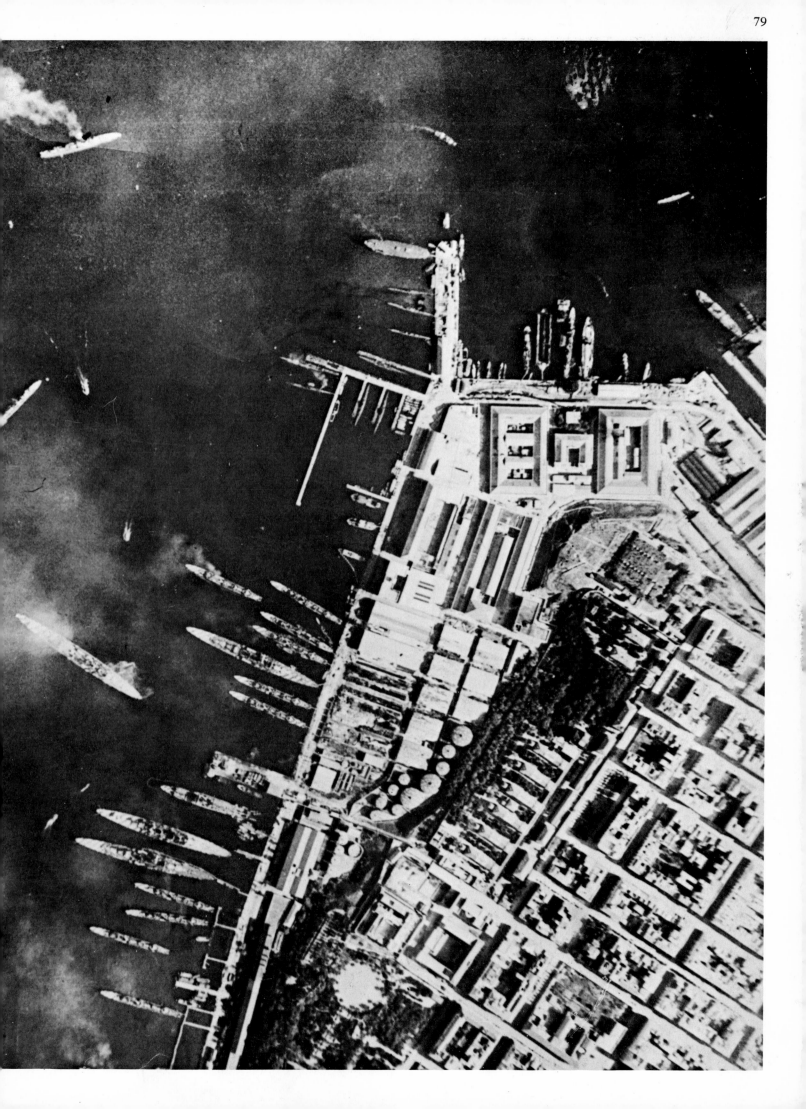

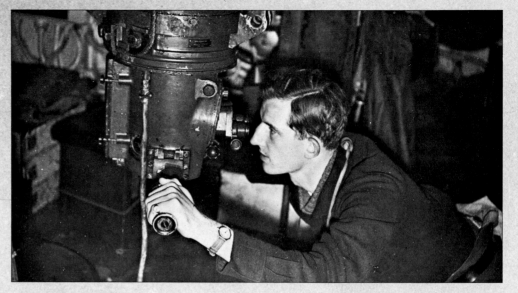

reconnaissance aircraft which had frustrated British moves. One squadron of Fulmars in *Illustrious* accounted for over 20 Italian shadowers and bombers, all for the loss of one aircraft, and from September 1940 to January 1941 no major British unit was damaged in a daylight air strike by Italian aircraft. This task was the one for which the British armoured deck carriers had been designed, and the *Illustrious* performed superbly in achieving local air superiority in the face of a land-based air force.

In November, just two weeks after Taranto, Force 'H' and a strong escort for a fast convoy to Alexandria met the Italian Fleet off Cape Spartivento, to the south of Sardinia. The action was disappointing to Admiral Somerville, but the three vital merchantmen got through without damage. Clearly Malta was the key to British success in holding the Mediterranean, contrary to prewar suggestions that it should be abandoned. Astride the

route through the Central Mediterranean, Malta was a base which could provide defence for ship-movements as well as a springboard for attacking the vulnerable communications between Italy and her North African armies. With this in mind the British built up a force of submarines at Malta and built up the island's defences as rapidly as possible.

The invasion of Greece by Italy in October 1940 forced the British to transfer troops from Egypt to Greece, and to meet this new commitment the Royal Navy set

BELOW: The Bristol Beaufort torpedo bomber was widely used in the Mediterranean for strikes against Axis shipping.

up an advanced base at Suda Bay in Crete. The British Cabinet took on such a major commitment with little apparent thought about how thinly stretched their armed forces were. Miracles were achieved in the Mediterranean between July and December 1940, but it was surely folly to launch a major land operation in the Balkans when the naval and air forces were over-stretched. Just how stretched they were can be gauged by the fact that even allowing for the Mediterranean Fleet's depredations, the presence of a submarine flotilla at Malta and a number of strikes by land-based aircraft from Malta and Egypt, the Italians passed over 690,000 tons of shipping to North African ports, and lost under two per cent. The reason was that both aircraft and submarines were too few in numbers and unsuitable for the job; the submarines were large boats originally designed for the Pacific, and apart from their size, tended to leak oil from their external fuel tanks. Italian escorts sank ten out of 17 boats in six months. The shallow sunlit waters of the

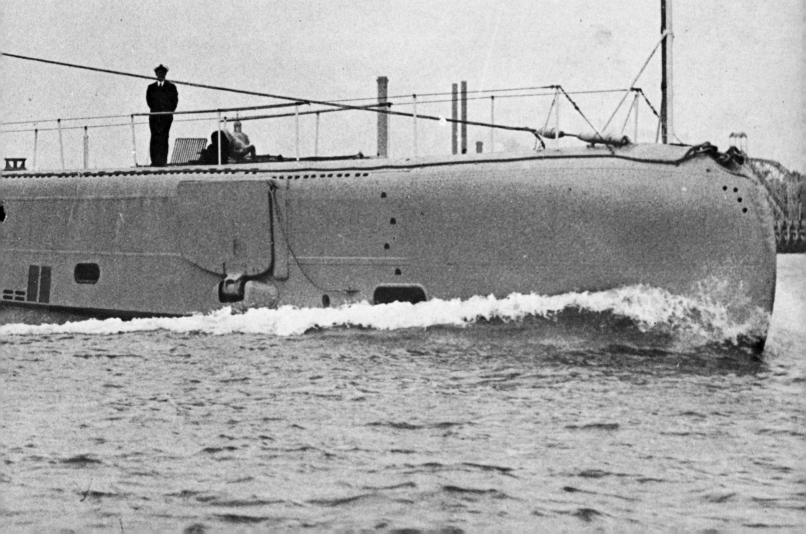

Mediterranean were dangerous for any submarine, but a gratuitous oil-slick made the enemy's job easier.

At the start of 1941 the British situation in the Mediterranean seemed favourable, with a strong probability of a successful onslaught on the Italians in East and North Africa and a strong naval offensive in the Central Mediterranean. But the Germans were watching the parlous state of their ally and, realising how important the Mediterranean was to the British, they decided to take a hand. A specially trained anti-shipping air group, *Fliegerkorps X*, was moved to Sicily to work with the Italians by attacking the British and knocking out their aircraft carriers. In itself this was a tribute to the success of the *Eagle*, *Illustrious* and *Ark Royal*, and also proof that when the Luftwaffe chose it was fully capable of learning how to sink warships. *Fliegerkorps X* jumped the *Illustrious* off Malta on January 10, 1941, and in a deadly co-ordinated attack with Ju-87 Stuka dive-bombers hit the carrier with six 500-kg armour-piercing bombs. The Germans calculated that two would suffice to sink a carrier, and there is no doubt that she was only saved by her armoured box hangar system and her high standard of fire precautions. Saved possibly, but ablaze, steering wrecked and unable to operate her aircraft, she crawled into Malta's Grand Harbour. She survived subsequent bombing attacks and was eventually patched up sufficiently to allow her to reach Alexandria for the long haul through the Suez Canal and across the Atlantic for a year's repairs in the United States.

As *Eagle* was too weak to supply air defence for the Fleet the situation was alarming, with the German Air Force in full control of the Sicilian Narrows and German and Italian land forces advancing against Egypt. Now for the first time the British control over the Middle East oil fields was threatened, and what had been an exercise in the peripheral use of sea power became a vital strategic struggle to prevent Germany from getting access to the oil which she needed. Fortunately another armoured carrier, HMS *Formidable*, was in the South Atlantic searching for surface raiders, a duty from which she could be spared. She passed through the Suez Canal in March, proof of how much the situation had worsened in only three months, for *Illustrious* had made the passage from Gibraltar in relative safety.

As soon as Cunningham had a fresh carrier he switched back to the offensive, and once again his boldness reaped a rich reward. On hearing that the Italians were heading for Crete he took the Fleet in pursuit from Alexandria. The Italian Fleet included only one battleship, the *Vittorio Veneto*, but first sighting reports indicated three more as well as a large force of cruisers. The presence of the *Formidable* was essential in resolving what at first appeared to be an alarming position. In the afternoon of March 28, 1941 her Albacore aircraft (an aircraft of only slightly more modern design than the Swordfish) had scored a torpedo hit on the *Vittorio Veneto*, slowing her down to 19 knots. At dusk the *Formidable*'s aircraft attacked again through intense flak, but instead of hitting the battleship they brought the cruiser *Pola* to a halt.

On board the flagship *Warspite* some 50 miles away, an argument took place between Cunningham and his staff, most of whom were reluctant to risk taking the three battleships west of Cape Matapan on the south-western extremity of the Greek mainland for fear of night attack by bombers.

Some indication of how Cunningham led his Fleet and followed Nelsonian principles is contained in a remark which he is alleged to have made at this meeting: 'You are a pack of yellow-livered skunks! I'll go and have my supper now and see after supper if my morale isn't higher than yours.' But what Cunningham was proposing was not a headlong rush attended by high risk, for he had many factors in his

LEFT: The mine deck of the fast
minelayer *Manxman* was used
to accommodate personnel as
well as supplies when
reinforcing Malta.

RIGHT: A fast minelayer unloads
much-needed food and stores in
Malta's Grand Harbour.

BOTTOM LEFT AND RIGHT: These
diagrams illustrate the basic
differences between shooting at
surface targets and air targets.

favour. For one thing his ships had radar, and for another his ships' crews were all highly trained in night-fighting. There were risks, particularly of firing on friendly ships, but it was unlikely that the Italian Navy would show anything like the same degree of skill in night-fighting. The gamble paid off, and at 2225 the battleships saw three Italian ships less than 4000 yards away. In a matter of minutes the heavy cruisers *Pola*, *Fiume* and *Zara* were on fire and sinking.

The Battle of Cape Matapan was unusual in that it was strategically decisive without even accomplishing its main objective. All that Cunningham had done was to sink a cruiser which had already been damaged and catch two sister ships which had been detached to rescue her (and two escorting destroyers). His main

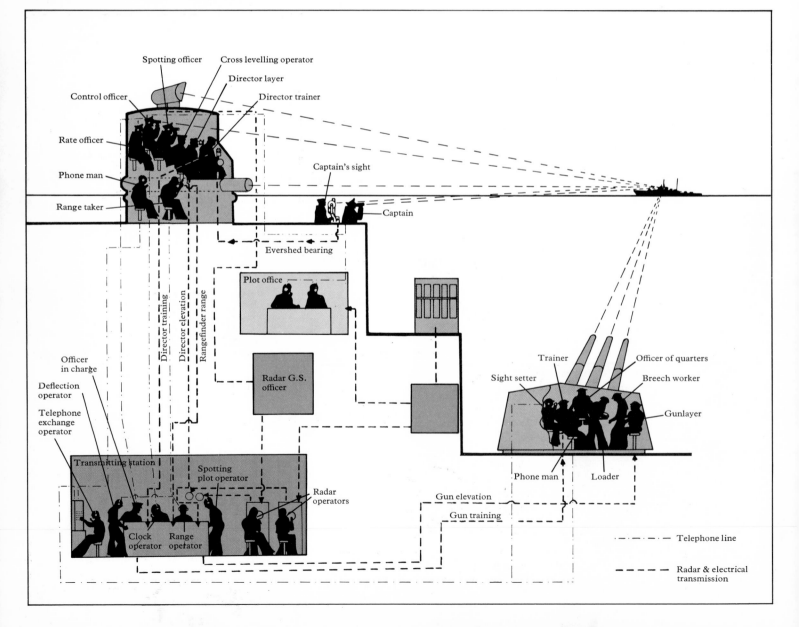

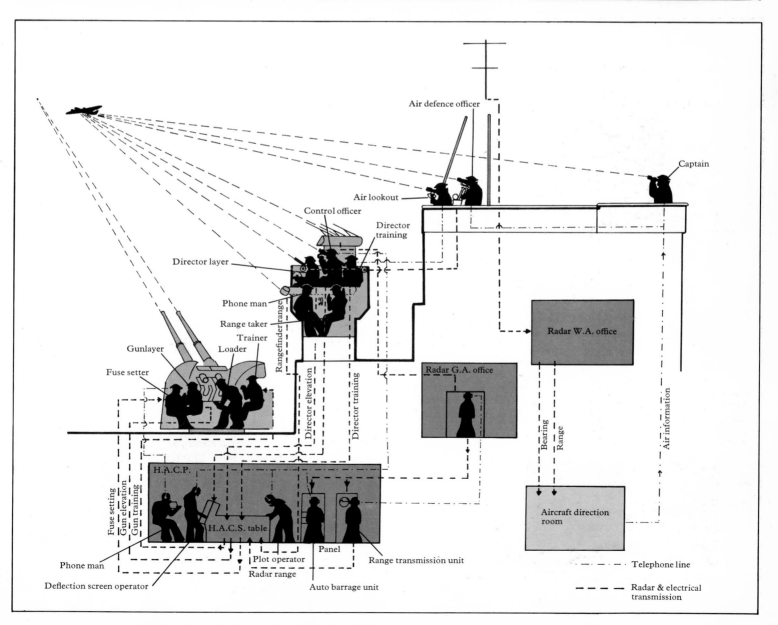

Air defence officer

Captain

Air lookout

Control officer

Director training

Director layer

Phone man

Range taker

Rangefinder range

Trainer

Gunlayer

Loader

Fuse setter

Director elevation

Director training

Radar W.A. office

Radar G.A. office

Bearing

Range

Air information

H.A.C.P.

Fuse setting

Gun elevation

Gun training

H.A.C.S. table

Panel

Range transmission unit

Aircraft direction room

Phone man

Deflection screen operator

Plot operator

Radar range

Auto barrage unit

Telephone line

Radar & electrical transmission

prey, the battleship *Vittorio Veneto*, escaped. In his own words, 'it was hardly a battle . . . two minutes of fierce night action', but those two minutes brought the British a priceless advantage in the months to come.

Germany had finally come to the rescue of her feckless Italian ally and on April 6, 1941, Greece was attacked by German ground and air forces. Within two weeks it was the fall of France all over again, with the Royal Navy called on to evacuate British and Greek forces. But the situation was much worse, with virtually no air defence available from Egypt and no well-equipped naval bases nearby to repair and refuel ships. Alexandria was 400 miles from Greece, and even though Crete was chosen as the new British base, no sooner had it been occupied than the Germans occupied all the principal islands.

The fall of Crete was not long delayed, and as expected it called for heavy sacrifices by the Navy. Indeed it has been called the supreme test of the war for the RN. The Mediterranean Fleet had two tasks; first, to prevent any seaborne landings, and later to try to evacuate as many troops as possible. In the first aim the warships proved highly successful, and on the

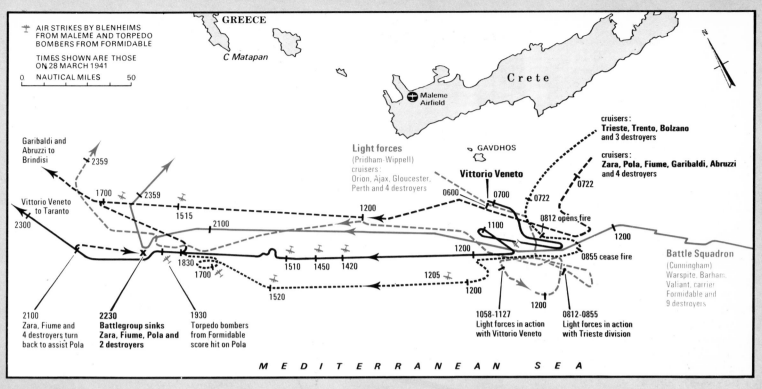

AIR STRIKES BY BLENHEIMS
FROM MALEME AND TORPEDO
BOMBERS FROM FORMIDABLE

TIMES SHOWN ARE THOSE
ON 28 MARCH 1941

0   NAUTICAL MILES   50

GREECE

C Matapan

Crete

Maleme
Airfield

GAVDHOS

Light forces
(Pridham-Wippell)
cruisers:
Orion, Ajax, Gloucester,
Perth and 4 destroyers

Vittorio Veneto

cruisers:
Trieste, Trento, Bolzano
and 3 destroyers

cruisers:
Zara, Pola, Fiume, Garibaldi, Abruzzi
and 4 destroyers

Garibaldi and
Abruzzi to
Brindisi

2359

1700   2359

Vittorio Veneto
to Taranto

2300

1515

2100

1200

0600   0700   0722

0722

0812 opens fire

1100

1200

1830

1510   1450   1420

1700

1520

1205

1200

1200

1200

0855 cease fire

1200

0812-0855
Light forces in action
with Trieste division

1058-1127
Light forces in action
with Vittorio Veneto

Battle Squadron
(Cunningham)
Warspite, Barham,
Valiant, carrier
Formidable and
9 destroyers

2100
Zara, Fiume and
4 destroyers turn
back to assist Pola

**2230
Battlegroup sinks
Zara, Fiume, Pola and
2 destroyers**

1930
Torpedo bombers
from Formidable
score hit on Pola

M E D I T E R R A N E A N   S E A

night of 21/22 May the cruisers *Ajax*, *Dido* and *Orion* and four destroyers slaughtered a convoy of light craft crowded with German assault troops and drove off the Italian escorts. Next morning a force of cruisers and destroyers forced another convoy to turn back, but when it fell back on the main fleet, it was heavily attacked by German bombers. The destroyer *Greyhound* and the cruisers *Gloucester* and *Fiji* were quickly sunk, and the *Warspite* was hit by a heavy bomb. Next day Lord Louis Mountbatten's famous 5th Destroyer Flotilla was attacked, and the *Kelly* and the *Kashmir* were sunk.

The decision on May 27 to evacuate Crete brought further losses, and a large number of ships were badly damaged, including the carrier *Formidable*. Yet once again ships had achieved a degree of success in the teeth of overwhelming enemy air superiority, with over half of the garrison of Crete rescued. The cruisers *Fiji* and *Gloucester* were only sunk because they had left the main fleet and after they had fired away every round of anti-aircraft ammunition. Throughout the entire operation the Italian Fleet had remained passive, allowing the British to concentrate on the immediate problems of survival and evacuation. Had the Italians made even a demonstration they might well have lured the Mediterranean Fleet away and speeded the capture of the island. But they did not, and the British reaped their reward for Matapan.

The lesson of the loss of Crete was a simple one. Warships by themselves could not dispute an amphibious assault over a short distance if the enemy had total air superiority. Crete was lost by an army unprepared for the swift German retaliation and by a Cabinet made overconfident by recent successes. Despite having had the island for six months, the British made no attempt to reinforce the RAF or to build up Crete as an advanced air base. The German glider-borne assault very nearly failed, and showed thereby how vulnerable paratroops are to counterattack, but at the same time it demonstrated what a more inspired defence could have achieved. Nevertheless the defence of Greece and Crete helped to delay the German timetable for the invasion of Russia, and virtually eliminated the German glider-borne and paratroop formations.

After the fall of Crete the British Mediterranean Fleet was forced on the defensive, but its submarines continued to harass the German and Italian supply-

BELOW: The old Italian armoured cruiser *San Giorgio* was damaged by British Air attack at Tobruk in January 1941. She was scuttled when Tobruk fell to the British.

BELOW: Admiral of the Fleet Sir Andrew Cunningham was C-in-C of the Mediterranean Fleet 1940–43. He more than any other was responsible for the annihilation of Italian sea power.

BOTTOM: Admiral Sir James Somerville held the independent command of Force 'H' at Gibraltar.

BELOW: The crew of a 40-mm Bofors anti-aircraft gun on 'B' turret of the cruiser *Manchester* enjoy a lull during the attacks on her convoy.

routes, and Malta became even more important as the only forward base from which any form of counterattack could be made. In mid-June two aircraft carriers flew off 47 Hurricane fighters to help the defence of the island, and later that month another carrier flew off a further 64 fighters. Submarines were used to run vital supplies in, to avoid the risk to surface ships. On the Libyan coast warships were also helping to supply the beleagured garrison of Tobruk, and as the supply-route lay just off the enemy coast it was soon christened 'Bomb Alley'. Yet for the loss of 25 warships and five large merchant ships, between April 1940 and December 1941 34,000 tons of stores and 34,000 men were sent into Tobruk.

In July 1941 a fast convoy was successfully sent into Malta in 'Operation Substance', and in September a further ferrying operation by the carriers *Ark Royal* and *Furious* added 49 Hurricanes to Malta's strength. The submarine strength was also reinforced, and Malta began to exert more pressure on the Germans and Italians. The RAF was able to mount bomber raids against North African con- voys, supplemented by Fleet Air Arm torpedo bombers. Between June and September over a hundred German and Italian merchant ships were sunk, a total of nearly 300,000 tons of scarce shipping. The German liaison staff in Rome regarded the situation as catastrophic and demanded the reinforcement of the Luftwaffe in Sicily. The continuing strain on the Italian land forces in North Africa was remedied by sending the Afrika Korps, but that only exacerbated the supply problem. In response to orders from the High Command six of the Atlantic U-Boats were sent from the Bay of Biscay to the Mediterranean in September, and a further four in November.

The presence of even a small number of battle-trained U-Boats in the Mediterranean was to bring about a dramatic reversal of fortunes. Hitherto the British had been able to cope with Italian submarine attacks and this had made them complacent. On November 13 the carrier *Ark Royal* was torpedoed and sunk by *U.81* only 25 miles from Gibraltar. Since September 1939 German propaganda broadcasts had asked plaintively: 'Where

BELOW: After many narrow escapes the carrier *Ark Royal* was finally sunk off Gibraltar in November 1941. Her loss was a heavy blow to British supremacy in the Mediterranean.

is the *Ark Royal*?', and it is ironic that when this famous ship was finally sunk German radio had to quote a British announcement to substantiate the claim. The loss of this fleet carrier was all the more unfortunate because it need not have happened. From the official enquiry it appears that the *Ark Royal* sank as a result of inadequate damage control measures and premature abandonment by her crew.

British surface forces were active, and in one outstanding action on November 13 the destroyers *Sikh*, *Legion*, *Maori* and *Isaac Sweers* (Royal Netherlands Navy)

BELOW: The American tanker *Ohio* brought a vital cargo of fuel into Malta in August 1942 and saved the island.

BOTTOM: The *Ohio* was so badly damaged that she was kept afloat by destroyers lashed alongside. Although she sank in Grand Harbour her vital cargo was intact, so that the aviation gasoline could be pumped ashore.

torpedoed the cruisers *Alberto di Guissano* and *Alberico da Barbiano* off Tunisia. So desperate was the supply position that the two cruisers were carrying a deck cargo of petrol. Then, on November 24, *U.331* torpedoed the battleship *Barham*, flagship of the 1st Battle Squadron. The old ship rolled over and then blew up with the loss of 862 of her crew, the only British battleship to be torpedoed by a submarine at sea throughout the war. On the night of December 14/15 the cruiser *Galatea* was torpedoed near Alexandria, and only five days later the Malta cruiser squadron, Force 'K', ran into a minefield off Tripoli. The flagship *Neptune* was sunk, the *Aurora* and *Penelope* were damaged, and the destroyer *Kandahar* was sunk trying to rescue survivors.

There is no clearer example of how naval operations can influence land campaigns. With British sea power neutralised, the Germans and Italians immediately ran two convoys through to North Africa and restored the situation for their armies. The Italian Navy, too, had a contribution to make by way of compensation for their previous performance. On the night of December 19 the submarine *Scire* launched two 'human torpedoes' against Alexandria, and they severely damaged the battleships *Queen Elizabeth* and *Valiant*. These *maiale* or 'pigs' were really midget submarines, ridden by two operators sitting astride the body. The warhead was detached and left clamped underneath the target, set for detonation by a time-fuse. The two British ships, the last capital units left to them in the Mediterranean, were as good as sunk, for they rested on the bottom of the harbour for months, but as they were in very shallow water and upright, aerial photographs gave no idea of how serious the damage was, and at the most crucial period the Italians could not exploit the major victory just won. The shadow of Matapan still hung over the Italian Fleet.

THE GERMAN NAVY

BELOW: The battleship *Tirpitz* keeps her lonely vigil in the Arctic.

German Shipyard Production

Programme 1935	Ships	Type	Completed	Programme 1936	Ships	Type	Completed
	Bismarck	Battleship	1940		*Tirpitz*	Battleship	1941
	Prinz Eugen	Cruiser	1940		*Peter Strasser*	Carrier	–
	Graf Zeppelin	Carrier	–		*Seydlitz*	Cruiser	–
					Lützow	Cruiser	–

RIGHT: German destroyers arrive at Narvik amid burning shipping. These destroyers were annihilated in the two battles of Narvik, although the vital port was finally recaptured by the Nazis.

The German Navy was caught in a very difficult situation at the start of the war, in the middle of a grandiose programme of expansion and somewhat muddled ideas on how to fight the war at sea. By a blend of hard work and duplicity the Kriegsmarine had been created out of the emasculated coast-defence force allowed to Germany under the Treaty of Versailles, but as matters stood at the outbreak of World War II it was ill-balanced.

The new German Navy was the inspiration of Admiral Raeder, who saw its main offensive purpose as the destruction of enemy commerce. In practice this meant British or French commerce, and Raeder hoped to create a balanced fleet of battleships, aircraft carriers, cruisers and destroyers which could tie down the British Fleet rather than engage it in major actions, disrupt the convoy system and give his U-Boats a free hand. The first step in this plan was the building of the pocket battleship *Deutschland* under the

1929 Programme, but it took a new turn in 1933. The building of up to six of the *Deutschland* type was permitted under the treaty, but in 1933 the fourth of the type was dropped and replaced by a battlecruiser. Her tonnage was deliberately understated by nearly 20 per cent, but in any case the announcement constituted an open violation of the Treaty which went unchecked by the guarantors, on the dubious grounds that she was needed to match the French *Dunkerque* Class. But the eight submarines secretly ordered under the same programme were absolutely forbidden by the treaty, and a year later a further battlecruiser was ordered in total secrecy, with two heavy cruisers and sixteen large destroyers, all in defiance of the Versailles Treaty.

Germany was not only defying the Treaty of Versailles but also falsifying the tonnage of the ships, so it is hardly surprising that her warship designers were able to incorporate heavier armament

and protection than their foreign contemporaries.

Following the repudiation of the Treaty of Versailles and the Anglo-German Naval Agreement of 1935 the German Navy was to be 35 per cent of the Royal Navy's total tonnage. In practice this figure was hard to achieve as German shipyards were incapable of stepping up production of large ships.

Between 1935 and 1941 the British completed three battleships, three aircraft carriers and 16 cruisers, in addition to modernising three capital ships and numerous other vessels. In 1938 the German Navy presented its 'Z' Plan to Hitler as a blueprint for securing dominion of the oceans, but in the light of the figures already quoted we can see just how unrealistic it was. Under this plan the German Navy would build:

Six battleships (56,000 tons) to complete by 1944

Four heavy cruisers to complete by 1943

BELOW: The battlecruiser *Scharnhorst* was armed with nine 11-inch and twelve 5.9-inch guns. After a successful career as a commerce raider in the Atlantic, followed by her daring daylight dash through the English Channel in 1942, she was sunk in the Battle of the North Cape in December 1943. The forward superstructure (left) bristled with anti-aircraft guns, some of them specially mounted for the Channel dash.

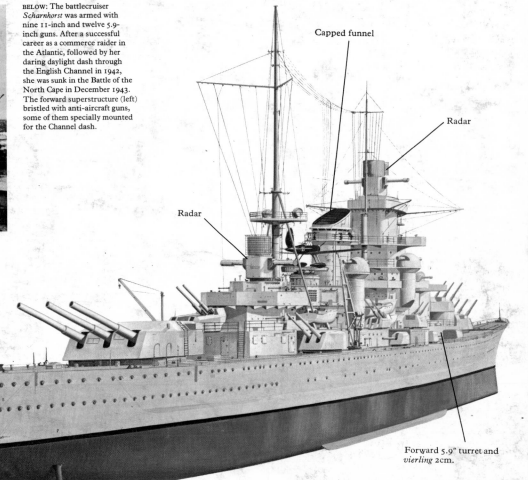

Capped funnel

Radar

Radar

Forward 5.9" turret and *vierling* 2cm.

RIGHT: The *Scharnhorst* in a heavy Atlantic swell.

BELOW: When the captain of the *Graf Spee* received orders from Hitler to scuttle his ship, demolition charges turned the once-proud pocket battleship into a burning hulk. The wreckage in the foreground is an entire 11-inch gun turret blown sideways.

Four heavy cruisers to complete by 1945
Four light cruisers to complete by 1944
13 light cruisers to complete by 1948
Two aircraft carriers to complete by 1941
Two aircraft carriers to complete by 1947
128 submarines to complete by 1943
95 submarines to complete by 1947

The 'Z' Plan was subsequently modified, but at best it was a pipedream which relied on the British doing absolutely nothing. As it was the British proved more than adequate to match the German building programme on a ratio of two-to-one and more. Had war been delayed until 1944 as Admiral Raeder hoped, the contest would have been long and bitter, but it is hard to avoid the conclusion that the result would have been the same.

Capital Ships

The two battlecruisers *Scharnhorst* and *Gneisenau* were handsome 32,000-ton ships armed with nine 11-inch guns in triple turrets, and capable of 32 knots. They were based on the World War I *Mackensen* Class, which were not completed. It was hoped to arm them with six 15-inch guns in twin turrets, but instead they utilised the six triple 11-inch mountings which had been ordered for the cancelled pocket battleships. This was an unsatisfactory feature, giving these large ships an armament considerably inferior to their likely opponents. In 1942 *Gneisenau* was taken in hand for rearming and reconstruction, but the time for such luxuries was past, as there was neither the

Strength Of The German Navy In September 1939

Figures in parentheses indicate ships under construction.

2 Battleships (+11)[1]
2 *Scharnhorst* Class, completed 1939

[1] Only 2 *Bismarck* Class launched; remainder cancelled 1940.

3 Armoured Cruisers (later re-rated as heavy cruisers)
1 *Deutschland* completed 1933
2 *Admiral Scheer* Class completed 1934-36

2 Heavy Cruisers (+3)[1]
2 *Admiral Hipper* Class completed 1939

[1] 1 improved type completed 1940, 1 sold to USSR incomplete 1940 and 1 never completed.

6 Light Cruisers (+6)[1]
1 *Emden* completed 1925
3 *Königsberg* Class completed 1929-30
1 *Leipzig* completed 1931
1 *Nürnberg* completed 1935

[1] Only 3 in hand, and all cancelled.

22 Destroyers (+12)[1]
16 *Leberecht Maass* Class completed 1937-39
6 *Diether von Roeder* Class completed 1938-39

[1] None yet launched.

20 Torpedo Boats/Small Destroyers (+13)
6 *Möwe* Class completed 1926-29
6 *Wolf* Class completed 1928-29
8 *T.1* Class completed 1939

59 Submarines (+50)
6 Type IIA (*U.1-6*) completed 1935
18 Type IIB (*U.7-24*) completed 1935-36
2 Type IA (*U.25-26*) completed 1936
10 Type VIIA (*U.27-36*) completed 1936-37
7 Type IXA (*U.37-43*) completed 1938-39
11 Type VIIB (*U.45-49, U.51-53*) completed 1939
5 Type IIC (*U.58-62*) completed 1938-39

labour nor the manpower to spare, and work stopped in 1943.

The battleships ordered in 1935–36 were named *Bismarck* and *Tirpitz*, two names which are immortal in naval history. Although announced as 35,000-tonners, they displaced 7000 tons more and were the largest battleships built at the time. It is still widely believed that they were very heavily armoured, and even that they had some novel type of armour, but the facts are more mundane. Like the *Scharnhorst* design, that of the *Bismarck* Class was updated from an existing World War I design, that of the *Baden* Class, completed in 1916. The reason for this paradox, a new navy prepared to cheat in order to achieve superiority over its rivals and yet forced to use 20-year-old designs, is simply the lack of an experienced design team during the period 1919–1929. The hurried expansion under Hitler caught not only the shipbuilders but the naval architects off balance, and there was no time to carry out the exhaustive tests and evaluation of competitive sketch designs that the British, Americans and Japanese were working on throughout the 1920s and early 1930s. The *Bismarck* was by no means the most

heavily armoured battleship of her day, and compared badly with her American and British contemporaries in her underwater protection against mines and torpedoes. Her machinery was complex, and yielded only 29 knots' sea speed for 27 per cent more power than the British *King George V* needed for $28\frac{1}{2}$ knots. Her main armour belt was 12·6-inch thick as against 14/15-inches in the British ship, and deck armour was a maximum $4\frac{1}{2}$-inches as against 6-inches; the British ship was 5000 tons smaller, as well.

The six 56,000-ton ships were to have had 16-inch guns, and were to have had twelve diesel motors driving three shafts, the most powerful diesel installation ever planned. Only the unnamed 'H' and 'J' (German warship names were never announced until the launching) were laid down and they were stopped in 1940. Other designs, positively megalomaniacal in their scope, were drawn up between 1942 and 1944, starting at 83,000 tons and rising to 122,000 tons, armed with eight 20-inch guns; in the words of a British naval architect, the designers seemed intent on avoiding service on the Eastern Front by showing how busy they were, and these projects should not be taken

seriously. Three projected battlecruisers of similar size to the *Scharnhorst*, but armed with six 15-inch guns, were also dropped in 1940.

The *Scharnhorst* and *Gneisenau* operated for most of their short lives as inseparable twins, and were known to the British as 'Salmon and Gluckstein'. In November 1939 they sank the British Armed Merchant Cruiser *Rawalpindi* southeast of Iceland, and during the Norwegian campaign they trapped the aircraft carrier *Glorious*. Early in 1941 they made another foray into the Atlantic and sank 115,000 tons of shipping and returned, not to Germany, but to the French port of Brest. Here they were a constant worry to the British, who mounted an endless series of bomber raids against them. What is hard to understand about the German Navy is the way in which these two powerful ships were put off their stroke on more than one occasion by the sight of an elderly British battleship escorting a convoy. Hitler's orders were definite, however, and his admirals were not to risk damage in action with British heavy units.

The most famous exploit of the two battlecruisers actually took place early in 1942, but as it brought the 1941 phase of

BELOW: The battlecruiser *Gneisenau* could always be distinguished from her sister *Scharnhorst* as she had her mainmast stepped against the funnel.

FAR LEFT: The battlecruisers *Gneisenau* and *Scharnhorst* in a 1939 naval review.

LEFT: A heavy cruiser of the *Admiral Hipper* Class was armed with eight 8-inch guns. The funnel cap has been removed by the German censor.

RIGHT: The old battleship *Schleswig-Holstein* had been used as a gunnery training ship in the prewar period.

BELOW RIGHT: The battleship *Schlesien* sinking after striking a mine off Swinemünde in May 1945.

German naval operations to an end it can be touched on here. This was 'Operation Cerberus', Hitler's plan to extricate the two ships from Brest, where it was only a matter of time before they were destroyed by aerial bombing. Once again Hitler demonstrated his uncanny intuition, for against the advice of his naval staff he demanded a daylight run through the English Channel as the safest way back to Germany. Hitler's contributions to naval warfare were generally disastrous, but this time his hunch that the British would be caught napping was correct. The *Scharnhorst*, *Gneisenau* and *Prinz Eugen*, with a huge umbrella of aircraft and an escort of destroyers and torpedo boats, swept past the Dover Straits and brushed aside attacks from coastal guns, destroyers, motor torpedo boats and aircraft. The British

BELOW: The battleship
Bismarck at sea four days before
her encounter with HMS *Hood*
and *Prince of Wales* in which
Hood was sunk. Three days
later the *Bismarck* was caught
and disappeared below the
waters of the Atlantic.

BELOW: *S.4* was one of the early
German motor torpedo boats.

BOTTOM: British personnel
examine a surrendered
'*Seehund*'-type midget
submarine, desperately
designed to save the flagging
chances for survival of the
Third Reich in 1944.

were enraged by this affront to their dignity, and a full-scale enquiry into the causes was ordered by Parliament; not for 300 years had an enemy fleet got so close to English soil without suffering some sort of retribution.

The reasons for the success of 'Cerberus' are complex, however. For a start, the RAF had vehemently protested that its torpedo-bombers were more than adequate to deal with any surface ships in the Channel, and had pooh-poohed any suggestion that destroyers, motor torpedo boats or even coastal guns were needed to back them up. In the event RAF aircraft were found to have an unbelievable number of malfunctioning radar sets, while torpedoes were kept at airfields some distance from the aircraft, etc. etc. Clearly the likelihood of large ships in the Channel had receded to the point where nobody was seriously guarding against it, what might be called the 'Pearl Harbor Syndrome'. When other arms were committed to battle they were thrown in piecemeal. Motor torpedo boats attacked unsupported and were driven off; Swordfish torpedo-bombers attacked without the promised fighter escort; four destroyers got within 4000 yards but the German ships dodged their torpedoes; finally the Dover coastal guns were forbidden to open fire until the ships were at extreme range and disappearing into the haze. Had a co-ordinated attack taken place something might have been achieved, but each separate attack was too weak, and Hitler's gamble paid off. But the British could draw comfort from the fact that the *Scharnhorst* struck a mine at the end of her

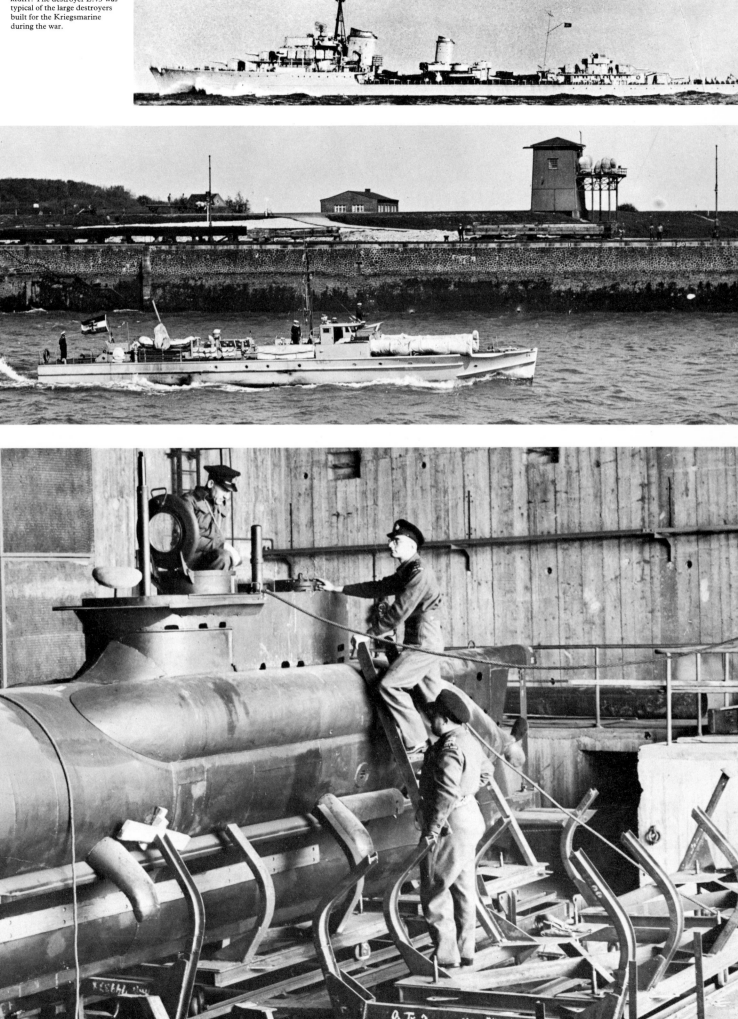

RIGHT: The destroyer *Z.43* was typical of the large destroyers built for the Kriegsmarine during the war.

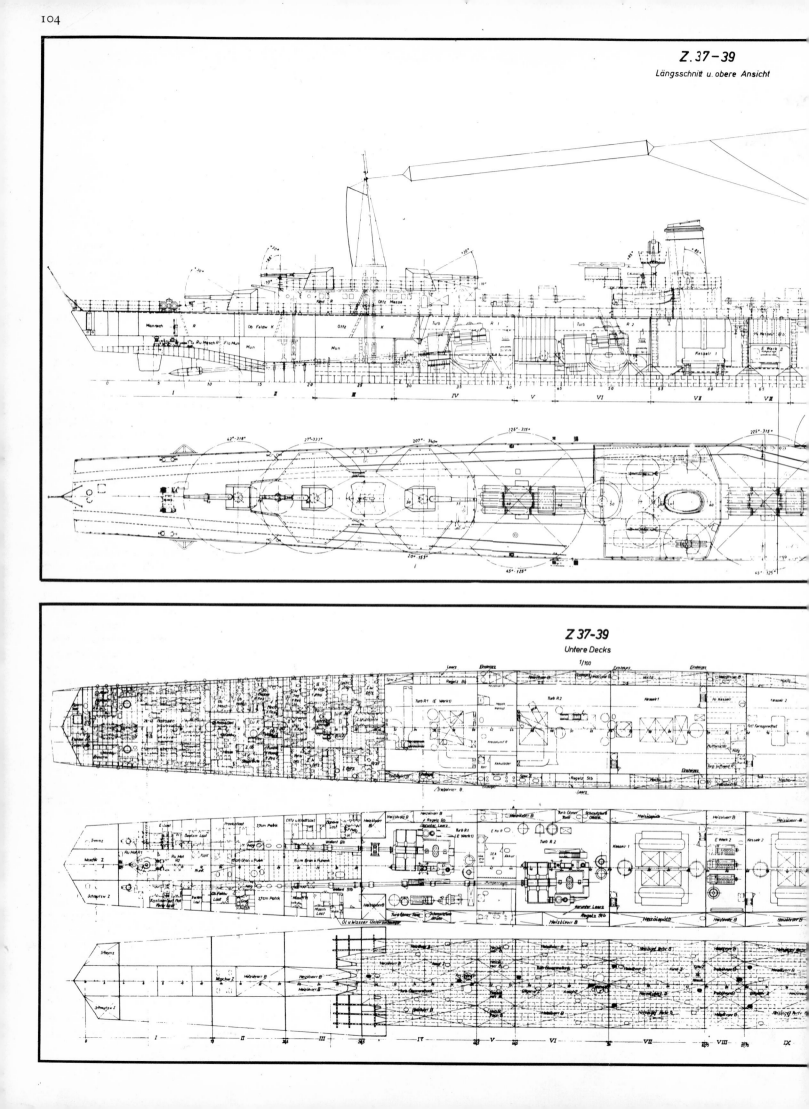

Z. 37–39
Längsschnitt u. obere Ansicht

Z 37–39
Untere Decks

1/100

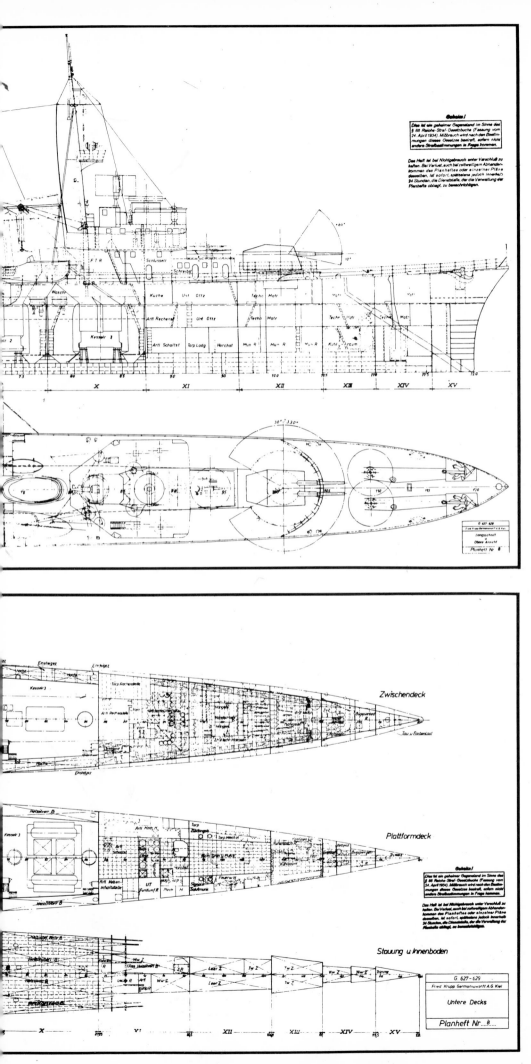

LEFT: Official plans of German destroyers Z.37-39. Their profile and deck plan appear above, and the internal decks below.

voyage and was damaged. But in the long run the Channel Dash, however gratifying to the German Navy, was at best a strategic withdrawal which was of more help in easing the British situation in the Atlantic. In home waters the three German ships were far less dangerous than they had been on the western coast of France, and they never again posed such a threat to Allied sea power.

The *Bismarck* was ready for action in April 1941, and she and the heavy cruiser *Prinz Eugen* sailed from Bergen on May 21 in a bold attempt to achieve what Admiral Raeder longed to do, and *Scharnhorst* and *Gneisenau* had failed to do; to disrupt the entire North Atlantic convoy system. This was always easier in theory than in practice, but the threat was real enough, for the *Bismarck* and *Prinz Eugen* could destroy the escorts and then pound the virtually defenceless merchantmen with gunfire, using their superior speed to catch any trying to escape. The problem for the British was first to locate the enemy ships, and then to intercept them. The aircraft with sufficient range to reconnoitre did not carry the weapons which could sink a battleship, while bombers lacked the ability to attack at extreme range. To complicate matters the RAF did not yet have a suitable heavy armour-piercing bomb capable of sinking a battleship. There were only two ways of sinking the *Bismarck* at any distance from the British Isles; a torpedo-attack by carrier aircraft or destroyers, or gunfire from another battleship.

The entire *Bismarck* episode lasted only six days, and was a classic operation in which all types of warships played out the role for which they had been designed. Battleships fought one another, cruisers reconnoitred for the battle fleet, aircraft carriers launched strikes against enemy surface ships, and destroyers attacked them with torpedoes. It should also be remembered that it took place at the same time as the evacuation of Crete, when the Royal Navy's situation was critical. The *Bismarck* operation was a turning point of the naval war, and both navies knew it. The Germans had only one more capital ship completing, the *Tirpitz*, whereas the British would soon have three more, as well as three more of the aircraft carriers which proved so dangerous in the Mediterranean. As time went by the British position was likely to improve, and raids by battleships in the Atlantic would become more risky.

The British cruisers on patrol in the

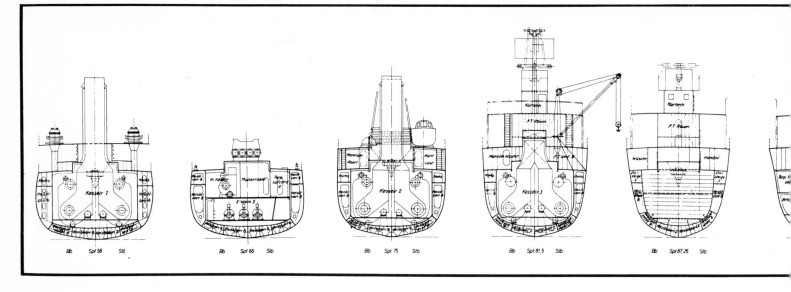

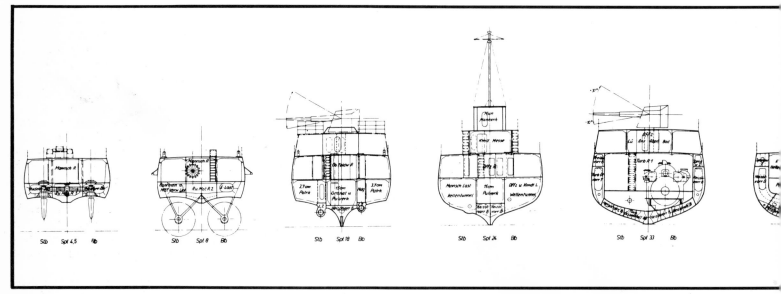

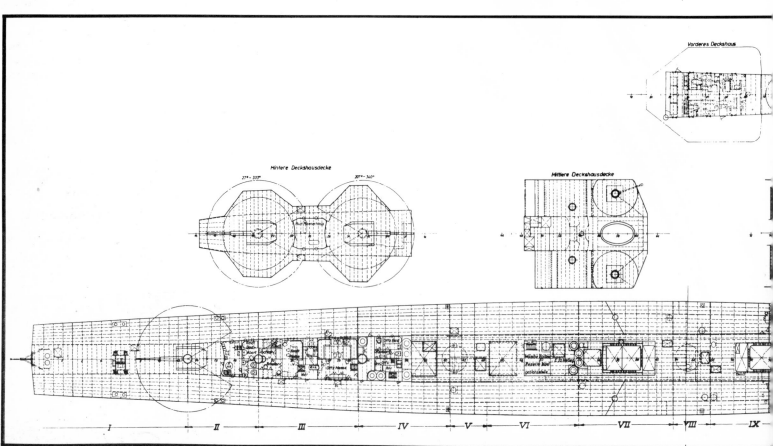

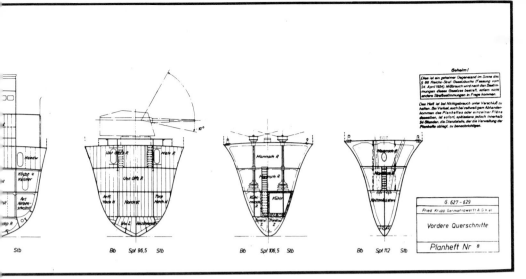

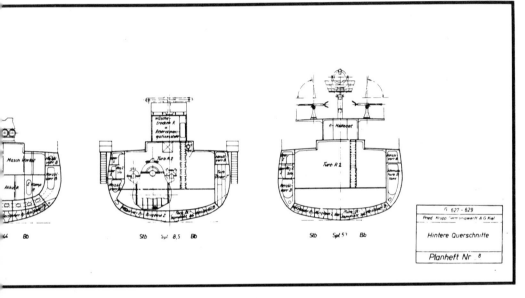

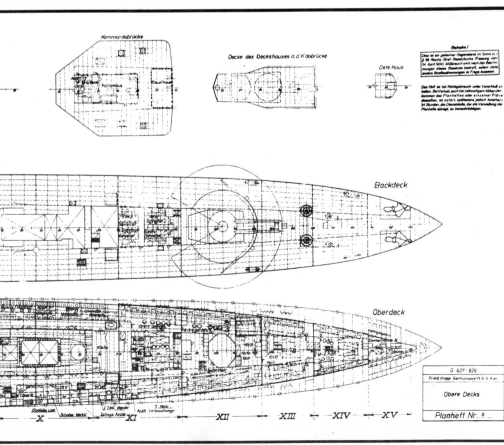

LEFT: Transverse sections of the destroyers Z.37-39 (top and centre); weather deck and platforms appear below.

BELOW: Guns of the *Tirpitz* at maximum elevation loom over a pocket battleship and other units in line ahead.

Denmark Strait between Iceland and Greenland were alerted by the Admiralty after intelligence reports confirmed the movement of the German ships out of the Baltic, and HMS *Suffolk* made the first sighting at 1922 on May 23. The *Hood* and *Prince of Wales*, which had sailed from Hvalfjord in Iceland, reached a favourable interception point early next morning, and Vice-Admiral Holland took his squadron into action at a range of about 25,000 yards (over 14 miles). Unfortunately when the British ships came into action they were on a fine bearing, presenting their bows to the German ships. Although this reduced the target area, it effectively halved the number of British guns which could bear, so that instead of matching the eight 15-inch and eight 8-inch German guns with his eight 15-inch and ten 14-inch guns, Holland could only bring four 15-inch and ten 14-inch guns to bear. To make matters worse, the *Prince of Wales* had only been completed two weeks before, and she had builders' workmen on board rectifying faults in the main armament; one gun in her forward turrets was certain to jam after one round, and this reduced her to only five guns in the opening stage.

What followed was the blackest moment of the whole war for the Royal Navy. Only eight minutes after the start of the action, and after firing three salvoes, the *Hood* was 'straddled' by the *Bismarck* and blew up shortly afterwards. In a matter of seconds, 1416 officers and men had

BELOW: The battleship *Bismarck* refuelling the heavy cruiser *Prinz Eugen* during their sortie in May 1941.

RIGHT: The inboard profile of the *Bismarck*. The 15-inch gun turrets and their magazines are separated by the triple shaft steam turbines and boiler rooms. She carried eight 15-inch guns in four twin mountings and twelve 5.9-inch guns. Her 41,000 ton hull was protected by a 12.6-inch belt of armour and heavy decks.

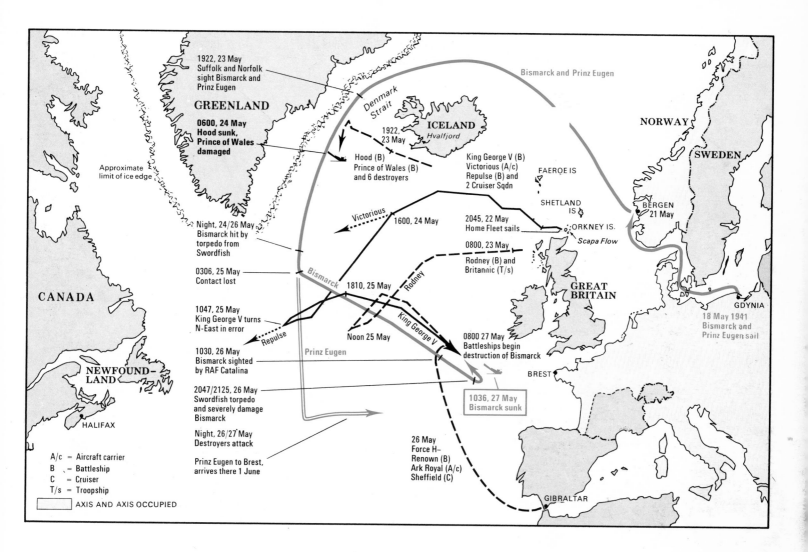

1922, 23 May
Suffolk and Norfolk
sight Bismarck and
Prinz Eugen

Bismarck and Prinz Eugen

GREENLAND

**0600, 24 May
Hood sunk,
Prince of Wales
damaged**

Denmark
Strait

ICELAND
Hvalfjord

1922,
23 May

NORWAY

SWEDEN

Approximate
limit of ice edge

Hood (B)
Prince of Wales (B)
and 6 destroyers

King George V (B)
Victorious (A/c)
Repulse (B) and
2 Cruiser Sqdn

FAERØE IS

BERGEN
21 May

Night, 24/26 May
Bismarck hit by
torpedo from
Swordfish

Victorious

1600, 24 May

SHETLAND
IS

2045, 22 May
Home Fleet sails

ORKNEY IS.
Scapa Flow

CANADA

0306, 25 May
Contact lost

Bismarck

1810, 25 May

Rodney

0800, 23 May
Rodney (B) and
Britannic (T/s)

GREAT
BRITAIN

GDYNIA

1047, 25 May
King George V turns
N-East in error

King George V

18 May 1941
Bismarck and
Prinz Eugen sail

Repulse

Noon 25 May

0800 27 May
Battleships begin
destruction of Bismarck

NEWFOUND-
LAND

1030, 26 May
Bismarck sighted
by RAF Catalina

Prinz Eugen

BREST

1036, 27 May
Bismarck sunk

2047/2125, 26 May
Swordfish torpedo
and severely damage
Bismarck

HALIFAX

Night, 26/27 May
Destroyers attack

26 May
Force H–
Renown (B)
Ark Royal (A/c)
Sheffield (C)

A/c = Aircraft carrier
B = Battleship
C = Cruiser
T/s = Troopship

Prinz Eugen to Brest,
arrives there 1 June

GIBRALTAR

AXIS AND AXIS OCCUPIED

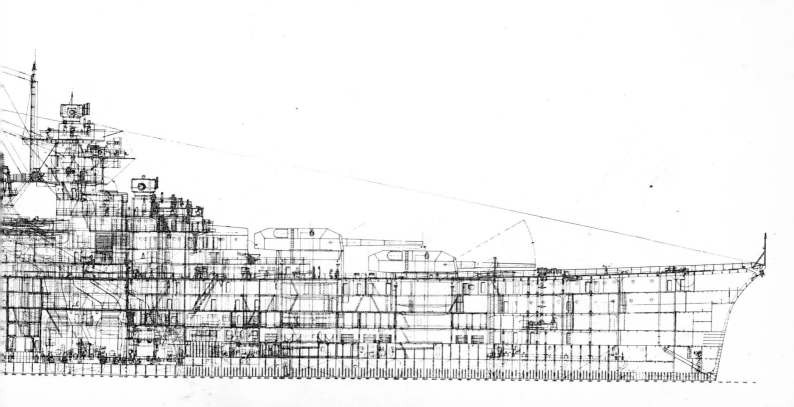

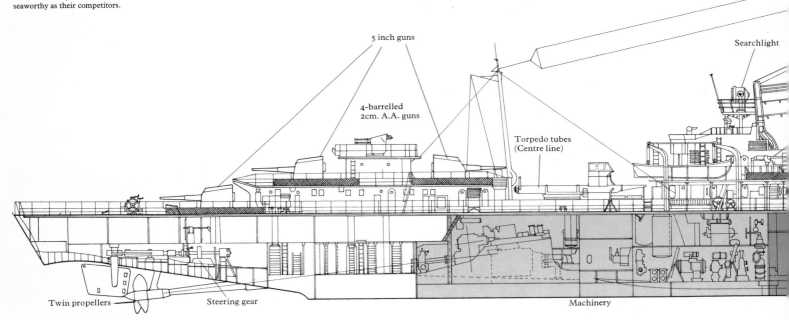

5 inch guns

4-barrelled 2cm. A.A. guns

Torpedo tubes (Centre line)

Searchlight

Twin propellers

Steering gear

Machinery

ABOVE: The quarterdeck and after superstructure of the *Scharnhorst*.

been wiped out, leaving only three survivors, and the largest ship in the Royal Navy had been sunk almost without trace. It was believed at the time that the *Hood*'s armour had been pierced by a 15-inch shell, but careful sifting of the scanty evidence indicates that a more likely cause was an ammunition fire among some anti-aircraft rocket projectiles stowed around the boat deck, which spread to the main magazine below. The *Hood* was not a modern ship, having been completed in 1920, and her magazine protection had never been updated. Examination of her plans shows no way in which a shell landing in the position of the last known hit could go straight into a main magazine.

The two German ships immediately shifted fire to the *Prince of Wales*, and scored a damaging hit on her bridge which killed or wounded all but her captain. She

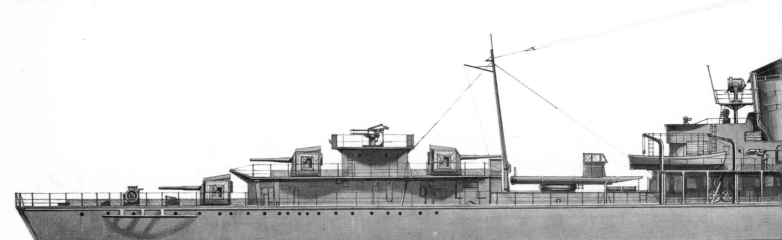

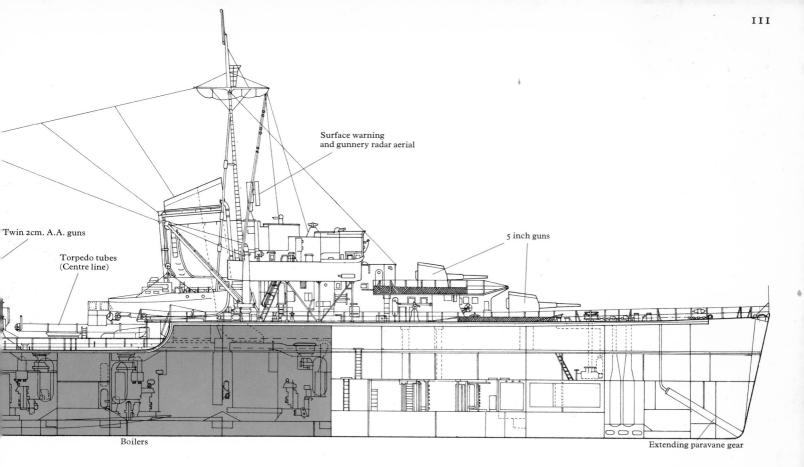

Twin 2cm. A.A. guns

Torpedo tubes
(Centre line)

Surface warning
and gunnery radar aerial

5 inch guns

Boilers

Extending paravane gear

was hit in all seven times, but stood up
remarkably well, and demonstrated the
toughness of the latest British battleship
designs. The sequence of hits was as follows:

No. 1. a 15-inch hit which passed
through the bridge without exploding – fragments of the bin-
nacle caused casualties, not the
shell.

No. 2. a glancing hit on the base of the
anti-aircraft control from a 15-
inch or 8-inch shell which did
not explode.

No. 3. a 15-inch shell which hit the
base of the after funnel but
detonated only partially.

No. 4. a hit from an 8-inch shell on the
boat deck; the shell did not explode and was thrown over-
board.

No. 5. a 15-inch shell which pitched
short and dived underwater and
penetrated the hull below the
armour without exploding; it
was located back in harbour and
defused.

Nos. 6 & 7 two 8-inch shells which
detonated only mildly on the
armoured deck aft without
penetrating.

ABOVE: The massive bow of the
Tirpitz, the sister battleship of
the *Bismarck*.

The only serious damage was caused by Hit No. 5, as the ship took on 600 tons of water, but this reduced her speed by only two knots and did not affect her fighting power. After the *Hood* blew up she fought back and obtained several straddles on the *Bismarck*. Two hits were scored, one of which caused a fuel leak and contaminated other tanks. This was sufficient to make Admiral Lütjens cancel the Atlantic raid, and showed how vulnerable surface raiders were to relatively slight damage.

The *Prince of Wales* broke off the action but continued to shadow with the cruisers *Norfolk* and *Suffolk* until forced to return to Scapa Flow to refuel. The British situation was bad, with their nearest heavy units over 300 miles to the south-east, but the Admiralty had ordered every capital ship, cruiser and carrier into the area. Down at Gibraltar Force 'H' under Admiral Somerville had anticipated orders as soon as the news about the *Bismarck*'s appearance had been received, and the *Ark Royal* and her escorting battlecruiser *Renown* were moving northwards. The battleship *Rodney* was 550 miles away with a convoy bound for Halifax, but she left, taking four destroyers with her. Although both these forces seemed too

far away to be any use, they ultimately proved vital to the operation.

The new Home Fleet carrier *Victorious* had hurriedly landed a cargo of RAF fighters bound for Malta, and had only nine Swordfish torpedo-bombers and six fighters on board when she sailed from Scapa Flow. In spite of the squadron's lack of experience a night attack succeeded in hitting the *Bismarck* with one torpedo. Unfortunately the 18-inch aerial torpedo carried too light a warhead to do more then superficial damage to the German ship's main armour belt, and her speed was not affected.

A dramatic sequence of events now ensued. First, on the evening of May 24 the *Bismarck* rounded on her pursuers to allow the *Prinz Eugen* to break away independently for Brest, and next morning HMS *Suffolk* lost radar contact. The British cruiser was zig-zagging at extreme radar range, and an alteration of course by the *Bismarck* took her out of range. The Home Fleet under Admiral Tovey was now only 100 miles away, but the German battleship was completely lost. The Admiralty was working on the assumption that the *Bismarck* would try to return to Germany, as indeed Lütjens' orders

stated, and many of the pursuers were in the wrong sector, but suddenly the *Bismarck* chose to break radio silence with a long transmission to Germany. This was immediately picked up by direction-finding stations in England, and one may wonder why such an elementary blunder was made by the German admiral. The answer is that his intelligence about the range of British surface warning radar was over-generous; his ship's radar-detector was picking up the *Suffolk*'s radar pulses, but he did not know that the pulses were too weak to travel back to the receiver, and so it was assumed that the *Bismarck*'s position was still known to the British.

A Catalina flying boat of RAF Coastal Command spotted the *Bismarck* at 1030 on the morning of May 26. The hunt was on again, but with the German ship heading for Brest each hour brought her nearer to the protection of shore-based aircraft which could then attack the British battleships.

Early the same afternoon the *Ark Royal* launched a torpedo-strike, but the fourteen Swordfish found the cruiser HMS *Sheffield* first, and in the bad visibility launched their torpedoes. These were fitted with magnetic exploders, and the weather proved too rough for them; the violent rise and fall took them into the earth's magnetic field and exploded them prematurely. The naval aircrew, puzzled at the lack of anti-aircraft fire from their target, flashed a message to the aggrieved *Sheffield*, 'Sorry for the kippers', but the mistake was fortunate, and the *Sheffield* radioed the *Ark Royal* to warn her of the behaviour of the torpedoes. When the second Swordfish strike took off three hours later their torpedo-exploders were set for 'contact' instead of 'non-contact', and this time they scored two hits on the *Bismarck*. The first did little damage, but the second was a deadly hit which wrecked her rudders, damaged the propellers and made her unmanoeuvrable. The giant ship turned circles while damage parties desperately tried to bring her back under control. Eventually she made off at reduced speed, steering erratically by using her engines. During the night she was attacked by destroyers and although the British claimed a hit the final evidence was too confused to confirm this, despite the controversy which has raged ever since.

The *Bismarck* died gamely next morning, under a withering fire from the *King George V* and the *Rodney*. The British ships manoeuvred independently at a range of 16,000 yards, and after half an hour the German ship was silenced and

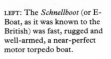

LEFT: The *Schnellboot* (or E-Boat, as it was known to the British) was fast, rugged and well-armed, a near-perfect motor torpedo boat.

BELOW: The 15-inch turrets and forward superstructure of the *Tirpitz*.

BOTTOM: Men of the *Tirpitz* clean one of her 15-inch gun barrels.

BELOW: The *Tirpitz* lies in Fettenfjord using the cliffs as a natural defence against air attack.

BOTTOM LEFT: The 15-inch guns of turret 'Caesar' at full elevation.

helpless. The *Rodney* closed to under 4000 yards, with orders to do maximum structural damage, while the C-in-C in the *King George V* stayed at maximum range to achieve plunging hits. The *Bismarck* was now so low in the water that it proved very difficult to penetrate her armoured decks, and although she was a wreck Tovey's ships could not sink her outright, so the cruiser *Dorsetshire* closed in and fired two torpedoes. At 1036 the *Bismarck* disappeared with her flag still flying, leaving only 110 survivors.

Thus ended the last attempt by the Germans to use their heavy surface units as ocean raiders, and the cherished idea of a foray by the *Scharnhorst, Gneisenau, Bismarck* and *Tirpitz* from Brest. The *Tirpitz* was to spend the rest of the war in Norwegian fjords, but with the avowed intention of tying down British forces rather than any aggressive role. In this role the *Tirpitz* succeeded admirably.

BELOW: A salvo from the after turrets of the *Tirpitz*.

BOTTOM: The *Tirpitz* achieved little during her career in the Norwegian fjords, but her presence tied down valuable Allied heavy units which could have been deployed elsewhere.

RIGHT: The torpedo boat *Tiger* was one of a series of small destroyers built during the prewar period.

CENTRE: The pocket battleship *Lützow* (ex-*Deutschland*) was renamed at the insistence of Adolf Hitler. He was afraid of the bad luck it would bring if a ship named Germany were sunk.

BOTTOM: *M.401* was typical of a large number of fleet minesweepers built before and during World War II.

Aircraft Carriers

The first German aircraft carrier, *Graf Zeppelin*, had been authorised in 1935 and launched in 1938, and a second, reported to be called *Peter Strasser*, was ordered in 1936. But the technical problems had proved too much, and endless wrangling with the Luftwaffe made it impossible to guarantee that any aircraft would be available. Marshal Göring's claim to control 'everything that flies' hampered the project at all stages, but the total lack of German experience in aircraft carrier design was as much to blame. *Graf Zeppelin* was suspended in April 1940 to allow detailed redesign; work started again in 1942 but was again suspended in 1943.

Two 12,000-ton carriers were planned before the war, but the failure with the two large carriers killed off the project. In 1942 the liners *Europa*, *Gneisenau* and *Potsdam* were selected for conversion to carriers, and the incomplete hull of the cruiser *Seydlitz* was taken in hand. In 1942–43 her superstructure was removed, but in 1945 she was scuttled at Königsberg and fell into Russian hands. To judge by the surviving plans of the *Graf Zeppelin* and the sketch designs for the conversions, none of these carriers would have been very successful, and they only demonstrate the extent to which the German Navy's desires outran performance, and how overstretched they were. Experiments in naval aviation were an expensive luxury which the Kreigsmarine could not easily afford.

Cruisers

Apart from the obsolescent training cruiser *Emden*, the Germans built three unusual light cruisers in the 1920s, but they played little part in wartime operations. As a class they were unlucky, with *Königsberg* sunk by dive bombers at Bergen and *Karlsruhe* torpedoed by HM Submarine *Truant* in April 1940; after an undistinguished career *Köln* was sunk at her moorings in Wilhelmshaven in 1945. Two later cruisers, *Leipzig* and *Nürnberg*, were rather more successful. Like the three 'Ks' they had an unusual gun arrangement, with only one triple 5·9-inch turret forward and two aft, but one cannot help thinking that the German Navy built these light cruisers largely because other navies had them; they had a modest endurance record and were not useful for ocean work.

Under the 1938 and 1939 Programme six 7800-ton vessels were proposed. With a speed of 35½ knots from a 3-shaft steam

and diesel plant and eight 5·9-inch guns they were intended to screen the new battle fleet. Like so much of the planned expansion, the class had to be cancelled, and the three laid down were replaced in 1941 by three *Spähkreuzer* or scout cruisers. This was a measure of desperation, caused by the fact that existing battle units had no suitable cruisers to act as a screen. They could outstrip the light cruisers in prolonged high speed steaming, while the heavy cruisers lacked endurance. But the loss of the *Bismarck* solved the dilemma,

and all three were stopped after only one had been laid down.

The two heavy cruisers in service were impressive ships, but their fighting qualities were achieved by a massive (40 per cent) increase over the 10,000-ton limit. Despite this margin they were hardly value for money, as they had only a theoretical endurance of 6800 miles at their economical speed. Nor could they claim great reliability in compensation, and *Admiral Hipper* was plagued by machinery problems. The *Prinz Eugen*

LEFT: Part of an incomplete German midget submarine surrendered in 1945.

BELOW: The powerful anti-aircraft armament of the Type VII C submarine *U.826*. She flies the white ensign after her surrender in 1945.

RIGHT: A Type VII C U-Boat sinks stern first during an aircraft attack.

BELOW: The torpedo recovery vessel *Raule*.

BELOW CENTRE: *Uj.2228* was the former Italian corvette *Euterpe*. Captured in 1943 by the Germans, she was scuttled in Genoa in April 1945.

BOTTOM: As a gesture of good will the Allies transferred obsolescent warships to the Soviet Navy. The battleship HMS *Royal Sovereign* was renamed *Arkhangelsk* in 1944.

BELOW: Flak gunners of *U.848* huddle for shelter south-west of Ascension Island when attacked by US Navy aircraft in November 1943.

was an improved sister, and a further pair, *Seydlitz* and *Lützow*, had originally been announced as light cruisers. *Lützow* was sold incomplete to the Russians in 1940, but without certain essential equipment to enable them to complete her. She was damaged by bombing at Leningrad in 1941–42, and was never completed. *Seydlitz* was nearly complete in 1942 when Hitler ordered her to be converted to an aircraft carrier.

Prinz Eugen had a lucky career. After being damaged by a magnetic mine in April 1941, she joined the *Bismarck* for her fatal sortie a month later, and escaped from the Battle of the Denmark Strait without damage. With the *Scharnhorst* and *Gneisenau* she went through the Channel in February 1942, and served in the Baltic. During the final evacuation of the East she rammed the *Leipzig* amidships and nearly cut her in half; finally she surrendered at Copenhagen in 1945 and was used as a target-ship at Bikini.

Destroyers and Torpedo Boats

Following the practice established before World War I, the German Navy referred to its small destroyers as torpedo boats, and construction of both types continued in parallel. The vessels built under the Versailles Treaty and later international

agreements were named, but from 1939 numbers were substituted, preceded by 'Z' for *Zerstörer* and 'T' for *Torpedoboot*. The prewar torpedo boats were 900-tonners, and were about 50 per cent over the permitted displacement. The destroyers were also oversized, and were handsome craft with two 5-inch guns forward and three aft. In both categories seakeeping qualities ranked below weight of armament, and they did not perform as well in service as their smaller contemporaries in the Royal Navy. To cite one clear example, in December 1943 *Scharnhorst*'s destroyers were sent back to base because the weather conditions were too rough, and yet she was torpedoed by smaller Home Fleet destroyers. The wartime destroyers, from *Z.23* onwards (known as the 'Narvik' Type) accentuated this problem by being armed with 5·9-inch guns. The weight of the mounting was too much for a light hull, and in any case the shell proved too heavy for hand-loading in a seaway. The usual problems with high-pressure boilers made them unreliable as well, so the bigger German destroyers must be considered as a failure.

The smaller torpedo boats fared better in the Channel and Baltic, where they were not exposed to such bad weather conditions. The *T.22* group were built in 1941–43 and were known as the 'Elbing' Type. They approximated to British pre-war destroyers in size and characteristics, and represented an altogether more useful type of medium-sized destroyer with reasonable endurance and armament.

BELOW: The *Marat* was one of three 25,000-ton battleships which had been built for the Czarist Navy before World War I. They were modernised between the wars and given suitable revolutionary names, but regained their former names in 1943.

ABOVE: The *Parizhskaya Kommuna* fires a salvo from her forward turret against German army positions around the fortress of Sevastopol. She was armed with twelve 12-inch guns and had a maximum speed of 23 knots.

BELOW: The German pocket battleship *Admiral Graf Spee* shows its camouflage scheme worn at the time of the Battle of the River Plate. She was armed with six 11-inch guns and had a speed of 26 knots.

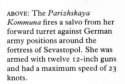

Motor Torpedo Boats

In their *Schnellboote* or S-Boats, known to the British for some strange reason as 'E-Boats', the Germans achieved near-perfection. The first S-Boats had been ordered in 1930, and later a contract was placed with MAN and Daimler-Benz for the development of a lightweight high-speed diesel engine. Research work proceeded on a novel hull-form as well, and by 1935 it was possible to treble the power without a corresponding increase in dimensions. No other country had made such startling progress, and in 1939 the new 20-cylinder V-form diesel appeared from Daimler-Benz. Large orders were placed during the war, and some 200 were completed by 1945.

Apart from a small success in sinking a Norwegian torpedo boat, S-Boats had their first success in May 1940 at the time of the fall of France. On the night of May 9/10 the destroyer HMS *Kelly* was torpedoed, and during the Dunkirk evacuation they sank three destroyers, the French *Jaguar* and *Sirocco* and the British HMS *Wakeful*. As more boats came into service the scale of operations in the Channel and off the English east coast were stepped up. For a long time the S-Boats completely outclassed the British MTBs in speed and firepower, and they sank large numbers of merchant ships with ease. The British retaliated with bigger and better MTBs and MGBs (Motor Gun Boats) and many bloody battles were fought.

In mid-1941 three flotillas of S-Boats were sent to the Baltic, and in October ten boats made a remarkable journey to the Mediterranean via the Rhine, the Rhine-Rhône Canal, the Doubs and the Saône and the Rhône. To cloak the operation in secrecy the boats were given funnels and the crews wore civilian clothes, but ironically a British MTB Flotilla had made the same journey the other way in 1939! Another flotilla made an even more unorthodox journey to the Black Sea in 1942, travelling via the Kiel Canal and the Elbe to Dresden, then by road to Ingolstadt and then down the Danube.

On the night of June 22/23, 1941, the German Navy took on a further commit-

LEFT: Siberian troops board the flotilla leader *Tashkent* on their way to reinforce Sevastopol in 1942.

RIGHT: Men of the Russian Navy load a torpedo. The old cruiser *Krasni Krim* (Red Crimea) lies in the background.

BELOW: The newly commissioned *Arkhangelsk* lies at Rosyth before leaving for Russian service in 1944. She was armed with eight 15-inch guns and had a speed of 22 knots.

LEFT: Russian boats deliver vital supplies to the besieged city of Leningrad across Lake Ladoga. Trucks were used in place of boats during the winter when the lake froze solid.

BELOW: The *Tashkent* unloads ammunition for the defence of Sevastopol. The *Tashkent* was built in Fascist Italy in 1937 for the Soviets.

BOTTOM: There was little genuine fraternisation between British and Russian sailors, for the British resented the fact that the Soviet Navy played such a small role in convoying food and military equipment to Murmansk and Archangel.

ment, the war against the Soviet Union. As we have seen three flotillas of S-Boats had already been transferred to the Baltic, and U-Boats and surface warships were similarly redeployed. The Soviet Navy was in a parlous state at this time, with many of its highest officers shot during the 1937–38 purges. Its older ships were obsolescent and the rapid expansion under Stalin had not been accompanied by an increase in competence. Fire control was poor and machinery was unreliable. Efforts had been made to use foreign expertise to remedy these deficiencies, and despite ideological differences Russian technical missions had approached the United States for help with battleship designs, Italy for help in building cruisers and destroyers, and Germany for help with submarines. The link between Germany and Russia was a particularly cynical relationship going back to the time before the abrogation of the Treaty of Versailles, when Russia had allowed essential testing of submarine components to take place on her soil, and in return received German help in eliminating

RIGHT: Vice-Admiral Golovko, C-in-C of the Russian Northern Fleet, decorates a sailor of the destroyer *Gremyashky*.

ABOVE: Two British subs, the *Sunfish* and *Ursula*, were handed over to the Soviet Navy in 1944.

ABOVE RIGHT: Russian sub chaser drops depth charges in the Barents Sea while a sailor takes a range.

RIGHT: The cruiser *Enterprise* sank a force of German destroyers with the *Glasgow* in the Bay of Biscay on December 28, 1943. This was the last major surface action in European waters.

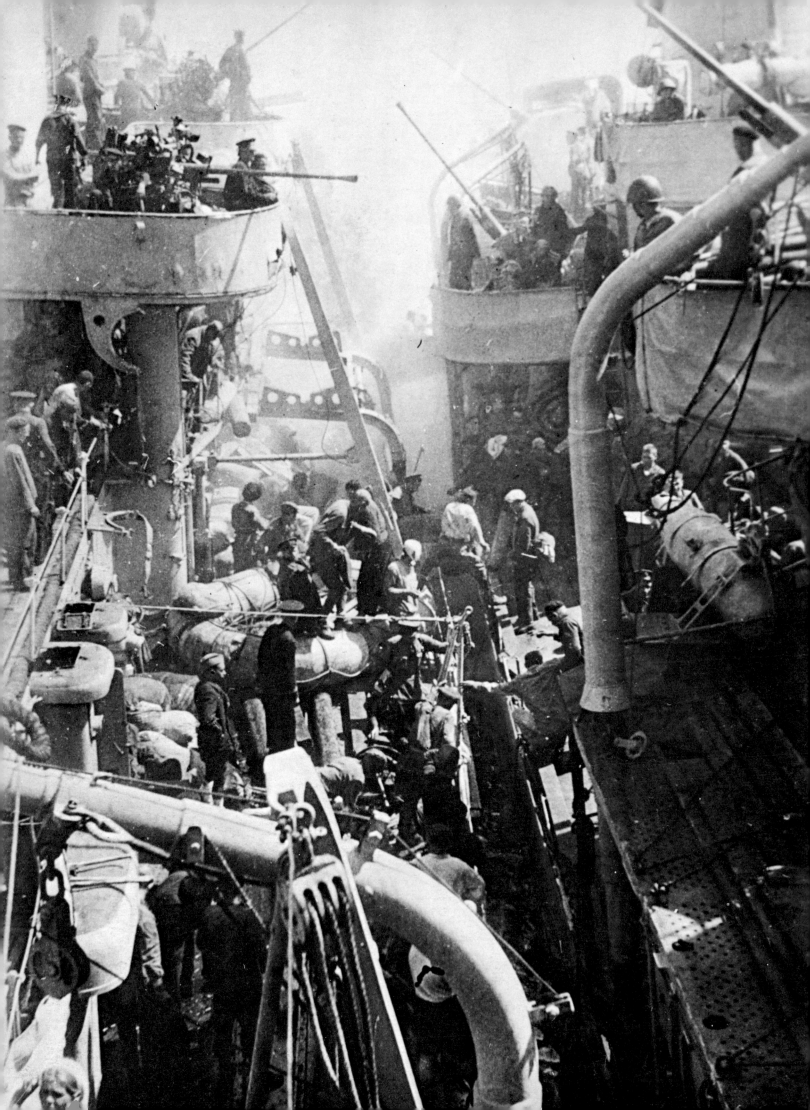

faults in her submarines. The Russian Navy was anxious to see the plans of the *Bismarck*, and as we have seen, bought the uncompleted cruiser *Lützow* in 1940 as part of the Molotov-Ribbentrop Pact. But the Germans had plans of their own for Russia, and procrastinated throughout 1940 and early 1941, with the result that very little information changed hands, and the *Petropavlovsk* (ex-*Lützow*) proved impossible to complete.

Despite the Russians' numerical superiority in the Baltic their lack of initiative allowed German forces much more access than they had hoped for. Because of the shallowness of the Baltic and the enormous number of mines laid by both sides, the majority of activity was limited to small ships, torpedo boats, gunboats and motor torpedo boats. As in the Channel and North Sea these actions were frequently bloody and confused. The Russians had a very large submarine force (it had been the world's largest in 1939), but it failed to produce proportionate results, whereas German and Finnish submarines sank a large number of Russian ships. However, the diversion of forces to the Baltic and Black Sea was an additional strain which the under-strength German Navy could not afford, however well it acquitted itself.

BELOW: Grumman Hellcat fighters crowd the flight deck of the US carrier *Hornet*, the second such craft given this illustrious name after the first was sunk at Santa Cruz in 1942.

THE US NAVY

132

BELOW: The *North Carolina* was the first of the new generation of battleships built for the US Navy before World War II. She was armed with nine 16-inch guns and steamed at 28 knots.

The United States had shown itself a true friend to the British as early as 1940, when after Dunkirk President Roosevelt had persuaded Congress to 'lend' fifty elderly destroyers to the Royal Navy to tide them over the losses and casualties incurred during the Dunkirk evacuation and the Norwegian Campaign. In March 1941 the Land-Lease Bill became law, and in exchange for a 99-year lease for bases in Newfoundland and the West Indies, the USA began to channel an ever-increasing amount of war matériel to Britain. President Roosevelt made no secret of his belief that a victory by Germany and Italy in Europe would be against American interests, but the United States was still committed to a policy of non-involvement in the European War, and aid to the British stopped short of provoking German retaliation for the time being.

The US Navy was limited to a nominal parity with the Royal Navy by international treaty, but differed considerably in its composition. Like the British the Americans relied on their battle fleet as the main striking force, with the aircraft carrier assigned a supporting role. Cruisers and destroyers had the same roles in screening the fleet, but the anti-submarine escort was conspicuous by its absence, despite the fact that the USN had entered World War I at the height of the U-Boat offensive of 1917, it had seen at first-hand the dire results of an offensive against shipping.

In one respect the US Navy was particularly well equipped. Unlike the Royal Navy naval aviation had never been hived off to a separate 'unified' air force, and although naval air power was not yet fully recognised as the main strength of the Fleet, a number of senior officers were air-minded and its aircraft were well designed. The American carriers were the best in the world, thanks to 20 years of steady development. The President's policy of giving the British maximum aid brought two priceless advantages which were not immediately obvious. First, the British passed on all their technical and operational experience, particularly about their own weapons and those of the enemy. Second, from April 1941 the repair facilities extended to British warships in US Navy Yards gave those yards a wealth of experience in coping with battle damage and brought them to a peak of efficiency which would be desperately needed sooner than anyone had imagined.

In 1940 Congress had approved the 'Two-Ocean' Navy Bill, an increase of

Strength Of The US Navy In December 1941

Figures in parentheses indicate ships under construction.

16 Battleships (+16)[1]

1 *Arkansas*[2] completed 1912
2 *New York* Class completed 1914
2 *Nevada* Class completed 1916
2 *Pennsylvania* Class completed 1916
3 *New Mexico* Class completed 1917-19
2 *California* Class completed 1920-21
3 *Colorado Class* completed 1921-23
1 *North Carolina* Class[3]

[1] A second *North Carolina* Class, 4 *South Dakota* Class, 6 *Iowa* Class and 5 *Montana* Class under construction. [2] A sister-ship had been converted to a target ship. [3] The second ship due for completion March 1942.

7 Aircraft Carriers (+11)[1]

2 *Lexington* Class completed 1927[2]
1 *Ranger* com.1933   1 *Wasp* com.1941
3 *Yorktown* Class completed 1937-41.

[1] *Essex* Class. [2] Converted from battlecruiser hulls.

18 Heavy Cruisers (+8)[1]

2 *Pensacola* Class completed 1929-30
6 *Northampton* Class completed 1930-31
2 *Portland* Class completed 1932-33
7 *Minneapolis* Class completed 1934-37
1 *Wichita* completed 1939

[1] *Baltimore* Class.

19 Light Cruisers (+32)[1]

10 *Omaha* Class completed 1923-25
7 *Brooklyn* Class completed 1938-39
2 *Helena* Class completed 1939

[1] *Cleveland* Class.

6 Anti-Aircraft Cruisers[1]

[1] 4 launched, and 1 (*Atlanta*) nearly completed.

171 Destroyers (+188)[1]

1 *Allen* completed 1917[2]
71 *Wickes*/*Clemson* Classes[3], com 1918-22
8 *Farragut* Class completed 1934-35
12 *Mahan* Class completed 1936-37
7 *Selfridge* Class completed 1936-37
5 *Somers* Class completed 1938-39
2 *Dunlap* Class completed 1938
19 *Gridley* Class completed 1938-40
8 *Anderson* Class completed 1939-40
38 *Benson* & *Livermore* Classes com.1940-41

[1] *Benson/Livermore* and *Fletcher* Classes. [2] Sole survivor of the *Sampson* Class. [3] Known as the flush-deckers, of which 50 were lent to the RN, 46 were serving on subsidiary duties and the remainder scrapped.

114 Submarines (+79)[1]

8 "O" Class completed 1918
19 "R" Class completed 1918-19
38 "S" Class completed 1919-24
3 *Barracuda* Class completed 1924-25
1 *Argonaut* minelayer completed 1928
2 *Nautilus* Class completed 1930
1 *Dolphin* completed 1932
2 *Cachalot* Class completed 1934
10 "P" Class completed 1935-37
16 "S" Class completed 1937-39
12 "T" Class completed 1940-41

[1] *Gato* Class.

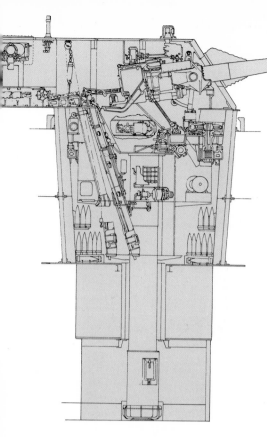

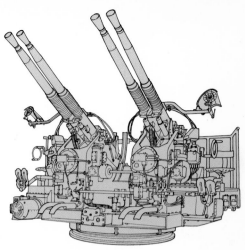

1,325,000 tons of major warships to the authorised strength. This meant that the USN began World War II with a ship-building industry already warmed up and geared for mass-production in all categories. This, combined with the steady expansion of the refitting capacity of the naval yards and the growth of mercantile shipbuilding capacity to meet British requirements meant that America did not enter World War II totally unprepared.

But the US Navy's position in other respects was not so healthy. Carrier tactics were not as good as they might be, and anti-submarine tactics and equipment were dangerously outdated. Contrary to all lessons of 1917–18, the US Navy set its face against the use of convoy, and firmly believed in so-called 'offensive patrols' as a means of protecting shipping. This stemmed from a reluctance to tie warships down to what was seen as the humdrum task of escorting convoys. To add to the problem, developments in Sonar had not matched British progress with Asdic. Radar was under development, but the practical applications owed much to British experience.

Battleships

The bulk of the American battle fleet was of World War I vintage, but the older ships had been rebuilt and modernised. The first new ships were ordered in 1937, the *North Carolina* and *Washington*, and were roughly comparable in size to the British *King George V* Class, with heavier armament and lighter armour. Like the British ships they adopted a dual-purpose secondary armament to save weight, and they were designed for the same speed, 28 knots. The next four ships had a better system of underwater and deck protection, but adopted a shorter and wider hull. This meant more horsepower to maintain the same speed as the *North Carolina* Class to overcome the drag of the wider hull. But by concentrating the superstructure more room was left for a well-laid-out anti-aircraft armament.

The next class, six 45,000-ton *Iowa*s, were ordered in 1940, and took advantage of the end of the tonnage limitations under the international treaties. The armament was the same as in the *North Carolina* and *South Dakota* Classes, but with over 50 per cent more horsepower and finer lines they were much faster. Although impressive ships they were an extravagant design by comparison with their immediate predecessors. For all their extra power they only achieved a sea speed of 30 knots, two knots faster than the *South Dakota*, and no extra protection. For years they were credited with massive 18-inch armour belts and a speed in excess of 33 knots, but their armour was overstated by a factor of 50 per cent and their speed exaggerated. The rationale of the design seems to have been a belated realisation of the Bureau of Ships that its new aircraft carriers were faster than the new battleships. The *Iowa* Class were rushed through the design stage, and armour protection had to be subordinated to a massive increase in power, with no time allowed for redesign to economise on space. As things turned out the first pair were not ready until 1943, by which time the likelihood of a fleet action against Japanese battleships had receded, and the four completed made superb escorts for carrier task forces. The last two *Iowa*s were not completed, while the 60,000-ton *Montana*s were suspended in 1941 and cancelled in 1943 to avoid the diversion of resources from other ships.

Aircraft Carriers

The US Navy's original carrier, the ex-collier *Langley*, had been re-rated as an aircraft transport in 1937, so the oldest carriers in commission in 1941 were the *Lexington* and *Saratoga*, which had been converted from the hulls of two 33,000-ton battlecruisers cancelled under the Washington Treaty. Like the World War I battleships they had turbo-electric propulsion rather than the standard steam turbines in other navies. Steam drove four giant turbo-generators, which supplied power to eight 16,500-kw electric motors. Although hailed as an engineering masterpiece in its day, 'electric drive' was very weighty for the power developed, and it was never repeated in large American warships.

The *Lex* and *Sara* were the world's largest carriers when completed in 1927, and they carried 90 aircraft. They were thus able to play a decisive role in the evaluation of naval airpower in prewar fleet exercises and war games, and the US Navy was fortunate in getting so many of the answers right in its first operational carriers. The next ship, the *Ranger*, was

FAR LEFT: Trainee pilots learned to land on two Great Lakes paddle steamers, the *Wolverine* and the *Sable* (right).

LEFT: The USS *Enterprise* (CV.6) was the greatest US carrier in World War II. The Big 'E' fought in every major action from Pearl Harbor to Okinawa.

RIGHT AND FAR RIGHT: The *Sable* was used on Lake Michigan throughout the war as a training carrier.

BELOW: The new *Hornet* was the fourth unit of the *Essex* Class fast carriers which came into service in 1943. She displaced 27,100 tons and carried 100 aircraft.

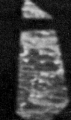

138

LEFT: The USS *Lexington* (CV.2) during the Battle of the Coral Sea a short time before she was destroyed by a series of internal explosions. Note that no 8-inch gun turrets appear; they were removed in July 1941 for coastal defence.

BELOW: The battleship USS *California* (BB.44) was sunk at Pearl Harbor, yet was raised and docked only four months later. She was completely rebuilt and re-commissioned in May 1944.

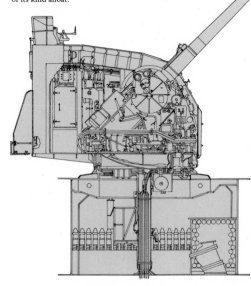

BELOW: The 5-inch/38-cal. dual-purpose gun was the standard US Navy anti-aircraft weapon in the war, probably the finest of its kind afloat.

BOTTOM: The USS *Lansdowne* (DD.486) was a destroyer of the *Livermore* Class, armed with four 5-inch guns and ten 21-inch torpedo tubes, had a top speed of 37 knots.

much smaller, and although she carried 86 aircraft her drawbacks only tended to confirm the value of greater size. Although another small carrier, the *Wasp*, was built just before the war, the next class went up to the maximum allowed under the treaties. This was the *Yorktown* Class, which proved highly satisfactory and were used as the model for future construction.

The *Enterprise*, *Hornet* and *Yorktown* were to become household names before long. They differed considerably from contemporary British carriers, and had more in common with Japanese carriers. The main difference from British practice was in having an 'open' hangar as opposed to the 'closed' or armoured box hangar of the *Illustrious* Class. This meant that the hangar was limited in area only by the ship's side, and was kept weatherproof by roller shutters. In British carriers the hangar was totally enclosed by compartments and had to be entered through a fireproof lobby. The American system allowed a much greater aircraft capacity but offered a much greater fire hazard, particularly as the hangar ventilation was linked to the ship's main ventilation system. In addition the main armour protection was on the hangar deck, and not on the flight deck. This was to prove crucial later on, but the US Navy and its designers were fundamentally right in thinking that the carrier's aircraft were its main defence. To back up this concept the aircraft handling arrangements were designed to allow flight deck crews to launch, recover, strike down, refuel and rearm aircraft faster than any other navy.

The eleven *Essex* Class under construction in 1941 incorporated all the ideas developed in earlier carriers, but with no limits on tonnage. Two more were ordered a week after the outbreak of war, and a further eleven of slightly modified design were ordered during the war, one of which was suspended at the war's end and another two were cancelled. The first of the class, the USS *Essex*, was commissioned almost exactly a year after the outbreak of war, and there is no doubt that the US Navy had judged the margin too finely in its provision for aircraft carriers.

Heavy Cruisers

The 8-inch gunned cruisers built under the Washington Treaty compared favourably with foreign equivalents, and achieved a good balance of fighting qualities without exceeding the tonnage limits. Unlike foreign cruisers they abandoned torpedo-tubes. The design of the last heavy cruisers tended to merge with that of light cruisers, apart from the different gun-calibre; the *Wichita*, completed in 1939, was a modification of the 6-inch gunned *Brooklyn* type, and the 1940 Programme *Baltimores* were very similar to the contemporary *Clevelands*. Apart from simplifying the superstructure and trunking the twin funnels into one to allow better fields of fire for the anti-aircraft armament, no further changes were made in the war-built cruisers.

Light Cruisers

With only ten 'scout' cruisers of antiquated design even when they were completed in the early 1920s, the US Navy had not shown much interest in 6-inch gunned cruisers. In 1933–34 seven *Brooklyn* Class cruisers were ordered as a reply to the Japanese *Mogami* Class, followed by a slightly different pair, the *Helena* Class. Their most unusual feature was a flush deck with two catapults and an aircraft crane right aft. A hangar for four floatplanes was sited underneath the stern, which for the first time in any cruiser was squared off, a so-called 'transom' stern. Although much admired abroad this arrangement of housing floatplanes proved to be more trouble than it was worth, and it was never repeated. The *Brooklyns* copied the layout of the *Mogami* Class, with an extra triple 6-inch turret between the bridge and the two forward turrets – a position with very restricted arcs of fire and therefore of negligible or little use.

The next class, the *Clevelands*, recognised the shortcomings of the *Brooklyns*, and dropped the fifth turret in favour of better anti-aircraft fire. Thirty units were ordered, making them the largest single class of cruisers ever built. It will be seen later how useful this class was in remedying the shortages of aircraft carriers in the early stages of the war.

Anti-Aircraft Cruisers

In 1939 the first of a unique group of cruisers was ordered, the *Atlanta* Class. Bearing no resemblance to any other USN cruiser design, these ships were similar in conception and layout to the British *Dido* Class. They were intended to work with destroyers, and had an armament of twin 5-inch guns and torpedo-tubes. Although intended for the ultra-high speed of 38 knots, they proved disappointing in service and lacked endurance for the Pacific. However, when operating as screening vessels for task forces, their heavy battery of sixteen 5-inch guns proved valuable.

Destroyers

At the start of the war the US Navy's destroyer strength was ill-balanced, with too many obsolescent vessels built at the end of World War I. These 'flush-deckers' had been mass-produced to meet

the desperate needs of the Allies in 1917, but the existence of such large numbers prevented the construction of new improved types. No new destroyers were laid down until 1932, by which time foreign destroyer design had overtaken American ideas, but by hard work and careful design a lot of leeway had been made up. In 1941 the excellent *Fletcher* Class was under construction, 2000-tonners armed with five 5-inch dual-purpose guns and ten torpedo-tubes. Although not as powerful on paper as their Japanese opponents, the *Fletcher*s had the endurance and seaworthiness needed, and they rank as possibly the best destroyers produced by any navy in World War II.

BELOW: *Salt Lake City* (CA.25), *Pensacola* (CA.24) and *New Orleans* (CA.32) at Pearl Harbor on October 31, 1943. The prewar heavy cruisers bore the brunt of the fighting in the South Pacific throughout 1942.

RIGHT: USS *Marblehead*
(CL.12) at Brooklyn Navy Yard
in May 1942, home for repairs
from her ordeal in Dutch East
Indian waters in February.

BELOW LEFT: The basic US wartime destroyers of the *Fletcher* Class were designed well but added gunpower and endurance were achieved by the expanded *Allen M. Sumner* Class portrayed here.

CENTRE LEFT: A Japanese pilot's eye-view of Pearl Harbor at the moment of attack, as Battleship Row is hit at around 0800, December 7, 1941.

BOTTOM LEFT: The new destroyer USS *Nicholas* (DD.449) runs her speed trials late in 1942.

BELOW RIGHT: US Submarine *Tinosa* (SS.283) returns to Pearl Harbor from a war patrol in 1944. The *Gato* Class boats proved to be exceptionally well designed for Pacific operations.

The war between the United States and Japan began at the US Navy's Pacific Fleet base, Pearl Harbor, in the Hawaiian Islands. On Sunday, December 7, 1941, at 0800 bombers and torpedo-bombers from a Japanese carrier striking force attacked without warning and knocked out the battleships of the Pacific Fleet. It was a repetition of Taranto, with one significant exception; the aircraft carriers *Saratoga*, *Lexington* and *Enterprise* and thirteen cruisers were not in harbour at the time, and so, although the Japanese achieved their aim of destroying the American battle fleet, they left the most dangerous strike element untouched.

By any standards the situation was bad, with the *Arizona* and *Oklahoma* wrecked beyond repair, the *West Virginia* and *California* sunk, and the *Tennessee* and *Nevada* seriously damaged. The attackers had escaped without serious loss. Anti-aircraft fire had inflicted casualties on the second wave, which had failed to destroy the fuel storage tanks on which any future fleet operations depended. The debacle is hard to comprehend, for a severe diplomatic crisis existed between the United States and Japan, vital intelligence about the impending attack was withheld from the commanders of the forces in Hawaii.

However brilliant the planning of the Pearl Harbor attack may have been, it did not have the anticipated effect of cowing the Americans and forcing them to abandon the Far East to Japanese hegemony. The United States swung behind its President and immediately began to arm itself for the struggle. In a mad moment Adolf Hitler chose to declare war on the United States in support of Japan, and so what had been a purely European war was now joined to the Pacific War, and became truly a World War. Thanks to the foresight of Franklin D. Roosevelt the US was much stronger than it had been two years earlier, but much of its armed strength was still unrealised.

At the 11th hour the British, Australians and Dutch threw in their lot with the United States, but it was too late. British plans had always emphasised the risk of a war in the Far East, but, of course, by the end of 1941 the disasters in the Mediterranean had disposed of the ships which might have been sent to the Pacific. After July 1941 Russia was fully committed against Germany, and so the Japanese Army could spare troops from Manchuria. By December Japanese troops had invaded Thailand and were clearly poised for an attack on Malaya as part of their

Naval Strength In The Pacific, December 1941

	British & Empire	US	Dutch	Free French	Japanese		British & Empire	US	Dutch	Free French	Japanese
Capital Ships	2	9	–	–	10	Light Cruisers	7	11	3	1	18
Carriers	–	3	–	–	10	Destroyers	13	80	7	–	113
Heavy Cruisers	1	13	–	–	18	Submarines	–	56	13	–	63

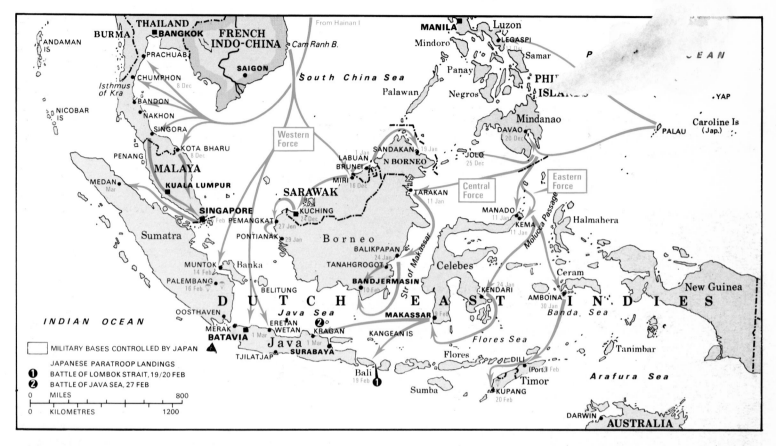

drive southwards to take over the rubber and oil fields of the East Indies. Although the Netherlands Navy had the bulk of its surface fleet and some submarines in the East Indies, the main defence against the Japanese would be the British and Australian naval forces based on the fortress of Singapore.

In October 1941 Winston Churchill hatched an ill-considered plan to send the modern battleship *Prince of Wales* and the old battlecruiser *Repulse* to 'overawe' the Japanese and to deter them from attacking Malaya. The plan was ill-conceived because it overrode the Naval Staff's contention that only a balanced fleet (with at least one aircraft carrier to provide cover) was worth sending. Division of force is an unsound military principle, and it is interesting to consider what the effect on Japanese plans might have been if the two British capital ships had been sent to join the US Navy. Although outnumbered the combined Allied forces in the Pacific would have made a powerful fleet in every category except aircraft carriers.

Admiral Phillips, the new British Commander-in-Chief, had time to discuss a joint plan with Admiral Hart, commanding the US Asiatic Fleet in the Philippines, just before the Pearl Harbor attack, but thereafter the situation deteriorated so rapidly that there was little planning apart from extemporised defences. Simultaneous attacks were launched by the Japanese on Hong Kong, the Philippines, Siam and Malaya, as well as individual islands across the Pacific. Pearl Harbor and the virtual extinction of

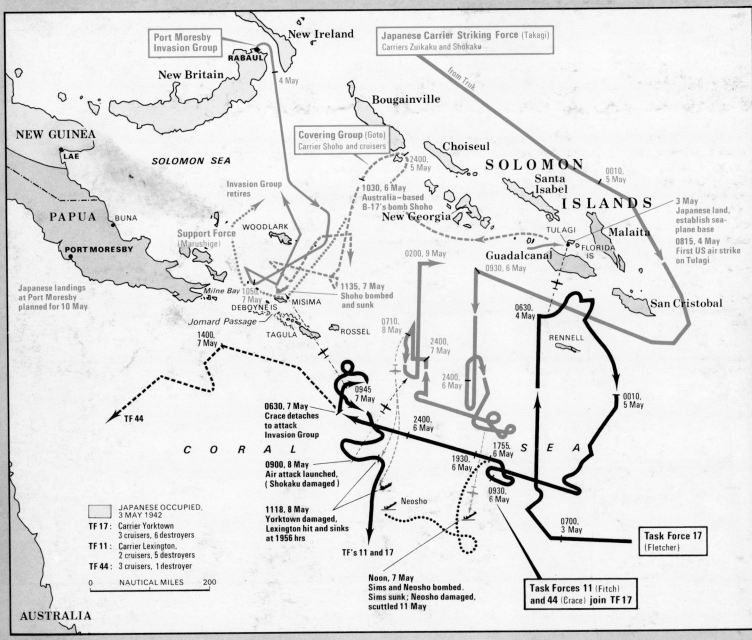

Port Moresby Invasion Group

New Ireland

RABAUL

New Britain

Japanese Carrier Striking Force (Takagi)
Carriers Zuikaku and Shokaku

4 May

Bougainville

from Truk

NEW GUINEA

LAE

SOLOMON SEA

Covering Group (Goto)
Carrier Shoho and cruisers

2400, 5 May

Choiseul

SOLOMON

Santa Isabel

0010, 5 May

ISLANDS

PAPUA

BUNA

Invasion Group retires

1030, 6 May
Australia–based
B-17's bomb Shoho

New Georgia

3 May
Japanese land, establish sea-plane base

PORT MORESBY

Support Force (Marushige)

WOODLARK

TULAGI

Malaita

0815, 4 May
First US air strike on Tulagi

Japanese landings at Port Moresby planned for 10 May

Milne Bay 1050, 7 May

MISIMA

0200, 9 May

Guadalcanal

FLORIDA IS

San Cristobal

1135, 7 May
Shoho bombed and sunk

0930, 6 May

0630, 4 May

DEBOYNE IS

1400, 7 May

Jomard Passage

TAGULA

ROSSEL

0710, 8 May

2400, 7 May

RENNELL

0010, 5 May

TF 44

0945 7 May

0630, 7 May
Crace detaches to attack Invasion Group

2400, 6 May

2400, 6 May

1755, 6 May

1930, 6 May

C O R A L

S E A

0900, 8 May
Air attack launched,
(Shokaku damaged)

Neosho

0930, 6 May

0700, 3 May

Task Force 17
(Fletcher)

1118, 8 May
Yorktown damaged,
Lexington hit and sinks
at 1956 hrs

JAPANESE OCCUPIED,
3 MAY 1942

TF 17: Carrier Yorktown
3 cruisers, 6 destroyers

TF 11: Carrier Lexington,
2 cruisers, 5 destroyers

TF 44: 3 cruisers, 1 destroyer

TF's 11 and 17

Noon, 7 May
Sims and Neosho bombed.
Sims sunk; Neosho damaged,
scuttled 11 May

Task Forces 11 (Fitch)
and 44 (Crace) join TF 17

0   NAUTICAL MILES   200

AUSTRALIA

LEFT: The US carrier *Lexington* under attack during the Battle of the Coral Sea, May 8, 1942. She was sunk later that same day.

American seapower left the South-West Pacific completely isolated, and inevitably the British capital ships, *Prince of Wales* and *Repulse*, fell victim to overwhelming air attack on December 10. The two ships were caught while steaming off the eastern coast of Malaya to intercept a reported invasion force, and both ships went down in quick succession to skilful bomb- and torpedo-attack. Next to fall was the so-called 'impregnable' fortress of Singapore, which had been built to support a strong Far Eastern Fleet, and with it went the last hope of a unified defence of South-East Asia.

Late in December 1941 the ABDA Command (American-British-Dutch-Australian) was set up with Admiral Hart, USN, in command. Its first job was to ensure that supplies got through to Singapore while the fortress still held out, and the new ramshackle force achieved this admirably. But the real test was still to come. On January 24, 1942 ABDA ships inflicted casualties on a Japanese invasion force off Balikpapan in Borneo, but could not slow down the advance. Bali and Timor were attacked on February 19 and 20, and at the same time a carrier force raided as far south as Australia, inflicting heavy damage on Darwin. It must be remembered that simultaneously Japanese forces were overrunning the Philippines, and the situation was so fluid that it was

ABOVE: US Fleet sub of the *Gato* Class in 1944.

LEFT: Crewmen of the light cruiser *Marblehead* examine bomb damage after the ship limped into Tjilatjap in Java in February 1942.

BELOW: USS *Erie* (PG.50) beached off Curacao in the Dutch West Indies in November 1942.

146

BELOW AND BELOW RIGHT: The
USS *Yorktown* (CV.5) reels
under a bomb hit during the
Battle of Midway. Refitted after
Coral Sea in only three days,
her appearance at Midway
startled the Japanese. Although
the crew brought the fires
under control, the luckless
vessel was torpedoed by a
Japanese sub and finally sank.

RIGHT: Douglas SBD Dauntlesses
over the burning Japanese
heavy cruiser *Mikuma* during
the Battle of Midway: June 6,
1942.

impossible to organise any sort of co-ordinated defensive strategy.

On February 27 the surviving warships of ABDA fought the desperate Battle of the Java Sea. Under the Dutch Admiral Karel Doorman the heavy cruisers HMS *Exeter* and USS *Houston* and the 6-inch gun cruisers HNMS *De Ruyter* and *Java* and HMAS *Perth* were sunk by gunfire and torpedoes from Admiral Nishimura's heavy and light cruisers in a running battle over two days. In a space of less than three months the Allies had lost two capital ships, five cruisers, a seaplane carrier and 17 destroyers in the defence of South-East Asia, all to no avail. In the Central Pacific American seapower had not been wiped out quite so disastrously, but it had been neutralised, and there was little or nothing to prevent the Imperial Japanese Navy from overrunning the entire western half of the Pacific.

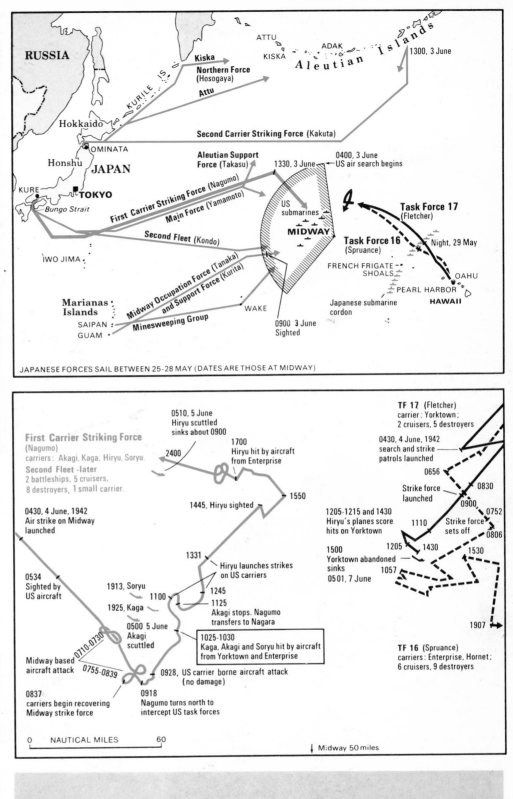

The first map:

RUSSIA

Kiska
Northern Force
(Hosogaya)
Attu

ATTU
KISKA
ADAK
Aleutian Islands

1300, 3 June

KURILE IS.

Hokkaido

OMINATA

Second Carrier Striking Force (Kakuta)

Honshu JAPAN

Aleutian Support Force (Takasu)

0400, 3 June
US air search begins

1330, 3 June

KURE
Bungo Strait

TOKYO

First Carrier Striking Force (Nagumo)
Main Force (Yamamoto)

US submarines

MIDWAY

Task Force 17 (Fletcher)

Second Fleet (Kondo)

Task Force 16 (Spruance)

Night, 29 May

IWO JIMA

FRENCH FRIGATE SHOALS

OAHU

Marianas Islands

Midway Occupation Force (Tanaka)
and Support Force (Kurita)

WAKE

PEARL HARBOR

HAWAII

SAIPAN
GUAM

Minesweeping Group

Japanese submarine cordon

0900 3 June Sighted

JAPANESE FORCES SAIL BETWEEN 25-28 MAY (DATES ARE THOSE AT MIDWAY)

The second map:

First Carrier Striking Force
(Nagumo)
carriers: Akagi, Kaga, Hiryu, Soryu.
Second Fleet -later
2 battleships, 5 cruisers,
8 destroyers, 1 small carrier.

0510, 5 June
Hiryu scuttled
sinks about 0900

2400

1700
Hiryu hit by aircraft
from Enterprise

1445, Hiryu sighted

1550

1331

Hiryu launches strikes
on US carriers

TF 17 (Fletcher)
carrier: Yorktown;
2 cruisers, 5 destroyers

0430, 4 June, 1942
search and strike
patrols launched

0656

Strike force
launched

0830

0900

0752

1205-1215 and 1430
Hiryu's planes score
hits on Yorktown

1110

0430, 4 June, 1942
Air strike on Midway
launched

0534
Sighted by
US aircraft

0710-0730

1913, Soryu
1925, Kaga

1100

1245

1125
Akagi stops. Nagumo
transfers to Nagara

1500
Yorktown abandoned
sinks
05 01, 7 June

1205

1430

Strike force
sets off

0806

1530

1057

1907

0500 5 June
Akagi
scuttled

1025-1030
Kaga, Akagi and Soryu hit by aircraft
from Yorktown and Enterprise

Midway based
aircraft attack

0755-0839

0928, US carrier borne aircraft attack
(no damage)

0837
carriers begin recovering
Midway strike force

0918
Nagumo turns north to
intercept US task forces

TF 16 (Spruance)
carriers: Enterprise, Hornet;
6 cruisers, 9 destroyers

0 NAUTICAL MILES 60

Midway 50 miles

THE IMPERIAL JAPANESE NAVY

The Japanese Navy was unique among the major navies of World War II. Under the threat of war against Russia in the early years of the century it had been expanded with considerable technical help from the British. The total annihilation of the Russian Fleet at the Battle of Tsushima in 1905 raised Japan to the role of a leading naval power, and by the end of World War I she ranked third. The naval limitation treaties were dismissed angrily by the Japanese as a 'Rolls-Rolls-Ford' ratio in place of the parity they wanted, and it was decided to build a navy which could dominate the Pacific when the time came, by any means, honest or dishonest.

From the end of World War I Japanese warship design took a direction all of its own, in pursuit of a doctrine which demanded absolute superiority in each category. Thus each cruiser class had to be superior to any foreign cruiser, and each destroyer had to match any foreign destroyer, with no great regard for what was needed. This produced a range of remarkable warships which astounded the world, but their qualities concealed many shortcomings. No navy has ever approached its problems of shipbuilding and tactics in such a dogmatic and doctrinaire fashion, and while no navy reached such high points, equally Japan's enemies never committed blunders of such magnitude.

Only the Japanese matched the progress made by the US Navy in naval aviation. The first carrier was completed in 1922, and many experiments were tried. Two large capital ship hulls were retained from the cancellations under the Washington Treaty, and when Japan announced her withdrawal from the treaties she pressed ahead with new big carriers. Their naval aircrew were without doubt the most highly trained, and with excellent aircraft as well, the naval air arm made the Japanese Navy a deadly foe.

The battle fleet had been limited by treaty, but the ships had all been modernised to an extent unknown in other navies to improve their fighting qualities. Because the 1930 London Treaty gave Japan a total tonnage allowance in proportion to the USA and Great Britain there was great emphasis on restricting displacement, but as high speed and gunpower were also required to maintain qualitative superiority, Japanese naval architects had great difficulty in staying within the limits. Many types of smaller ships suffered from lack of stability and structural weakness.

Japanese shipyards had been expanded

in World War I to meet British requirements for merchant ships, but they did not prove adequate in World War II. Little investigation was done into mass-production techniques until it was too late. Radar was not developed, and the dangers of submarine attack were not foreseen. Ultimately it was in the field of doctrine that the Japanese showed the most weakness, a point well illustrated by their failure in anti-submarine tactics. Despite her possession of a large fleet of submarines, with which she hoped to reduce the numerical advantage of the American Fleet, Japan did not foresee that her large mercantile fleet would be vulnerable to submarine attack. No escorts were planned, and no convoy organisation was even considered, largely because it was considered to be too defensive a measure for a fighting navy. Similarly submariners were encouraged to attack warships rather than merchant ships, a fact which saved the US Navy a great deal of trouble when sending troopships and transports through the Central Pacific.

Having said that, it must be remembered that the Japanese armed forces were tough, well-trained and determined fighters. Lacking radar, they developed a skill in night-fighting which was unmatched, and they showed a better appreciation of Pacific conditions than the Americans by developing torpedo-warfare to a high pitch. Their 'Long Lance' Type 93 24-inch torpedo was driven by oxygen, giving it a speed and range which came as a terrible surprise to the Allies. This was truly a 'secret weapon' which gave the Japanese a significant advantage in the first year of the war.

Battleships

The oldest battleships were the four *Kongo* Class, which had been completed at the beginning of World War I as British-designed battlecruisers of 27,500 tons, 8-inch armour and 27½ knots' speed. Between 1934 and 1940 they were rebuilt as fast battleships, displacing 32,000 tons, with the same scale of protection but

LEFT: The Japanese Fleet manoeuvring under attack from aircraft from the US light fleet carrier *Monterey* (CVL.26) in June 1944.

BELOW: Japanese heavy cruiser of the *Myoko* Class and merchant shipping under attack from the US Fifth Air Force at Rabaul in late 1943.

Strength Of The Imperial Japanese Navy In December 1941

Figures in parentheses indicate ships under construction.

10 Battleships (+3)[1]
4 *Kongo* Class completed 1913-15[2]
2 *Fuso* Class completed 1915-17
2 *Ise* Class completed 1917-18
2 *Nagato* Class completed 1920-21

[1] 3 *Yamato* Class, of which a fourth had been cancelled in 1941. [2] Ex-battlecruisers completely rebuilt as fast battleships 1934-40.

8 Aircraft Carriers (+8)[1]
1 *Hosho* completed 1922[2]   1 *Ryujo* completed 1933
1 *Kaga* completed 1928[3]
2 *Hiryu* Class completed 1937-39
2 *Shokaku* Class completed 1941[5]
1 *Akagi* completed 1927[4]

[1] *Shoho* and *Zuiho* converting from high speed oilers, and 6 liners and tenders about to begin conversion. [2] Brought back to front-line duties on outbreak of war but later relegated to training. [3] Ex-battleship. [4] Ex-battlecruiser. [5] Still working up.

18 Heavy Cruisers (+1)[1]
2 *Furutaka* Class completed 1926-27
2 *Aoba* Class completed 1926-27
4 *Myoko* Class completed 1928-29
4 *Takao* Class completed 1932
4 *Mogami* Class completed 1935-37[2]
2 *Tone* Class completed 1941[3]

[1] 1 *Ibuki* Class, not yet laid down. [2] Completed as 6-inch gunned cruisers 1936 but rearmed with 8-inch guns. [3] Designed as light cruisers but altered during construction to heavy cruisers.

20 Light Cruisers (+9)[1]
2 *Tenryu* Class completed 1919
5 *Kuma* Class completed 1920-21
6 *Natori* Class completed 1922-25
1 *Yubari* completed 1923
3 *Jintsu* Class completed 1924-25

[1] 3 *Katori* Class, of which 1 was cancelled, 4 *Agano* Class, 2 *Oyodo* Class.

108 Destroyers (+43)[1]
3 *Momi* Class com. 1920-22[2]   4 *Akatsuki* Class com. 1932-33
13 *Minekaze* Class 1920-22[3]   6 *Hatsuharu* Class com. 1933-35
7 *Wakatake* Class com. 1922-23   10 *Shiratsuyu* Class com. 1936-37
4 *Kamikaze* Class com. 1922-24   10 *Asashio* Class com. 1937-39
12 *Mutsuki* Class com. 1925-27   18 *Kagero* Class com. 1939-41
20 *Fubuki* Class com. 1928-31   1 *Yugumo* Class com. 1941

[1] 27 *Yugumo* Class and 16 *Akitsuki* Class. [2] Most others of class converted to patrol vessels by 1940. [3] 2 others converted to patrol vessels 1940.

BELOW: The Japanese battleship *Fuso* was built early in World War I, but she was modernised in 1936. She displaced 34,700 tons and was armed with twelve 14-inch guns.

152

RIGHT: A captured 'Shinyo' Class one-man suicide motor boat. About 6000 of these vessels were completed by the end of the war, but no Allied ship was seriously damaged by any of them.

FAR RIGHT: Wrecked 'Shinyo' Class litter the beach. Apparently some of the *Kamikaze* pilots of these boats were unable to complete their mission.

horsepower doubled to increase speed to 30 knots. All four served in the 3rd Battle Division from July 1941 and fought in the major actions of the early part of the war. The *Hiei* and *Kirishima* were sunk during the night actions off Guadalcanal in November 1942, but *Kongo* survived even the battle of Leyte Gulf and the Philippine Sea, only to be torpedoed by a US submarine. The *Haruna* fought in all the major actions, but she was finally sunk in Kure dockyard under the overwhelming weight of air attack which destroyed the Japanese Navy.

The *Fuso* and *Ise* Classes were also elderly units of World War I vintage which had been modernised in peacetime. In 1943 the two *Ise* Class were hurriedly converted into hybrid battleship-carriers, with a flight deck, hangar and catapults in place of their two after 14-inch gun turrets. They were designed to operate 22 floatplane bombers, and not only were the aircraft not available, but there were no pilots either, and so neither ship ever carried aircraft in combat. The *Mutsu* and *Nagato* had been completed after World War I, but they too had been completely rebuilt in the 1930s. Both ships saw a lot of action but *Mutsu* was sunk at anchor when her ammunition blew up in June 1943. *Nagato* survived the war in damaged condition and was sunk during the Bikini nuclear tests.

The last Japanese battleships were outstanding examples of the Japanese quest for individual superiority, for they were the largest battleships ever built and had the heaviest armament and protection ever given to a warship. The first plans were drawn up in 1935, and progressed through a series of changes to 1937, when the final design was approved. The result was a battleship of 64,000 tons, 863 feet long overall, nearly 128 feet wide and drawing 34 feet of water. Nine 18-inch guns were protected by $25\frac{1}{2}$-inch armour on the turrets and the deck armour was 9-inches thick; the only modest element was the speed, which was only 27 knots. The four ships ordered in 1937 were intended to outrange any battleship in existence and be proof against any bomb, shell or torpedo envisaged. The justification for this violation of international treaties was that Japan had announced her intention of withdrawing from her treaty obligations, and the ships were intended to be ready at the expiry of the last treaties in 1940. Of course, this was entirely opposed to the spirit of the treaties in that the Japanese began construction in total secrecy while still bound by the treaties. US and British intelligence sources had a shrewd idea of what was going on, but the political climate was such that neither government was prepared to make an issue of it.

Never before had there been such secrecy. The first three ships (the fourth was cancelled at the outbreak of war to save labour and materials) were built behind curtains of sisal to prevent even the bare hulls from being photographed. Even the allies of Japan, the Germans, were not let into the secret until the first, the *Yamato*, was launched in August 1940. The second ship, the *Musashi*, was launched three months later, and the third ship, the *Shinano*, was considerably delayed after December 1941. The *Yamato* was ready just after Pearl Harbor, and the *Musashi* eight months later, but the *Shinano* was redesigned as an aircraft carrier after the disastrous carrier losses at Midway, and did

BELOW: The destroyer *Yukikaze* was regarded as the lucky ship of the Imperial Japanese Navy. She was the only one of the 18 *Kagero* Class to survive the war. She was armed with six 5-inch guns and eight 24-inch torpedo tubes.

LEFT AND BELOW: The *Yamato* was the biggest battleship ever built. She displaced 64,170 tons and was armed with nine 18.1-inch guns. She was built in flagrant violation of the international naval limitations treaties to outclass any battleship which could have been conceivably built by the US Navy. The close-up shows the massive 18.1-inch gun turret which was protected by 25½-inch thick armour.

BOTTOM: The *Kirishima* was one of four World War I battlecruisers of British design reconstructed as fast battleships in 1930–36. She was armed with eight 14-inch guns and steamed at 30 knots.

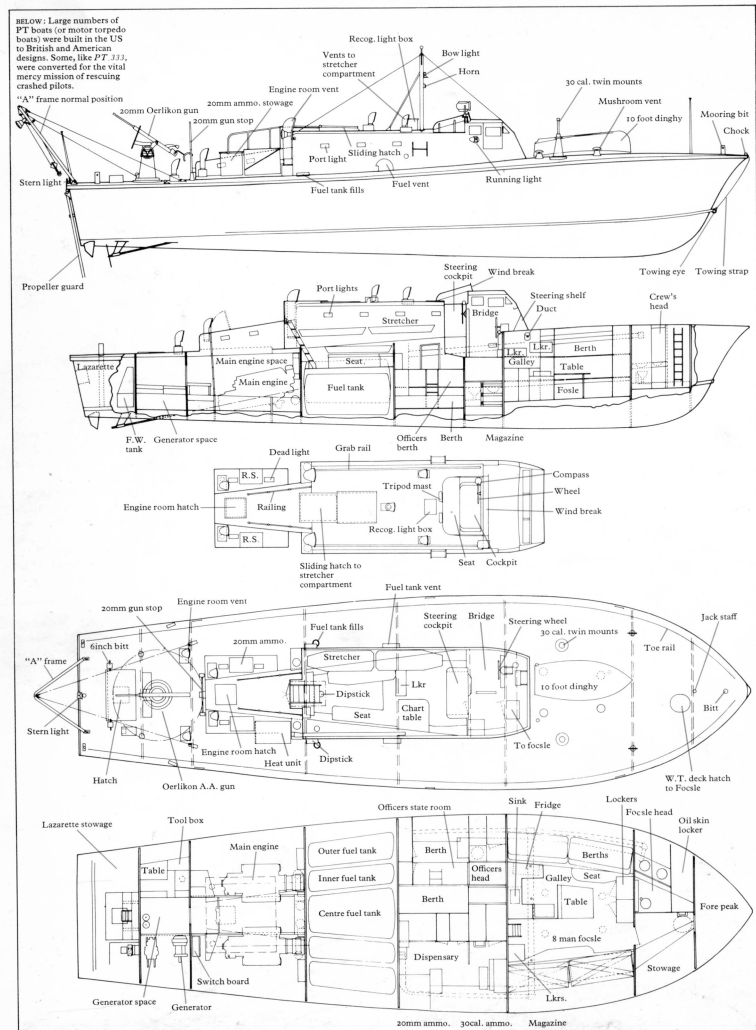

BELOW: Large numbers of PT boats (or motor torpedo boats) were built in the US to British and American designs. Some, like *PT.333*, were converted for the vital mercy mission of rescuing crashed pilots.

"A" frame normal position

Recog. light box
Vents to stretcher compartment
Bow light
Horn
30 cal. twin mounts
Mushroom vent
10 foot dinghy
Mooring bit
Chock

Engine room vent
20mm ammo. stowage
20mm Oerlikon gun
20mm gun stop

Port light
Sliding hatch
Running light

Stern light
Fuel tank fills
Fuel vent

Towing eye
Towing strap

Propeller guard

Steering cockpit
Wind break
Port lights
Steering shelf
Duct
Crew's head

Bridge
Lkr.
Lkr.
Galley
Berth
Table
Fosle

Stretcher
Seat

Main engine space
Main engine

Lazarette

Fuel tank

F.W. tank
Generator space
Officers berth
Berth
Magazine

Dead light
Grab rail
Compass
Wheel
Wind break

R.S.
R.S.
Engine room hatch
Railing
Tripod mast
Recog. light box
Seat
Cockpit

Sliding hatch to stretcher compartment

Fuel tank vent
Steering cockpit
Bridge
Steering wheel
30 cal. twin mounts
Jack staff

20mm gun stop
Engine room vent
Fuel tank fills
Toe rail

6inch bitt
20mm ammo.
Stretcher
Lkr.
10 foot dinghy
Bitt

"A" frame
Dipstick
Seat
Chart table

Stern light
To focsle

Engine room hatch
Heat unit
Dipstick
W.T. deck hatch to Focsle

Hatch
Oerlikon A.A. gun

Officers state room
Sink
Fridge
Lockers
Focsle head
Oil skin locker

Lazarette stowage
Tool box

Main engine
Outer fuel tank
Berth
Berths

Table
Inner fuel tank
Officers head
Galley
Seat

Berth
Centre fuel tank
Table
Fore peak

8 man focsle

Dispensary
Stowage

Switch board
Lkrs.

Generator space
Generator

20mm ammo.
30cal. ammo.
Magazine

not take the water until October 1944. She then suffered the ignominious fate of being torpedoed by a US submarine before she had even been completed.

Aircraft Carriers

The oldest carrier, the little *Hosho*, was hardly an effective unit of the fleet, and soon reverted to training duties, but the two ex-capital ship conversions *Kaga* and *Akagi* were formidable carriers. Like the American *Lexington* and *Saratoga* they had the anachronistic 8-inch gun armament allowed under the Washington Treaty. Their aircraft capacity was smaller than the American carriers, as they were smaller ships, but they adopted the same philosophy of maximum capacity. Both ships were sunk during the Battle of Midway, and with them went the cream of Japanese naval aircrew.

The next carrier, the *Ryujo*, was smaller in order to take advantage of a clause of the Washington Treaty which excluded carriers of less than 10,000 tons' displacement. As with other Japanese warships she could not be kept to her designed tonnage, and the excess tonnage was simply concealed from the outside world. She was found to be unstable and unseaworthy, and had to be modified twice after completion. The next pair, *Hiryu* and *Soryu*, were larger to allow the faults of the *Ryujo* design to be eliminated, and *Hiryu* shared with *Akagi* the distinction of having her island superstructure on the port side instead of the starboard side favoured in all other carriers. Two more even larger carriers, the 25,000-ton *Shokaku* and *Zuikaku*, were completed just

before the outbreak of war, and proved far more successful. In many ways they can be considered the most successful warship design produced by the Japanese, and possibly the most successful carriers after the American *Essex* Class.

To evade the restrictions on carrier tonnage imposed by the London Naval Treaty Japan ordered a series of auxiliaries which could be converted to carriers later, the *Tsurugizaki* Class high speed oilers, the submarine tender *Taigei* and the *Chitose* Class seaplane tenders. Thus the Japanese Navy gained the carriers *Shoho* and *Zuiho* by conversion between December 1940 and January 1942, the *Ryuho* in November 1942 and the *Chitose* and *Chiyoda* between October 1943 and January 1944. In 1940 work began on converting the first of three liners to escort carriers, eventually named *Taiyo*, *Chuyo* and *Unyo*, and a number of improvised conversions were attempted during the war. The most famous of these was the ex-battleship *Shinano*, which had been started in mid-1940, but was only proceeding very slowly throughout 1941. After the carrier losses at Midway she was redesigned as an armoured deck carrier and was almost complete in November 1944. To avoid damage from air attack she was ordered to steam from Yokosuka dockyard round to Matsuyama in the Inland Sea, but en route she was torpedoed four times by the submarine USS *Archerfish*. Manned by an inexperienced crew and still only partially complete, she did not survive as well as she might have, and sank after seven hours.

Another carrier was under construction

when the war started, the 29,000-ton *Taiho*. She had many features of the British *Illustrious* Class, including an armoured flight deck and an enclosed 'hurricane' bow for greater seaworthiness. During the Battle of the Philippine Sea in June 1944 she was torpedoed by the US submarine *Albacore*, and as with the *Shinano*, relatively light damage sufficed to sink her. Her ventilation system flooded the ship with avgas fumes, and when an electric pump was started the ship was literally blown apart by the explosion which followed. The only other fleet carriers begun were the six *Unryu* Class, which were repeats of the *Hiryu* Class; only three were completed by the end of the war, but they saw no active service.

Heavy Cruisers

If any class of Japanese warships attracted attention and bolstered the reputation of their designers, it was the heavy cruisers completed from 1926 onwards. The first were the two *Furutaka* Class, which purported to displace only 7100 tons while carrying six 8-inch guns and steaming at

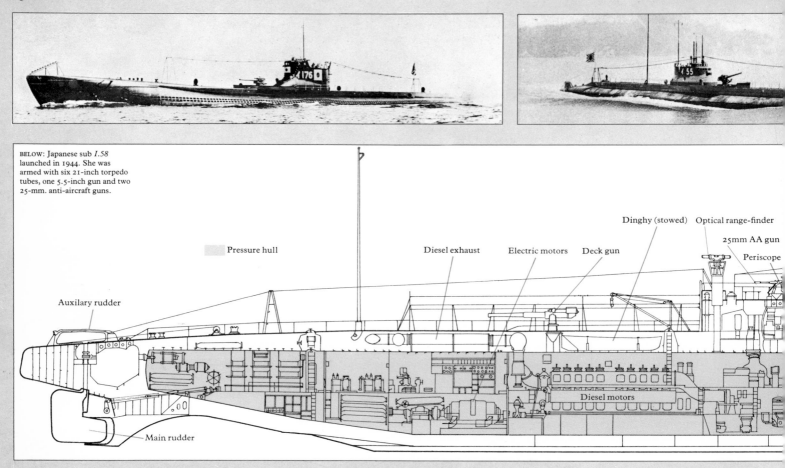

BELOW: Japanese sub *I.58* launched in 1944. She was armed with six 21-inch torpedo tubes, one 5.5-inch gun and two 25-mm. anti-aircraft guns.

Pressure hull

Dinghy (stowed)   Optical range-finder

Diesel exhaust   Electric motors   Deck gun

25mm AA gun

Periscope

Auxilary rudder

Diesel motors

Main rudder

$34\frac{1}{2}$ knots. In fact they displaced another 1000 tons, and after reconstruction they displaced over 9000 tons and speed dropped considerably. Two more ships were completed to the revised design, but still the tonnage exceeded the design figures by more than 25 per cent, a discrepancy which would have ensured the dismissal of the head of BuShips or the Director of Naval Construction in the USN and RN!

The succeeding classes were bigger and carried ten 8-inch guns, and they compared very favourably with British and American cruisers. But the tonnages were again understated, and the ships did not meet their original specification by a wide margin. The *Mogami* Class were the worst

RIGHT: The *I.73* was launched in 1935 and lost in January 1942. Her sister *I.70* was lost in the Pearl Harbor attack, and *I.68* sank the US carrier Yorktown and a destroyer at Midway.

example, for when the first two were completed in 1935 with five triple 6·1-inch gun turrets, it was found that the hull was distorted through defective welding and the stresses of firing the guns. The ships were taken in hand for drastic reconstruction which included widening the hulls, lowering the centre of gravity and riveting over the split welds. In 1939 all four ships were converted from light cruisers into heavy cruisers by replacing their five 6·1-inch gun turrets with twin 8-inch mountings, by which time their displace-

ment had risen from a nominal 8500 tons to 12,400 tons. Two later sisters, the *Chikuma* and *Tone*, were completed in 1938-39 to a modified design, with four twin 8-inch turrets forward and catapults and launching ramp for five floatplanes aft. The only other heavy cruisers were the *Ibuki* Class, of which only the name ship was launched in 1943, but she was immediately taken over for conversion to an aircraft carrier.

Light Cruisers
A large number of light cruisers had been built at the end of World War I, modelled on contemporary British vessels which acquitted themselves very well in action. In

2 0

FAR LEFT: The Japanese submarine *I.176* was launched in 1941 and lost in 1944. Armed with six 21-inch torpedo tubes, she was photographed here in Hiroshima Bay in 1942.

LEFT: Japanese sub *I.55* was completed in 1927 and was renumbered *I.155* in 1942. She was relegated to training by the end of the war.

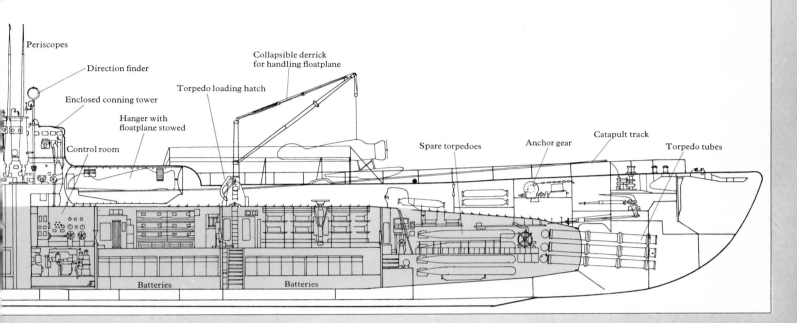

Periscopes — Direction finder — Enclosed conning tower — Control room — Hanger with floatplane stowed — Torpedo loading hatch — Collapsible derrick for handling floatplane — Spare torpedoes — Anchor gear — Catapult track — Torpedo tubes — Batteries — Batteries

1941 two were taken in hand for a unique conversion to torpedo cruisers. The *Oi* and *Kitakami* were fitted with no fewer than ten quadruple 24-inch torpedo-tube mountings, five on each side, which gave them the heaviest torpedo-armament ever mounted. This interesting arrangement was never tested in action, as both ships were converted for other duties.

In 1923 the *Yubari* ushered in a new concept in cruiser-design, with six 5·5-inch guns and a speed of 35½ knots on only 2890 tons. Although construction of light cruisers did not continue many of the ideas tried in this ship were used in the heavy cruisers. Apart from the big *Mogami* Class, which were nearer to heavy

cruisers, no more light cruisers were begun until 1940. The 6600-ton *Agano* Class with six 5·9-inch guns, followed by the slightly improved *Oyodo* Class, were completed by 1944.

Destroyers

After World War I a large number of destroyers had been built, using German designs as a basis. Many of these boats were re-rated as patrol vessels in 1939–40, but a number saw service with the Fleet. They were all 1200–1300-tonners armed with four guns and six torpedo-tubes, but from 1923 Japanese destroyer design took a completely new turn. To conform to the new philosophy of total superiority over

any foreign contemporary, the new 'Special Type' or *Fubuki* Class carried six 5-inch guns and nine 24-inch torpedo tubes on a displacement of 1750 tons. When completed in 1928–31 they ranked as the most powerful destroyers in the world, and they were immediately followed by further vessels of the same type. But when the Fourth Fleet ran into a typhoon in September 1935 so many of the new destroyers suffered structural damage that the whole class had to be strengthened and modified to improve their stability.

Despite these problems Japanese destroyers were formidable craft particularly with the 24-inch 'Long Lance' torpedo. The *Fubuki*s and their successors

were unique in having rapid-reloading gear, with provision for six or nine spare torpedoes. This gave them a great advantage in night fighting, and during the desperate fighting around Guadalcanal in 1942 their practice of firing torpedoes before firing their guns took the Americans by surprise on several occasions. Often it was assumed that Japanese destroyers were in full retreat, whereas they were merely retiring to reload their tubes, and were just as dangerous as before.

In common with the USN and RN the Japanese Navy began to plan specialised anti-aircraft vessels in the late 1930s, but chose a large destroyer-type in preference to the *Atlanta* or *Dido* type of cruiser. The resulting 'Type B' destroyer displaced 2700 tons and was armed with eight high-velocity 3·9-inch (100-mm) anti-aircraft guns in four twin mountings. Sixteen of these unusual vessels were in hand when war broke out, and as the *Akitsuki* Class they came into service from June 1942 onwards. They had one large funnel, and because of their great size were mistaken for the light cruiser *Yubari*, which had a similar silhouette. American Naval Intelligence was puzzled at first to hear reports of the *Yubari* appearing in so many places at the same time!

One other remarkable destroyer was in hand in 1941, the large, fast destroyer *Shimakaze*. Although similar in layout to earlier destroyers her high-pressure steam plant developed over 75,000 horsepower and she exceeded 39 knots. But expensive ships of this kind were not the sort of ship needed on the eve of a war, and a further order was cancelled in 1942.

RIGHT: The heavy cruiser *Takao* displaced 13,160 tons and carried ten 8-inch guns. She was attacked and crippled in Singapore by a British midget submarine in July 1945.

Stemming the Japanese Advance

The main problem for the Allies in the Pacific was how to prevent the Japanese from moving down into the Solomon Islands and New Guinea, from where they could then attack Australia and New Zealand. Well to the west, in the Indian Ocean, the British began to rebuild their shattered forces and had already started building up bases in Madagascar, the Seychelles and Mauritius, while in the South-West Pacific the Americans, Australians and New Zealanders reinforced the island garrisons in the New Hebrides, New Caledonia, New Guinea and Fiji. By May 1942 this process of stabilisation was well advanced, for the Allies were re-learning an ancient lesson, that seapower can only function with secure bases; the brilliant improvisation of a fleet base at Espiritu Santo in the north-western New Hebrides, to the east of Australia, was to prove vital within a few months.

A new command structure took effect in April, with General MacArthur as Supreme Allied Commander, South-West Pacific, and Admiral Nimitz as C-in-C, Pacific – a command stretching from New Zealand to the Aleutian Islands off Alaska. The naval command was sub-divided into North, Central and South Pacific areas, with the South Pacific theatre under Admiral Ghormley including Australian and New Zealand naval forces. The reorganisation had little time to settle down, for the Japanese were still driving all before them. On April 20 an invasion force left the new fleet base at Truk in the Caroline Islands, and it was this move which brought on the Battle of the Coral

BELOW: The *Hatsuharu* Class destroyers were ordered in 1931 to achieve the maximum armament possible under the tonnage restriction of the London Naval Treaty of 1930. They proved unstable and had to be heavily modified, losing a set of torpedo tubes.

Sea on May 6–7. The most important feature of this battle was that for the first time opposing aircraft carrier forces launched air strikes against each other's fleets – the aircraft carrier could decide an action without a gun being fired. American tactics in the battle were not as effective as the Japanese, for they split up their carriers into separate task forces, with little attempt at co-ordination. The Japanese operated on the same principle as the British, believing in the greater defensive value of a single anti-submarine and anti-aircraft screen for the carriers. As it was strikes on the Japanese ships were not co-ordinated, despite the obvious value of doubling the enemy's defensive problems in so doing.

BELOW: The destroyer *Shiranuhi* in dock at Maizuru in July 1942. This was all that was left after a torpedo hit from the US Submarine *Growler*.

CENTRE: The *Yamato* was sent on a *kamikaze* mission at Okinawa. She was sunk by an overwhelming air attack after having been given only enough fuel for a one-way trip.

American carrier aircraft sank the *Shoho*; torpedo-bombers put two torpedoes into the *Lexington* and set her on fire. After burning for hours she blew up and sank. But *Shokaku* had been sufficiently damaged to keep her out of the next battle. Tactically the Coral Sea was a drawn battle, but strategically it went to the US Navy by preventing the Japanese from capturing Port Moresby and getting a foothold in southern New Guinea. The loss of the *Lexington* was worrying, and Admiral Nimitz immediately sent the *Hornet* and *Enterprise* southwards as reinforcements.

Two weeks after the Coral Sea battle the naval war switched back to the Central Pacific, with the news from intelligence

sources that the next Japanese objective was Midway Island, the so-called 'Sentry to Hawaii'. The Japanese plan was to provoke an American attack by seizing Midway, and then destroy their fleet piecemeal by a combination of air, surface and submarine attack. To this end they mustered the carriers *Kaga*, *Akagi*, *Hiryu*, *Soryu*, *Hosho*, *Zuiho*, *Ryujo* and *Junyo*, and the seaplane carriers *Chitose*, *Kamikawa Maru* and *Kimikawa Maru*, backed up by eleven battleships and cruisers, destroyers and submarines. A total of 272 aircraft were embarked in the carriers, and the battleships included the giant *Yamato*. Against this force the Americans had no battleships at all and only three carriers. The *Wasp* was just returning from a trip to the Mediterranean to ferry aircraft to Malta, the *Saratoga* had only just completed repairs after being torpedoed by a submarine in January, while the *Yorktown* was still under repair after damage received in the Coral Sea. The British were unable to meet an American appeal to lend them a carrier, as the request did not reach the Admiralty until May 19, by which time it was too late for a carrier to make the 11,000-mile trip from Kilindini in East Africa to Pearl Harbor via South Australia. But Admiral Nimitz had one priceless advantage, for the same brilliant cryptographic team which had learned of the Pearl Harbor strike but had not passed the news to the Commander-in-Chief in time, now gave the Fleet full details of Admiral Yamamoto's battle plan. This enabled Nimitz to ignore the force heading for the Aleutians, including

the carriers *Zuiho*, *Ryujo* and *Junyo* and four battleships.

The odds were still heavy, for the American carriers mustered only 233 aircraft in all, as against the Japanese 272. But armed with the knowledge of Japanese intentions the Americans were able to take several precautions which evened the odds. Apart from establishing strong air and submarine patrols around Midway to give warning of the Japanese approach, Nimitz sent Admiral Spruance to a rendezvous position 350–400 miles northeast of Midway by June 2. This prudent measure preceded the establishment of a Japanese submarine patrol line and so robbed them of vital intelligence regarding the position of the US carriers.

The Battle of Midway began on the morning of June 4, 1942, when the Japanese Striking Force under Admiral Nagumo was at last sighted. The Japanese carrier aircraft launched a successful strike against Midway Island, but the Japanese admiral made a crucial blunder by ordering the aircraft held in readiness to attack the American carriers, to re-arm with bombs for a second strike against Midway. At that very moment the *Enterprise* and *Hornet*'s aircraft were already airborne, but a further mistake made matters worse; a Japanese floatplane spotted Spruance's carriers launching their aircraft but reported seeing only five cruisers and five destroyers.

The first attack waves fared badly against the Japanese carriers and they sustained heavy losses without any success, but eventually three squadrons made

a concentrated attack which wrecked *Akagi*, *Kaga* and *Soryu* in quick succession. *Hiryu* was still fully operational, however, and she launched a counter-strike which crippled the *Yorktown*; nearly three hours later another strike hit her with two torpedoes, which eventually sank her. Incredibly, the Japanese now assumed that they had hit *two* carriers, and as their intelligence assessment put the US Pacific Fleet's carrier strength at only two carriers, *ipso facto* there were no more American carriers left. The *Enterprise* and *Hornet* had very few aircraft left, but they were still full of fight.

Enterprise and *Hornet* launched a last desperate strike late in the afternoon, and they caught the *Hiryu* as she was preparing a dusk strike. Within minutes the carrier was on fire, and she too was doomed to burn for hours before sinking. With her went the Japanese hopes of capturing Midway, although for some hours Yamamoto continued to plan for a night action to destroy the American task force. He ordered all his forces to concentrate, and theoretically his small carriers might have mustered more aircraft than the decimated squadrons of the *Enterprise* and *Hornet*, but in practice there was insufficient time to bring the ships together over such vast distances. The most powerful battleship force in the world dared not press on without air cover, and at 0255 on June 5 Yamamoto ordered the withdrawal of his invasion force.

After only six months the Japanese Navy was stopped decisively at Midway. Not only stopped but beaten, for the

LEFT: A US Navy Avenger
torpedo bomber over Tinian in
the Marianas.

ABOVE: The Aichi M6A1 Seiran
floatplane bomber was designed
to operate from the giant *I.400*
Class Japanese submarines. Its
main purpose was to bomb the
locks of the Panama Canal.

flower of Japanese naval aviators died in
the four fleet carriers, and they would
never again have so highly trained a striking force. All the lessons of Taranto, Matapan and the sinking of the *Bismarck* pointed to the power of the carrier, but the
Battle of Midway, coming so soon after
the Coral Sea, showed that a fleet of
battleships could not stand against a
fleet of carriers. The strategic situation
was transformed overnight and the ulti-
mate result of the Pacific War was decided.

ABOVE: The destroyer USS
Buchanan (DD.484) with
mottled camouflage as used in
the South Pacific in 1942. She
displaced 1630 tons, carried an
armament of four 5-inch guns
and five 21-inch torpedo tubes.

BELOW: The captured *U.505* with the USS *Guadalcanal* (CVE.60) in the background. The *U.505* can be seen today in Chicago's Museum of Science and Industry

THE BATTLE OF THE ATLANTIC

BELOW: Two Canadian minesweepers preparing to sweep in pairs.

BOTTOM: The ex-American destroyer HMS *Georgetown* was a typical four-stacker transferred to the RN in the destroyer-base deal of 1940. She was completely rearmed for anti-submarine work in the Battle of the Atlantic.

BELOW RIGHT: The long-range escort destroyer HMS *Wanderer* replenishes her depth charges from an oiler in mid-Atlantic.

BOTTOM RIGHT: Units of the British 1st and 6th Minesweeping Flotillas have their quarterdecks covered with marker buoys and other sweeping gear.

ABOVE: A seaman aboard an escort destroyer with a 4-inch shell.

The Battle of the Atlantic has already been discussed, but as it ran from the summer of 1940 right through to the end of the war in Europe, it spanned almost the entire Second World War. What started as a simple confrontation between the maritime power of Great Britain and Germany became the most vital strategic battle, for it was the link between what would otherwise have been two separate wars – a Pacific War and a European War. If the Atlantic lifeline had been severed at any time after December 1941 not only would Great Britain have been defeated but the Americans would have been isolated. The pressure on Russia might have been enough to force her to make peace, leaving Germany, Italy and Japan in control of a vast part of the world's resources.

Paradoxically the United States was involved in the Atlantic battle almost from the beginning. In September 1940, fifteen months before Pearl Harbor, the transfer of fifty old destroyers to the Royal Navy showed where American sympathies lay. Iceland had been occupied in July 1940 by the British to prevent a German takeover, and a year later, after the occupation of Greenland, US troops took over garrison duties to release British and Canadian troops and to preserve the fiction that Iceland was under 'protection' rather than occupation. The acquisition of Iceland was far-sighted, for its refuelling facilities and air bases played a vital role in 1941 and 1942.

The passage of the Lend-Lease Bill in March 1941 allowed further warships to be transferred to the Royal Navy to ease the critical shortage of escorts, and a month later it was announced that the so-called Defence Zone, in which American merchant ships were escorted regardless of whether they were carrying war material to Britain or not, was to be extended to 26° West. At the signing of the Atlantic Charter by Roosevelt and Churchill in August 1941 it was agreed that American warships could escort ships not of US registry, and Canadian warships could similarly escort US merchant ships. The US Navy was already providing escorts for certain convoys to Mid-Ocean Meeting Points, or MOMPS for short, and by shifting them to about 22° West, 58° North the British escorts of Western Approaches Command could return without refuelling in Iceland. This allowed the escorts to be diverted to strengthen other convoys from Gibraltar or Freetown, Sierra Leone if needed, and a great deal of fuel was saved.

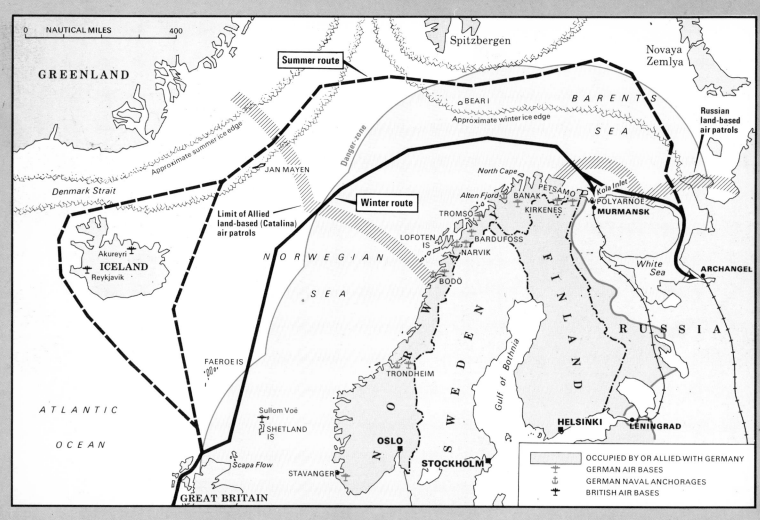

The big problem for escorts was lack of endurance. Corvettes had a reasonable endurance on account of their economical machinery but destroyers had been designed for high speed dashes in surface actions, and their machinery was not economical. In January 1941 the first of 20 World War I 'V&W' Class destroyers was taken in hand for conversion to a Long Range Escort to meet this specific problem. By removing the foremost boiler and funnel space was found for an extra oil bunker and about 80 tons more fuel. This increased their endurance at economical speed (12 knots) to nearly 3000 miles but still left them with a maximum speed of $24\frac{1}{2}$ knots, more than enough to chase a U-Boat or catch up with a convoy. The next step was to design a proper escort to meet all the requirements of North Atlantic escort work and to perfect weapons carried by ships and aircraft. The result was the 'River' Class, originally called High

Endurance Escorts or Twin-Screw Corvettes, but later given the title of frigates. The first, HMS *Rother*, was not launched until November 1941 and entered service early in 1942, and she reflected all the lessons learned in 1940 and 1941. She had a large quarterdeck uncluttered by obstructions, to allow the depth-charge crews room to reload the throwers, shelters in which gun-crews could sit and rest during the long cold watches, drying-rooms to dry soused clothing, and above all, ample fuel stowage. New weapons were also available. The 'Hedgehog' spigot mortar which fired a cluster of 32-lb contact bombs ahead of the ship, thus enabling the ship to attack while holding contact with her Asdic set, the 'Huff-Duff' direction-finder to home on U-Boats' messages, and the 1-ton depth-charge to attack deep-diving U-Boats 900 feet below the surface.

As we have already seen 1941 was a

critical year for the British as the shipping losses rose higher and higher, despite rising output from America, Canadian and British shipyards. At the end of 1939 a total of 755,000 tons of shipping had been sunk, while 1940 saw the loss of more than a thousand ships totalling 3,991,000 tons. But 1941 was even worse, with just under 1300 merchantmen sunk by all forms of enemy attack, totalling 4,328,000 tons. Even the imminent entry of the United States in the war would not be enough to offset this staggering drain on the world's shipping resources, quite apart from the value of cargoes lost.

Under the new arrangements for Anglo-American naval co-operation in mid-Atlantic it was only a matter of time

BELOW: The ex-US Coast Guard cutter HMS *Walney* sank during the Torch landings at Oran.

TOP: The depth charge remained the standard weapon against submarines despite the development of more sophisticated methods of attack.

ABOVE LEFT: The crumpled bow of the destroyer HMS *Viscount* after she rammed and sank *U.69* in February 1943.

ABOVE: Another ex-American escort destroyer HMS *Lincoln* in March 1943. These ships were named after towns common to the US and the British Empire.

Y04

before the US Navy was involved in an incident with the U-Boats. The US Navy had to escort ships to supply its garrison in Iceland, and as Iceland was also used by British escorts U-Boat commanders could easily be tempted to attack the wrong ship, especially as the British were using ex-American destroyers. It was indeed one of the old 'flush-deckers', the USS *Greer*, which was attacked by a U-Boat on September 4, but the old destroyer counterattacked with depth-charges. On October 17 the USS *Kearny*, a new destroyer but one with a silhouette not unlike British prewar destroyers, was torpedoed by *U.568*. Fortunately the *Kearny* managed to limp into an Icelandic anchorage, but two weeks later the flush-decker *Reuben James* was torpedoed by *U.562*. Despite an outcry in the United States this was not

sufficient provocation to make the United States declare war, nor was it enough to make the President reverse his policy, but in any case Pearl Harbor was only five weeks away.

In parallel with the effort to provide the warships and the weapons to fight submarines was the steady build up of maritime airpower. When the war began Coastal Command had been the Cinderella of the RAF, second only to the RN's Fleet Air Arm. The 500-lb anti-submarine bomb was more lethal to the aircraft that dropped it than to any U-Boat, for it had a nasty habit of bouncing up from the surface of the water. The first solution to this was to produce a modified aerodynamic version of the Navy's Mark VII depth-charge, and although this met requirements it was only a stopgap until

a properly designed aerial depth-charge was introduced.

The first airborne ASV (Air to Surface Vessel) radar sets were in use as early as January 1940, and although it was too crude to be effective against submarines it proved useful in helping aircraft to find convoys. A much improved ASV Mark II set was designed but proved very slow in production, but another invention was pushed through with great rapidity, the Leigh Light. This was basically a powerful searchlight carried under an aircraft's wing, and it enabled aircraft to bring to an end the immunity that U-Boats had enjoyed at night.

But whatever new weapons were produced there were still too few maritime

LEFT: USN escort carriers of the *Casablanca* Class, known as a 'baby flat-tops', were derisively named 'Woolworth carriers' by the British, since they were converted from merchant hulls. Nevertheless 52 were built and fought in both the Atlantic and Pacific.

LEFT: The *Evarts* Class destroyer escorts were the first of the US Navy's crash programme to remedy its desperate shortage.

RIGHT: The veteran World War I carrier HMS *Furious* remained with the Home Fleet until 1944. Her aircraft attacked the *Tirpitz* and she operated in the Norwegian campaign.

RIGHT: The USS *Intensity* (PG.93), formerly the Canadian-built corvette HMS *Milfoil*, was transferred to the USN in the spring of 1942.

BELOW: The 'River' Class frigate was the first escort designed primarily for the Battle of the Atlantic. In addition to a strong anti-submarine armament, she had high endurance and adequate habitability, important in the gruelling conditions in the North Atlantic.

RIGHT: The destroyer USS *Kearny* (DD.432) was torpedoed by *U.568* off Iceland in October 1941. Lying alongside the repair ship USS *Vulcan* at Reykjavik, the *Kearny* did not sufficiently arouse American public opinion against the Axis despite this act of war.

LEFT: USS *Guadalcanal* (CVE.60), whose support group captured *U.505* in June 1944.

BELOW LEFT: Swordfish on the deck of a MAC-ship. These ships carried grain or oil but also carried aircraft on an extemporised flight deck.

BELOW: USS *Martin H. Ray* (DE.338) was manned by a Coast Guard crew in the Battle of the Atlantic 1944–45.

aircraft available; in mid-1941 RAF Coastal Command had only 400 aircraft, about a third more than in September 1939. The aircraft were getting better – Lockheed Hudson bombers, Whitleys and Wellingtons, and Sunderland and Catalina flying boats – but, just as the Admiralty found with its destroyers, the worst problem was lack of endurance. The best were the flying boats; the Sunderland could fly for about two hours at about 600 miles from its base, while the Catalina in the same time could range 800 miles out because of its long wing-span. Late in 1941 Coastal Command equipped its first squadron with a new and vastly more potent aircraft, the American-built Liberator four-engined bomber. With its big fuel load it could patrol for three hours a thousand miles away from its base. Known as VLR (Very Long Range) Liberators, these aircraft were to play an ever <u>more</u> important part in the Battle of the Atlantic as they became available, but in 1942 any diversion of Liberators away from night-bombing over Europe was resisted by

Bomber Command. The RAF's strategic doctrine had for years stressed the overriding and indeed invincible claims for the bombing of cities, and it was hard to realise that bombers might not have fuel to take off if oil-tankers were not able to reach the United Kingdom.

The entry of the United States into the war on December 7, 1941 did not relieve the strain in the Atlantic, for despite all the warnings of what was happening to the British in 1941 the USN had not developed any workable anti-submarine tactics for protecting its East Coast shipping. The Germans had been waiting for the inevitable state of war and had plans to attack American shipping. On December 12, only five days after Pearl Harbor and the day after Germany's declaration of war on the US, Admiral Dönitz ordered 'Operation Drumroll' (*Paukenschlag*), the movement of U-Boats to the western Atlantic. These U-Boats arrived on station by the middle of January, and soon they were revelling in the return of the 'Happy Time', as they sank merchantmen sailing

Escorts

In March 1942 a joint British and American review assessed the Allied requirements for escorts as follows:

	British	American	Total
Available	383	122	505
Required	725	590	1215
Shortfall	342	468	720

BELOW: A Swordfish from a British escort carrier circles over the convoy in search of enemy subs.

BELOW: *PC.551* drops a depth charge in 1943. PCs were small, steel-hulled coastal escorts.

RIGHT: The British ASDIC was a retractable underwater transducer which emitted a sonic beam through a quartz plate. By measuring the time taken for the bounce of its echo against an enemy sub, its range and bearing could be calculated. The device remained totally secret until the fall of France in June 1940, and it still is in use for underwater detection.

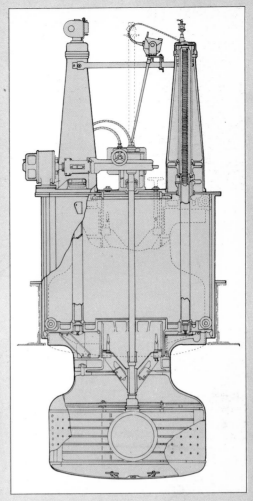

unescorted and giving their positions over the radio 'in clear'. There was no coastal blackout, and even the lighthouses and buoys and beacons were left lit. The constant radio chatter gave the listening U-Boats any further information that they needed. The only opposition was occasional 'offensive patrol' or hunting group of destroyers which raced over the horizon belching smoke, but the U-Boats simply waited until the group had disappeared, knowing full well that it would not be back until it had reached the end of its patrol line.

Not until April 1942 did the US Navy reluctantly adopt convoying as a countermeasure to the U-Boats, and the reason for the delay seems to be that the plodding, patient qualities demanded of escort commanders were considered to be alien to the American naval officer's outlook. It was held that 'taking the offensive' was more in keeping with American attitude of mind, although the British had resisted the introduction of convoy in 1916–17 for much the same reasons. It was not realised

that offensive patrolling relied completely on luck in striking a U-Boat that happened to be on the patrol-route, whereas the vicinity of a convoy was the likeliest place to find U-Boats – in other words, sooner or later the U-Boat must approach the convoy. Part of the misunderstanding about the success of convoy as a countermeasure is the failure to comprehend that its prime purpose was to protect and conserve shipping and the cargoes that are carried. Sinking submarines was only of secondary importance, and convoys were frequently re-routed to take them clear of concentrations of U-Boats.

The British transferred ten corvettes to ease the immediate shortage of coastal escorts, and a further 15 were ordered from Canadian shipyards, in one of the rare examples of 'Reverse Lend-Lease'. In addition two of the new 'River' Class frigates were earmarked for the USN. In March 1942 a joint British and American review assessed the Allied requirements for escorts as follows on the chart (left).

An order for 300 destroyer escorts had

already been placed by the British in the US, but they were not expected in service until the end of 1943. More were ordered, making an eventual total of over 1000 hulls, but as the British had found, it was one thing to build hulls and quite another to provide machinery. The shortage was due not so much to the inability of the United States to manufacture machinery as a conflict of strategic requirements.

The US Army entered the war with two aims, the defeat of Japan and the liberation of Europe. As President Roosevelt made it clear that priority was to be given to the defeat of Germany, the approach was one of Clausewitzian simplicity. Europe must be invaded at the earliest opportunity, and work must begin immediately on building the landing craft needed for that purpose. The British were reluctant to agree with this over-optimistic plan, although there was strong pressure in Britain for a Second Front to take the pressure off the Russians. It is now accepted by all but Russian commentators that an invasion of Europe late

BELOW: The 'Flower' Class corvette *Montbretia* was manned by the Royal Norwegian Navy. The corvette was developed from a whale-catcher design as a stop-gap anti-submarine escort.

in 1942 or in 1943 would have courted disaster of such magnitude that it might have prolonged the war considerably and jeopardised the Allies' grand strategy. But in the spring of 1942 the priority given to landing craft had already absorbed the labour, steel and above all engines which might have boosted the escort programme. The shortage of engines proved the most acute, and the DEs were equipped with a hotchpotch of diesel-electric, turbo-electric and diesel machinery.

Although the Americans eventually agreed reluctantly to drop plans for a Second Front in 1943, they continued to press for offensive action somewhere in the European theatre. In July 1942 the decision to invade North Africa was taken, and although 'Operation Torch' would only affect the naval situation in the Mediterranean by eliminating German and Italian air bases on the African coast, the whole invasion scheme diverted scarce resources from the Battle of the Atlantic. The defence of Malta called for a massive operation to get desperately needed supplies through, 'Operation Pedestal'. This was the greatest convoy battle of all, with only fourteen fast cargo ships escorted by two battleships, three large carriers, seven cruisers and 20 destroyers. Between August 10 and 13 the 'Pedestal' convoy braved attacks from aircraft, U-Boats and motor torpedo boats, and lost nine merchantmen, a carrier and two cruisers; the carrier *Indomitable* and two cruisers were badly damaged as well. But the five ships which crept into Grand Harbour, including the tanker SS *Ohio* with her precious cargo of aviation fuel for Malta's fighters, carried 32,000 tons of cargo, and the island was saved.

With Malta safe planning for the 'Torch' landings could proceed, but to land 70,000 men between Casablanca and Oran would require large numbers of ships and supporting warships. Six advance convoys and four assault convoys, 250 ships in all, left the United Kingdom and a further 136 ships in four convoys

RIGHT: Oerlikon 20-mm. anti-aircraft gun crews on board the escort carrier HMS *Trumpeter*.

OPPOSITE TOP: An Avenger torpedo bomber ready for shipment from the US to the UK. This rugged aircraft, built by Grumman, became the standard strike plane aboard British and American carriers.

OPPOSITE CENTRE: Grumman Hellcats aboard an escort carrier in freezing weather off Newfoundland.

PQ. 17 Cargoes Delivered and Lost

	Vehicles	Tanks	Aircraft	Other Cargo
Delivered	896	164	87	57,176 tons
Lost	3,350	430	210	99,316 tons

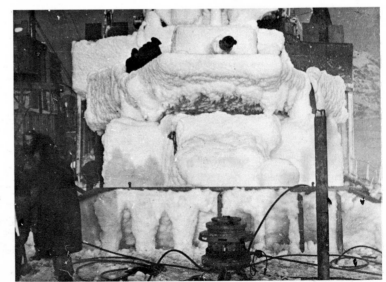

RIGHT: The forward guns of the destroyer HMS *Witch* are completely covered in ice after a patrol in the North Atlantic.

FAR RIGHT: The 'River' Class frigate *Mourne*, one of 120 which came into service in late 1942. They quickly established themselves as the most successful escorts in the Atlantic.

sailed directly from the United States, representing a heavy responsibility in terms of escorts and air patrols necessary to ensure their safe arrival. With the ships needed for controlling the actual landing and providing gunfire support, the 'Torch' landings required six battleships, five fleet carriers, seven escort carriers, 15 cruisers, 81 destroyers and 38 escorts of various types. Unfortunately the bulk of these escorts and the escort carriers were withdrawn from the Atlantic, where they were sorely missed.

In July 1942 the situation in the Atlantic was critical, for the losses on the American side were still worrying, and escorts were needed for the convoys to North Russia, a necessity of political rather than military significance. Russia was demanding a Second Front, and although the Allied leaders could not accede to this, they felt that the supply of war matériel would help the Russians to defend themselves and show the Russians that they were allies in more than name. The North Russian convoys became in effect an extension of the main Atlantic battle, with all the extra hazards involved in a journey past German air and naval bases in Norway. The *Bismarck*'s sister ship *Tirpitz* and other heavy surface units lurked in the fjords, a constant threat to convoys. The worst of these convoys, *PQ.17*, epitomises the dangers. The Admiralty, believing the *Tirpitz* to be at sea, ordered the convoy to scatter, and although the *Tirpitz* never made contact, U-Boats and aircraft sank 24 out of 37 merchantmen and rescue ships. This also illustrates how much war material was lost when merchantmen were sunk.

In the autumn of 1942 the Allies introduced more innovations. In September the first Support Groups were formed, groups of escorts which were not tied to any convoy in particular but were free to roam at will and harass the U-Boats. They differed from the old discredited idea of offensive patrols in one important respect: they operated in support of the convoy system, and were available to reinforce any hard-pressed convoy's escort. The first American-built escort carriers were also arriving, and with the support groups promised to put the U-Boats under strong pressure, but now the Allies had to pay the price of their ambitions, and the support groups and escort carriers were diverted to cover the North African invasion forces. At a time when they were needed more than ever the reinforcements were taken away from the battle.

RIGHT: Vice-Admiral Sir Bruce Fraser as C-in-C of the Home Fleet. He led the attack on the *Scharnhorst* in the Battle of the North Cape, December 1943.

BOTTOM: The destroyers HMS *Onslow* and *Ashanti* in the Arctic. The *Onslow* led her flotilla against the *Hipper* and *Lützow* in the Battle of the Barents Sea, December 1942.

The U-Boats were quick to sense the slight slackening of the offensive against them, and they attacked strongly. Losses rose again to 619,000 tons in October and 729,000 in November. Although losses fell in December nothing could alter the fact that 1942 had been a bad year for the Allies at sea, with the loss of 1664 ships totalling 7,790,000 tons. As the Allies had only built seven million tons of new ships, there was a deficit of nearly a million tons in addition to the losses incurred in 1940 and 1941. All this had been done in a year in which the U-Boat construction rate had been 15 per cent *lower* than planned. Although the Allies had sunk 190 German and Italian U-Boats, the total of U-Boats operational at the end of 1942 was 312 as against 91 a year earlier.

As 1943 opened it was clear to both antagonists that the Battle of the Atlantic was reaching a decisive climax. The shipping losses had reached such a level that the whole Allied war effort in the West was in jeopardy, no matter what victories were won in North Africa and the Mediterranean, or how many bombs were dropped on German cities. It must also be remembered that it was not just a question of steel ships, but also a question of human stamina and morale. The British Merchant Navy lost nearly 33,000 seamen out of 185,000 in World War II, a casualty rate of 17 per cent as against 9·3 per cent for the Royal Navy, 9 per cent for the Royal Air Force and 6 per cent for the British Army. These men, like the Americans, Canadians and other nationalities among the world's seamen were civilians, untrained for war, and had their morale cracked under the strain, the entire edifice of Allied seapower would have toppled. Yet, despite appalling weather and the risk of death by drowning, burning or even starvation in an open boat, there is no record of a merchant ship's crew refusing

to set sail. Nor for that matter did morale among the U-Boat personnel flag, even when they suspected that they were the victims of new and more sinister electronic devices.

The convoy battles in the first months of 1943 were even more ferocious than before. In March convoy SC.121 [SC and HX denotes slow and fast convoys from Halifax, Nova Scotia to the United Kingdom] was pursued by 17 U-Boats for four days and lost thirteen ships (about 62,000 tons). Shortly afterwards four ships of HX.228 were sunk, and the senior officer of the escort was lost after ramming a U-Boat. While lying disabled his destroyer was torpedoed by a second U-Boat, but this one was then sunk in her turn by a French corvette. Forty U-Boats attacked the convoys SC.122 and HX.229 and sank 21 ships, despite the fact that the two convoys joined together to strengthen the escort. Only heavy support from shore-based aircraft finally forced the U-Boats to give up, but they had sent 141,000 tons of shipping to the bottom. For the first time the British Admiralty lost its implicit faith on the convoy system, and the Naval Staff in London seriously considered abandoning it in the face of the unprecedented scale of attack. Never, it was said, did the Germans come so near to disrupting communications between America and Britain as in the first 20 days of March 1943, when more than *half a million* tons of shipping was sunk.

Help was at hand, for the support groups, escort carriers and long range aircraft which had been removed to cover the 'Torch' landings at the end of the previous year now came back into the Battle of the Atlantic. In the second half of March the scale of losses slackened, and then suddenly swung violently in favour of the Allies, with half the March total being sunk in April. There were now five support

groups working in the North Atlantic, two with an escort carrier each, and over 30 VLR Liberator bombers were available. Six U-Boats were sunk in the Atlantic in January, 19 in February, and 15 in March and another 15 in April, but in May no fewer than 41 were sunk.

At this point the German U-Boat Command suffered the effect of a series of mistakes which cost Germany the Battle of the Atlantic and eventually the war. To combat the use of ASV radar the Germans had introduced a radar search receiver known as 'Metox' in August 1942, and this gave U-Boats some respite from night attacks from aircraft fitted with Leigh Lights. But the Allies produced a new ASV Mark III set working on centimetric wavelengths, as opposed to the metre-wavelength ASV Mark II, and its signals were not detectable by the Metox. A 10-cm radar set fell into the German hands in January 1943, revealing for the first time how far ahead Allied radar had advanced, and immediately work started on a radar search receiver, code-named 'Naxos', but it was too late to stem the tide. Production difficulties held up Naxos production for months, and thus contributed to the next mistake. Because they knew of the existence of centimetric radar the Germans failed to spot the existence of 'Huff-Duff', the high-frequency direction-finding set which had been at sea in Allied escorts for a year. Losses of U-Boats were attributed to phenomenal performance of Allied radar, far in excess of its actual capabilities.

Ironically, German scientists had investigated centimetric wavelengths at the beginning of the war, but had decided on theoretical grounds that they would not work. With 'Huff-Duff' there was less excuse, as the evidence of its existence was already in German Intelligence files, picked up from monitored ship-to-ship messages. Evidence from agents at Al-

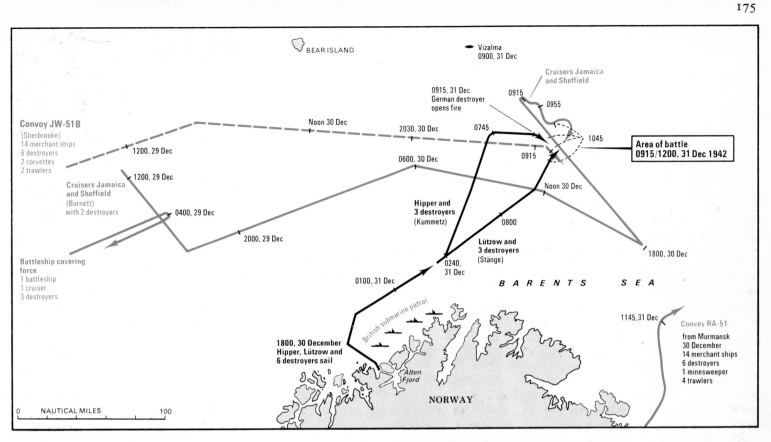

BEAR ISLAND

Vizalma
0900, 31 Dec

Cruisers Jamaica
and Sheffield

0915, 31 Dec
German destroyer
opens fire

0915
0955

Convoy JW-51B
(Sherbrooke)
14 merchant ships
6 destroyers
2 corvettes
2 trawlers

Noon 30 Dec
2030, 30 Dec
0745
1045

**Area of battle
0915/1200, 31 Dec 1942**

1200, 29 Dec
0600, 30 Dec
0915

**Cruisers Jamaica
and Sheffield**
(Burnett)
with 2 destroyers

1200, 29 Dec
Noon 30 Dec

0400, 29 Dec

**Hipper and
3 destroyers**
(Kummetz)

2000, 29 Dec
0800

**Lützow and
3 destroyers**
(Stange)

**Battleship covering
force**
1 battleship
1 cruiser
3 destroyers

0240,
31 Dec

0100, 31 Dec
1800, 30 Dec

B A R E N T S   S E A

1145, 31 Dec

British submarine patrol

Convoy RA-51
from Murmansk
30 December
14 merchant ships
6 destroyers
1 minesweeper
4 trawlers

**1800, 30 December
Hipper, Lützow and
6 destroyers sail**

Alten
Fjord

NORWAY

0   NAUTICAL MILES   100

FAR LEFT: The destroyer HMS
Cambrian takes aboard a
refuelling hose in heavy
weather.

LEFT: A 4-inch gun of the escort
carrier *Trumpeter* fires a salvo
under the overhang of the flight
deck.

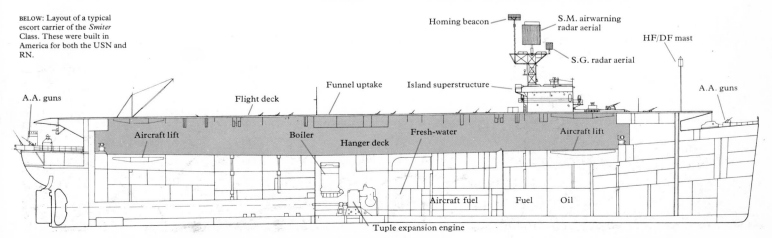

BELOW: Layout of a typical
escort carrier of the *Smiter*
Class. These were built in
America for both the USN and
RN.

Homing beacon
S.M. airwarning
radar aerial
HF/DF mast
S.G. radar aerial
A.A. guns
Funnel uptake
Island superstructure
Flight deck
A.A. guns
Aircraft lift
Boiler
Fresh-water
Aircraft lift
Hanger deck
Aircraft fuel
Fuel
Oil
Tuple expansion engine

geciras, who had photographed British warships fitted with the device, had been 'doctored' to remove the telltale Rock of Gibraltar from the background. Unfortunately the censor's brush also deleted the 'Huff-Duff' aerial!

By May 22 Admiral Dönitz was forced to admit defeat by withdrawing his U-Boats. Although he maintained that the withdrawal was only a temporary one to reduce losses the U-Boat Arm had suffered a decisive defeat. Six months later they returned to the battle with new equipment and deadlier weapons, but the Battle of the Atlantic never again reached

such a peak of ferocity. After 45 months of constant struggle the Allies had thrown off an all-out attempt to cut their communications and in the process had inflicted crippling losses in ships and men. Although U-Boat crews' morale remained high to the end, they never again showed such determination as they had in March 1943. Four months later Allied shipbuilding finally overtook the total of tonnage sunk, and it became possible for the Allied leaders to plan their long-awaited counter-offensive against Germany.

In the Arctic the convoy situation also improved. In December 1942 a force of

eight destroyers fought off an attack by the heavy cruisers *Hipper* and *Lützow* (the latter once rated as a pocket battleship or armoured cruiser). By holding the two German heavy units off, the escort delayed them long enough to allow two British cruisers to intercept. Leaving a luckless destroyer to be blown out of the water, the *Hipper* and *Lützow* departed as fast as they could. When Hitler learned of this humiliating action he raged at the cowardice and incompetence of the *Kriegsmarine*, ignoring the fact that his directives forbade any risk of serious damage to his ships in action. When Hitler followed

BELOW: The battlecruiser HMS *Hood*, which was sunk by the *Bismarck* in May 1941 with the loss of almost her entire crew. She was armed with eight 15-inch guns and had a speed of 31 knots.

FAR LEFT: A D-Day convoy with British escorts. An ex-American 'Captain' Class frigate appears in the foreground, with a 'Hunt' Class destroyer astern.

LEFT: A Seafire fighter aircraft aboard HMS *Furious*, with the battleship *Duke of York* in the background.

BELOW: RAF Beaufighters attack a German convoy off the Norwegian coast in August 1944. On both sides a salvo of four rockets each can be seen hurtling toward their target.

BOTTOM LEFT: The quarterdeck of a typical British escort, showing depth charges on their throwers and 20-mm. anti-aircraft guns on the platform.

BOTTOM RIGHT: The 'Squid' was the deadliest weapon used against U-Boats. Introduced late in 1943 it fired three full-sized depth charges ahead of the attacking ship.

his imprecations with a threat to scrap the entire surface fleet and mount its guns ashore as coastal batteries, Admiral Raeder resigned. Admiral Dönitz immediately accepted the post, but despite his overriding faith in the U-Boat as the only war-winning weapon, he persuaded Hitler to reprieve the Fleet on account of its usefulness in tying down Allied naval strength.

On December 26, 1943 the last major surface action in European waters eliminated the *Scharnhorst*, making an ill-judged foray against a Russian convoy. In vile weather she attempted to attack the convoy but was foiled by its escorting cruisers. Aerial reconnaissance by the Luftwaffe had passed on the news that the Home Fleet had been sighted, but the vital phrase 'including what may be a battle-ship' were excised from the teleprinter message to the Navy to conform with the golden rule that only verified facts were to be passed to another service! It therefore came as a shock to Admiral Bey when his flagship was hit by the first salvo of 14-inch shells from the battleship HMS *Duke of York*. The Battle of North Cape was unusual in that it was fought on the British side completely on information provided by the radar plots in the *Duke of York* and

her cruisers. Not only was the battle fought in darkness but also in such bad weather that nobody even saw the *Scharnhorst* sink.

With the *Scharnhorst* went the last serious threat to Allied shipping, for the *Tirpitz* had been damaged by midget submarines in September 1943 and was not ready for sea. In April 1944 she was damaged again by a massive air strike launched from the British carriers *Victorious*, *Furious*, *Emperor*, *Searcher*, *Fencer* and *Pursuer* in 'Operation Tungsten'. In all fourteen hits were obtained and extensive damage and casualties were caused, for

ABOVE: The 10,000 cruiser HMS *Sheffield* dips her bow into a mighty wave in the Arctic. Even the massive 6-inch gun turrets had to be trained on the beam to avoid damage in such weather.

RIGHT: The battleship HMS *Howe* and a 'County' Class heavy cruiser in the Arctic in 1943.

RIGHT: The final act in the Atlantic. A British 'Castle' Class corvette escorts surrendered U-Boats to a Northern Ireland anchorage.

FAR RIGHT: Scuttled Type-XXIII U-Boats in a German floating dock in May 1945. Almost a thousand of these coastal submarines were ordered by the German Navy, but few were completed.

the loss of only three aircraft. Further strikes were launched against the *Tirpitz* in July and August but without success. Throughout her lively but inactive career the *Tirpitz* owed her immunity more to nature than to any superlative resistance to damage, for the Norwegian fjords provided a superb defensive position, against which aircraft had great difficulty in carrying out a conventional bombing run. Finally she left the security of the Norwegian fjords and was moved south to Tromsö to repel the Norwegian invasion that Hitler felt was coming. By now she was unable to steam and was to be a *schwimmende batterie* or floating coast defence gun position. But she was now within range of bombers from the UK, and on November 12, 1944 a force of Lancasters sank her with 12,000-lb 'earthquake' bombs which ruptured her hull.

U-Boats remained lethal to the end. Later in 1943 they made another effort to attack the North Atlantic convoys, this time using acoustic homing torpedoes to sink escorts, pattern-running torpedoes to comb the tracks of the convoy, and other ingenious devices. To avoid the risks of air attack the *schnorchel* was introduced, an air-induction mast to allow the U-Boat to re-charge her batteries while running submerged. The homing torpedoes were beaten by a variety of countermeasures, including towed noisemakers, and although the *schnorchel* was effective it proved of negative value and did not lead to increased sinkings.

Admiral Dönitz pinned his hopes on a revolutionary type of submarine, the Walther high-test peroxide boat which could run at high speed without using outside oxygen. As an interim measure there was also the Type XXI 'electro-submarine', a streamlined boat with enlarged battery capacity for short bursts of high speed. The Type XXI was much more dangerous for it was capable of mass-production, whereas the Walther boat had innumerable technical snags which delayed its production. The heavy bombing of German shipyards slowed submarine construction so that only three Type XXI boats were ready in May 1945. Which brings the whole story of the Battle of the Atlantic back to the Allied victory in the summer of 1943, for that victory allowed the build-up of land and air forces in Great Britain which resulted in the invasion of Europe. The pressure of demands on German industry could only be met at the expense of U-Boat construction.

AMPHIBIOUS WARFARE

THE ETO

BELOW LEFT: The diesel engine room of a British submarine.

BELOW RIGHT: Beach parties were a vital part of any amphibious landing. Sailors would make a reconnaissance of the shore, strip off their clothing, link hands and wade in the water in order to find obstructions such as submerged wire, etc.

CENTRE RIGHT: To replace the rolling stock devastated by air raids on northern France, the Allies had to ship locomotives and railway wagons to France in converted landing craft.

BELOW RIGHT: A massive parachute drop over southern France as part of the assault of Operation Anvil to secure the beachhead. C-47s of the USAAF dropped these men between Nice and Marseilles.

BOTTOM: LCAs (landing craft assault) of the British 8th Army put men ashore in Sicily in July 1943. Warships and transports appear on the skyline.

When war broke out in September 1939 amphibious warfare was under a cloud. The disastrous Dardanelles campaign of 1915 was regarded by most naval strategists as final proof that large-scale landings were no longer possible, particularly in the face of air power. True, the US Marine Corps had been experimenting with light assault craft for raiding, and the Japanese had actually built an 8000-ton infantry landing ship for amphibious operations in China, but these developments were largely ignored until the war. Therefore it is all the more extraordinary that the outstanding feature of the naval side of World War II should be the use of seapower to land large armies on potentially hostile or enemy shores.

The first amphibious operation of World War II was the often ignored movement of the British Expeditionary Force to France in the autumn of 1939. The fact that it landed in friendly harbours should not conceal the fact that its supply-route was within striking distance of German motor torpedo boats and U-Boats, and yet an enormous quantity of ammunition, stores and vehicles was passed without interruption right up until the Dunkirk evacuation. But the first honours for a landing on a hostile coast must go to the Germans for their ingenious Norwegian landings. With only small covering forces, and under the noses of the British Home Fleet, the Germans transported six army divisions to seize the key Norwegian ports. This they achieved, despite the sinking of a troopship by the Polish submarine *Orzel*, which should have alerted the British.

The British, duly impressed by the German performance in Norway and imbued with the need to strike back at their enemies, set up a Combined Operations Command under Admiral of the Fleet Sir Roger Keyes in 1940 shortly after the fall of France. Work started immediately on the design of tank landing craft, and in this respect the British showed great ingenuity. In September 1939 a Landing Craft (Mechanised) or LCM was under construction, capable of landing one army truck or tank over a hinged bow ramp, so this was used as the basis for a much larger type to carry three 40-ton tanks. By adopting a cellular form of construction and a U-shaped hull the first TLC (later reversed as the LCT to give a constant 'L' prefix for landing craft) had a great reserve of stability. But its flat bottom and shallow draught made a landing craft sail like a tin tray, and its hasty welding could at times fail under the stress of bad weather. It was

BELOW: Tank landing craft were equipped with rockets for shore bombardment. This was a British LCT(R).

found that the idea of ramming a landing craft hard on the beach was so fundamentally alien to professional sailors that some of the best landing craft captains proved to be those happy-go-lucky 'hostilities only' ex-bank clerks and actors who took malicious pleasure in damaging Admiralty property. Ultimately the entire Allied maritime strategy came to depend on these ugly landing craft, for no invasion could be considered without having them in their hundreds.

The first raid in strength was in March 1941 against the Lofoten Islands in Norway, and showed what could be done with reasonable equipment and foresight. Like the later Vaagsö raid and the minor ones on the French coast through the summer of 1941 it was only a pinprick, partly to boost morale and partly to keep enemy troops in a state of alarm. But all these raids exercised troops and planners in the subtle art of inter-service co-operation. In the Mediterranean there was little opportunity for landings, but an Inshore Squadron was formed to run supplies from Alexandria to the beleagured garrison of Tobruk. Oddly enough, some of the vessels used were diesel-engined infantry landing craft dating from the Dardanelles campaign of 1915, the first powered landing craft ever designed.

In March 1942 a much bolder raid was launched against the French Biscay port of St Nazaire. The object was to destroy or damage the giant Normandie lock gate and so deny to the *Tirpitz* any dock on the coast of France big enough to take her. The winding estuary of the River Loire made any attack very difficult, for its five-mile length was heavily guarded and full of sandbanks. In addition St Nazaire was 400 miles from the nearest British anchorage, which meant that the light craft would face the hazards of an open-sea passage.

The attack was planned in two forms, an assault by commandos landed from motor launches to put the pumping stations out of action and distract the defences, and a straightforward ramming of the lock gate by a ship filled with explosives. The ship chosen was the old ex-American flush-decker destroyer HMS *Campbeltown* (ex-USS *Buchanan*), cleverly altered to look like a German torpedo boat. Flying a German ensign and flashing garbled signals the *Campbeltown* successfully avoided destruction from the coastal batteries and was able to imbed herself in the massive lock gate; twelve hours later the three tons of high explosive in her

bows blew up and totally destroyed the gate. The casualties totalled only 85 Navy personnel and 59 from the Army, a surprisingly small number for such a dangerous enterprise.

The entry of the United States into the war resulted in strong American pressure for an assault on Europe at the earliest opportunity. Fortunately the vociferous proponents of 'Operation Sledgehammer' were not able to sway military opinion from its view that the troops, the training and above all the landing craft did not exist for a landing on the powerfully fortified coast of Europe. Much of the 'Second Front Now' agitation was based on sympathy for the plight of Russia rather than military feasibility, and the Allied planners were only too well aware of the bloody and costly fiascos which had resulted from poorly planned amphibious operations in the recent past. But there were in the United Kingdom a number of highly trained troops, particularly Canadians, who had not yet seen any action, and it was felt that their morale would suffer if they did not see some employment soon. If a raid in strength could provide useful experience and at the same time force the Germans to divert more troops to the West rather than send them to the Eastern Front, then it might be militarily justifiable.

With such tenuous reasons for launching it, the Dieppe Raid did not look promising to the Combined Operations Staff under Lord Louis Mountbatten. Dieppe was chosen in April 1942 because it alone provided 'worthwhile' objectives and met other requirements such as being within

range of shore-based fighter aircraft. But Dieppe was heavily defended, with high cliffs overlooking narrow beaches. Rocky ledges formed a barrier to landing craft at anything but high tide, and a massive sea wall was a formidable anti-tank barrier. When the raid took place on August 19 all these drawbacks played their part in causing heavy casualties among the landing craft and assault troops. The tanks and troops never succeeded in getting off the beach, thanks to the sea wall, and they were gradually wiped out by the murderous fire from German pillboxes and gun-positions. The supporting destroyers could not make any impression on the concrete gun emplacements either, and so nothing could be done to secure the beaches. The Canadians and the commandos suffered some 5200 casualties killed, wounded or missing; the Royal Navy lost 550 men and 34 vessels, while the RAF lost a number of aircraft.

The Dieppe Raid caused a great public outcry, particularly in Canada, where it was felt that precious lives had been wasted needlessly. The Germans not unnaturally claimed that an attempt to open the Second Front had been repulsed, and in their own assessment of the operation maintained that the planning had been faulty. The reasons for the raid have been explained, but the mistakes made were serious, notably the failure to bomb the perimeter or to use paratroops to seize the flanks. In the long run, however, Dieppe was an invaluable dress-rehearsal for the Normandy landings two years later. On the one hand, the Allies learned that a landing should be preceded by a much

heavier bombardment than the destroyers had provided, and on the other, the Germans became obsessed with the notion that the Allies would try to seize a port as an essential prelude to landing. Dieppe is a good example of new weapons and ideas obscuring old truths: although enough fighter protection was provided over the beachhead, the fixed defences were left untouched.

The 'Torch' landing in North Africa was on a much larger scale. Although originally planned as an unopposed landing, it ran into heavy French opposition because the local garrisons did not support the claims of the American protegé, General Giraud, who had promised that the troops

would not disobey his orders. It has already been explained how the massive convoys were sailed from the United States and the United Kingdom, but it must be remembered that the assault convoys were divided into fast and slow groups which then had to be redivided to land in three widely separated sectors. Algiers was seized successfully on November 8, although the two destroyers sent in to prevent the French from wrecking the port were heavily punished by gunfire. A similar plan at Oran met with disaster, and both ships were sunk. But the two ports were safely in Allied hands within three days. The simultaneous American assault on Casablanca faced weaker defences but a

larger number of French warships, all of which were hostile. As in 1940 the French Navy fought with great gallantry in the full knowledge that their cause was hopeless. The battleship *Massachusetts* fought a brief one-sided duel against the *Jean Bart*, which had only one quadruple 15-inch gun turret mounted, but despite several hits from 16-inch shells the French ship was only temporarily disabled.

The collapse of French resistance in North Africa led to an even bigger disaster for the French Navy. The Commander-in-Chief, Admiral Darlan, in consultation with the British C-in-C Admiral Cunningham, urged the commander of the main French Fleet at Toulon to leave and

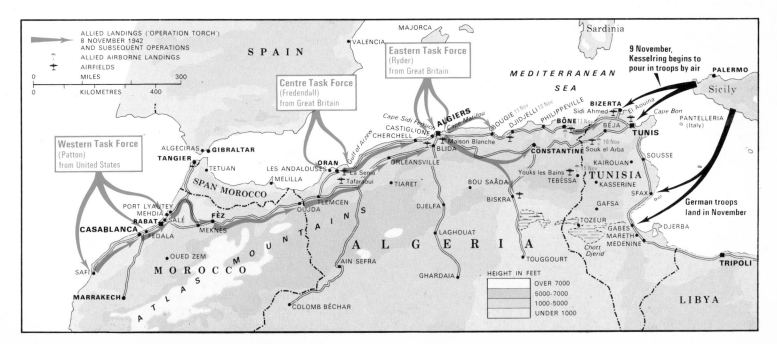

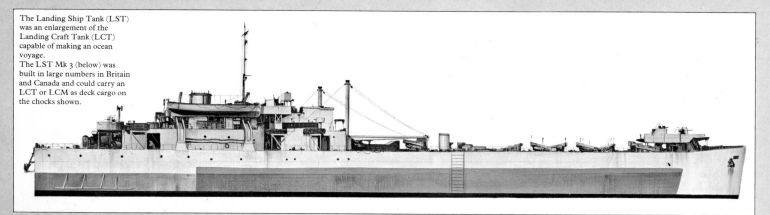

The Landing Ship Tank (LST) was an enlargement of the Landing Craft Tank (LCT) capable of making an ocean voyage.
The LST Mk 3 (below) was built in large numbers in Britain and Canada and could carry an LCT or LCM as deck cargo on the chocks shown.

RIGHT: LCTs of the British Eighth Army arrive in Sicily, July 10, 1943. British LSTs, Mark III, like the one pictured below, were larger and capable of making ocean voyages. LCTs could be carried as deck cargo on an LST.

bring his ships to North Africa. Privately Darlan admitted to Cunningham that Admiral de la Borde was too fanatically anti-British to accept such a proposal, even though the Minister of Marine under the Vichy Government was sympathetic. Darlan and Auphan rightly feared that the Germans would break their promise not to invade 'unoccupied' France before long, to deny the Toulon Fleet to the Allies and to quell any rebellious sentiments at Vichy. De la Borde vacillated, and on November 14, 1942, special Nazi assault troops tried to storm Toulon dockyard. By the time they had overcome resistance Darlan's 1940 promise had been kept and the pride of the French Navy had been scuttled. Three capital ships, seven cruisers, 30 destroyers and 16 submarines, 237,000 tons in all, were blown up and the dockyard had been wrecked.

With the North African air bases in Allied hands and a victorious 8th Army advancing westwards from Cyrenaica to link up, it was only a matter of time before the whole North African coast was occupied. In fact it took longer than expected, and it was not until May 1943 that the Allies could boast that they had taken the surrender of all German and Italian forces in Tunisia. 'Sink, burn and destroy. Let nothing pass' was Admiral Cunningham's order to his ships, and so destroyers and aircraft sealed off the escape routes. The stage was now clear for the invasion of Sicily, for the British wanted to knock

LEFT: The first British LSTs were shallow-draught tankers built originally for Lake Maracaibo in Venezuela, but they were soon replaced by properly designed vessels.

BELOW: Bombs are unloaded from LCTs in North Africa.

BOTTOM: The laden *LCT.355* passes a row of transports on D-Day in Sicily, July 10, 1943.

Germany's weak partner out of the war as soon as possible. This was agreed to by the United States, but only on condition that if their forces in Italy outnumbered those of the British their own strategy would be followed. Churchill wanted to strike the 'soft underbelly of the Axis', whereas Roosevelt wanted to drive the Germans out of France.

As a first step the islands of Pantelleria and Lampedusa between Tunisia and Sicily were captured in May and June, partly to remove hostile bases from the lines of communication but more important, to provide airfields for the Sicily landings, since Malta was too small to accommodate all the aircraft needed. The main assault plan was ready in May but 'Operation Husky' did not take place until July 10. Some 66,000 American troops and 115,000 British and Empire troops were landed on the south-eastern corner of Sicily, under cover of six battleships, two fleet carriers and fifteen cruisers, and an armada of Dutch, Greek, Polish, Belgian and Norwegian minor warships. Over 500 major landing craft (LSTs and LCTs) and 1200 minor landing craft were used. Losses were very small, and even air attacks proved lighter than expected; although troublesome they did not achieve any disruption of the invasion. By the first week in August Italian and German forces were escaping to the mainland by means of the 'Messina Straits Regatta', a massive rescue operation which the Allies failed to

disrupt effectively. In all 62,000 Italian troops and 39,500 Germans as well as nearly 10,000 vehicles were ferried across the Messina Straits, in what might be described as a brilliant amphibious operation in reverse.

'Operation Avalanche', the invasion of the Italian mainland, followed 'Husky' as quickly as possible, not least to foil the tendency in both Washington and London to regard the Mediterranean theatre as a supply depot. The previous warships

and landing craft which had made the Sicily landings so successful were earmarked for the 'Overlord' operation, the reconquest of France. Admiral Cunningham objected to this whittling down of his strength, even to the point of holding back units which he had been ordered to release. But the covering force was still massive, Force 'H', with the battleships *Nelson*, *Rodney*, *Valiant* and *Warspite*, and the carriers *Illustrious* and *Formidable*, with the US cruisers *Savannah*,

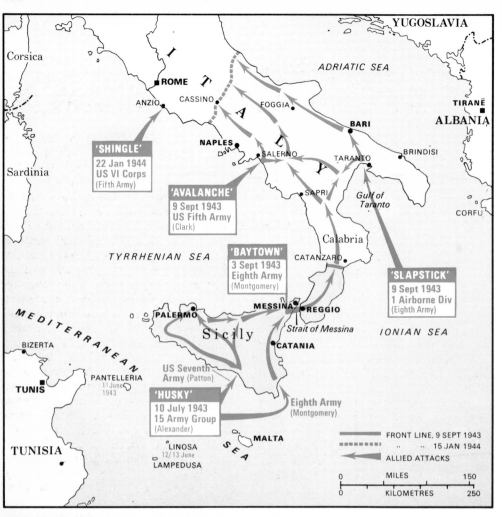

Boise, *Philadelphia* and *Brooklyn* and the modern battleships *Howe* and *King George V* as a reserve force if needed.

The unusual feature of the 'Avalanche' landings on September 9 was the complexity of the plan, demonstrating the Allies' growing confidence in the techniques of amphibious warfare. First the Fleet made a feint to give the impression that it was only exercising, and then passed through the Sicilian Channel into the Tyrrhenian Sea to begin a heavy bombardment of Reggio Calabria. The British 8th Army quickly seized Reggio, and then the 5th Army went ashore in the Bay of Salerno to hasten the capture of Naples. Because Salerno was so far from the airfields of Malta and Sicily, it was necessary for the first time to rely entirely on aircraft carriers for protection over the beachhead. In addition to the two big Fleet carriers the British provided the escort carriers *Attacker*, *Battler*, *Hunter*, *Stalker* and *Unicorn*, known as Force 'V'. Their Seafire fighters, aided by the ships'

radar and fighter direction facilities, maintained a constant umbrella over the landing zone. To achieve this 20 aircraft had to be launched every hour, and from dawn to dusk on the first day the five small carriers flew off 265 sorties; in all they carried 113 aircraft. Despite the exertions of the naval pilots the Montecorvino airfield was still in enemy hands at the end of the day, and so it was not possible to hand over to shore-based fighters for another day and a half, when the Americans improvised an airstrip at Paestum. This was to be a recurring feature of the landings in the Pacific, where the distances were always too great for shore-based air cover in the initial stages of the landing.

On the night before the assault dramatic news came from London: the Italian Government had sued for an armistice. Three years of attrition had brought Italy to its knees. Huge losses in North Africa had been accompanied by heavy losses at the hands of the British submarines,

aircraft and surface warships. And so, in conformity with the armistice terms the Italian Fleet, including the battleships *Roma*, *Vittorio Veneto* and *Italia* (formerly the *Littorio*), six cruisers and eight destroyers, left La Spezia on the west coast of Italy heading south for internment at Malta.

The Germans had no intention of allowing the Italians to make a separate peace with the Allies, and had already taken action to seize control from Italian ground forces. As the battleships headed for safety on September 9 they were attacked by eleven Do-217 aircraft. The German aircraft were about to launch the world's first guided missile attack on warships using the FX.1400, a 1400-kg radio-controlled armour-piercing bomb, and the results were devastating. The *Roma* and *Italia* were hit, and the *Roma* caught fire and blew up with heavy loss of life. The shaken survivors met HMS *Valiant* and *Warspite*, their opponents at Matapan, next morning, and joined the *Andrea*

Doria and *Caio Duilio* from Taranto at Malta. With justifiable pride Admiral Cunningham signalled, 'The Italian Fleet now lies under the guns of Malta.'

The defection of the Italians had no appreciable effect on German resistance at Salerno, thanks to the precautions taken as soon as news of the proposed armistice leaked out. The fighting on shore was bitter, and at one time it looked as if the invaders might be pushed back into the sea. At one stage German tanks were sighted close to the beaches, but they did not reckon with the lethal fire from destroyers lying only a few hundred yards off – a 4·7-inch (120-mm) high-velocity gun was found to be a superb tank-buster, as the Germans might have remembered from Boulogne in May 1940. Naval gunfire was a vital factor in holding the German counter-attacks, particularly from smaller warships such as destroyers.

Many experimental devices were tested at Salerno. The British used the first LSTs (Landing Ship, Tanks), the 5700-

LEFT: The 15-inch guns of the battleship *Warspite* bombard Catania. The *Warspite* was heavily damaged during the Salerno landings, but she was used to it; she fought at Jutland in 1916.

RIGHT: The *Nelson* fires her 16-inch guns in support of the Salerno landings. *Nelson* served in every theatre of operations in World War II.

RIGHT: The 6-inch gunned cruiser *Mauritius* firing at night in support of the US Fifth Army off the Italian coast.

ton freak craft *Boxer*, *Bruizer* and *Thruster*, which were designed with extending ramps. Rocket-firing LCTs were used for the first time, but although their drenching salvoes of rockets were good for the morale of the assault troops their value was much less than the proper gunfire support. More attacks were made by the Luftwaffe with FX.1400 radio bombs against the invasion ships, but skilful use of smokescreens kept the losses low. Four days after the initial landings a desperate call for support against a German tank thrust brought the battleships *Valiant* and *Warspite* at full speed from Malta to pour 15-inch shells into the beachhead. But on September 16 the *Warspite* was very badly damaged by three FX.1400 radio bombs. The old ship nearly sank, and needed seven tugs to tow her sideways through the Straits of Messina.

By the middle of October Allied ground forces were well-established ashore, and with the fall of Naples control of southern Italy passed into the hands of the Allies giving them unfettered control over the Mediterranean. Salerno reversed the verdict of Dieppe by proving that a well-planned assault could succeed even

against a prepared and aggressive enemy. The major mistake was the refusal to allow a preliminary aerial and naval bombardment to give maximum surprise, but as the Allies had powerful bombardment forces in reserve, this decision was not too costly.

The last major landing in the Mediterranean was not part of any preconceived strategic plan, but arose out of an attempt to outflank the German forces in Italy. This was the Anzio landing in January

1944, which was planned in an attempt to speed up the advance of the Allied armies up the spine of Italy. But from the start the planning was bedevilled by a shortage of shipping and landing craft, many of which had been withdrawn for the Normandy landings. Despite achieving surprise the Allied ground forces reacted very cautiously, and while they wasted precious hours digging in, the Germans rushed reinforcements into the beachhead. The German Navy also had ideas about how to deal with amphibious assaults, and rushed its 'K' units (*Kleine Kampfmittel* = small assault forces) to Anzio. These were mid-

get submarines of various types, and although a nuisance they did not achieve important results. Again the radio-controlled FX.1400 bomb was the worst threat, and for the first time a major warship, the cruiser HMS *Spartan*, was sunk while firing off the beaches. Jamming gear had already been fitted to three warships but the handlers were not fully accustomed to using the new equipment. As the Germans were close to the beachhead the

landing craft, transports and bombarding ships were under constant artillery fire.

The Anzio operation finally justified itself when in May the American and British forces broke out of the beachhead and headed for Rome. Instead of the planned bold flanking movement, it had become a drain on resources, but it also diverted six German divisions from the main front. Also, by using seapower once more the Allies showed that they could land where

they chose. Although other combined operations took place in the Mediterranean, the Allies were now free to turn the main weight of their attack on North-Western Europe.

The planning for the invasion of Europe can be said to have begun as the last soldier left France in June 1940, when Winston Churchill insisted that the Germans should not be left in undisputed possession of the Continent. But any ambitions of reconquest were mere pipe-dreams at the time, and it was not until late 1941 that the British Joint Planners produced a draft for 'Operation Round-up', a projected 1943 invasion.

The entry of the United States into the war in December 1941 altered everything, and by March 1942 the two Allies were working on 'Super-Roundup'. By the following June the Combined Commanders, including Lt.Gen. Dwight D. Eisenhower and the Chief of Combined Operations had chosen the Naval Commander Expeditionary Force. This was none other than Vice-Admiral Sir Bertram Ramsay, the same man who had so skilfully arranged the Dunkirk evacuation. As we have already seen, the Americans were eager for

BOTTOM LEFT: A column of ambulances re-embarks wounded over a floating roadway of the Mulberry harbour at Arromanches.

BOTTOM CENTRE: *LCT.710* unloads a locomotive in northern France.

BOTTOM RIGHT: An American LST with British troops aboard approaches the Normandy beaches in June 1944.

German Forces Available Mid-1944

On the Atlantic coast	On the Channel coast
49 U-Boats at Lórient, Brest, St Nazaire and La Pallice	5 torpedo boats
6 destroyers and torpedo boats	34 S-Boats (MTBs)
205 minesweepers and patrol vessels	220 minesweepers and patrol vessels
	42 artillery barges

an invasion that year, and it was not until President Roosevelt overruled his Chiefs of Staff that it was agreed that the requisite numbers of trained troops did not exist. The North African landings were the next choice, and the decision of the Casablanca Conference in January 1943 to land in Sicily meant a further postponement of the European invasion.

Not until May 1943 did the invasion plan to get the code-name by which it is better known, 'Operation Overlord' (with the associated naval operation named 'Neptune'), but the site, the stretch of the Normandy coast between the Rivers Orne and Vire, had been fixed much earlier. Many detailed changes were made from time to time, notably the decision not to invade the south of France simultaneously. The biggest headache for the British, particularly the Royal Navy, was manpower. It was estimated that 'Operation Neptune' would need 45,000 extra personnel, and this at a time when the Americans had been promised reinforcements in the Far East. To save manpower the Royal Navy decommissioned four old

battleships of the *Royal Sovereign* Class, five 'C' and 'D' Class small cruisers, 40 destroyers (all of them World War I veterans) and the last of the Armed Merchant Cruisers. Yet it was still necessary to draft personnel from the Army and Air Force to make up the numbers.

One fear which obsessed the 'Neptune' planners was a counter-attack by the German surface fleet. It was believed that the *Admiral Scheer*, *Lützow*, *Hipper*, *Prinz Eugen*, *Leipzig*, *Köln*, *Nürnberg* and *Emden* were still available for an attack on the invasion convoys in the English Channel, and of course the *Tirpitz* was still lurking in the Norwegian fjords, although she was under repair. In fact, by May 1944 the *Hipper* and *Köln* were still under repair and all the other ships were on training duties in the Baltic, some of them not fully operational. To watch this motley force the British kept three modern battleships, three fleet carriers and six cruisers, and it is not surprising that the Americans were unimpressed by British requests for reinforcements. But in fairness it should be remembered that the British had to run

convoys to North Russia, and if the *Tirpitz* had completed her repairs and made an attack, the Home Fleet would not be available to protect 'Overlord' further south. Accordingly Fleet Admiral King cancelled his objections and sent three battleships, two cruisers and 22 destroyers to the United Kingdom in April 1944.

The smaller German surface forces and the U-Boats were a much greater hazard to the invasion. In mid-1944 the Germans had available the above.

In addition there were the midget submarines and assault units tried out at Anzio. A new mine, the pressure-operated 'oyster' mine, which was almost unsweepable, was to prove the worst threat, but the Germans would not use it until the invasion started, to avoid betraying its secrets.

The U-Boats were countered by a large-scale anti-submarine operation to 'cork' both ends of the Channel, and a massive umbrella of aircraft made it virtually impossible for German surface forces to operate in daylight, or even

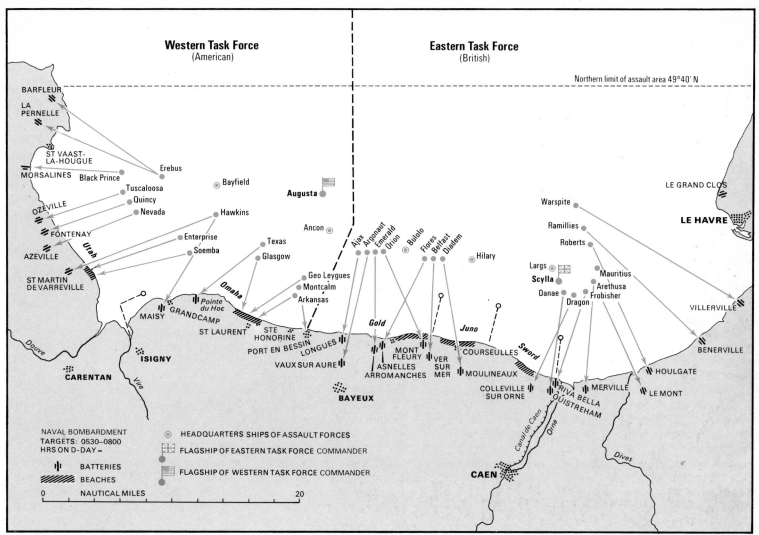

Western Task Force (American)

Eastern Task Force (British)

Northern limit of assault area 49°40′ N

BARFLEUR
LA PERNELLE
ST VAAST-LA-HOUGUE
MORSALINES
Black Prince
● Erebus
● Bayfield
● Tuscaloosa
● Quincy
OZEVILLE
● Nevada
● Hawkins
FONTENAY
● Enterprise
● Soemba
AZEVILLE
Utah
ST MARTIN DE VARREVILLE
● Texas
● Glasgow
● Geo Leygues
● Montcalm
● Arkansas
Omaha
MAISY
GRANDCAMP
Pointe du Hoc
ST LAURENT
STE HONORINE
PORT EN BESSIN
LONGUES
ISIGNY
VAUX SUR AURE
CARENTAN
Douve
Vire
BAYEUX

Ancon ◉
Augusta

Ajax
Argonaut
Emerald
Orion
● Bulolo
Flores
Belfast
Diadem
Hilary ◉

Gold
MONT FLEURY
ASNELLES
ARROMANCHES
VER SUR MER
Juno
COURSEULLES
MOULINEAUX
COLLEVILLE SUR ORNE
RIVA BELLA
OUISTREHAM
Sword
Canal de Caen
Orne
CAEN

LE GRAND CLOS
● Warspite
● Ramillies
LE HAVRE
● Roberts
Largs ◉
Scylla
Danae ●
● Dragon
● Mauritius
Arethusa
Frobisher
VILLERVILLE
BENERVILLE
HOULGATE
MERVILLE
LE MONT
Dives

NAVAL BOMBARDMENT
TARGETS: 0530–0800
HRS ON D-DAY—
◉ HEADQUARTERS SHIPS OF ASSAULT FORCES
⚑ FLAGSHIP OF EASTERN TASK FORCE COMMANDER
| BATTERIES
▨ BEACHES
⚑ FLAGSHIP OF WESTERN TASK FORCE COMMANDER
0 NAUTICAL MILES 20

LEFT: Churchill aboard HMS *Kimberley* during the Anvil invasion of southern France.

RIGHT: The massive invasion fleet leaves an Italian port prior to the Anvil landings.

CENTRE RIGHT: British and Indian troops of South-East Asia Command (SEAC) land at Rangoon in the final stages of the reconquest of Burma.

BOTTOM: A British LCT and assault craft land at Westkapelle on Walcheren Island in the Netherlands in November 1944. The operation was launched to free the approaches to the vital port of Antwerp on the Scheldt River.

moonlit nights. The pressure mine could only be countered by moving ships at very slow speed. The British produced one very peculiar countermeasure, a pair of giant trimaran craft named HMS *Cyrus* and HMS *Cybele*, designed for towing across a minefield to set up a pressure-wave which would explode pressure-mines in the vicinity. The idea worked but the gigantic framework of steel proved as difficult to handle as a battleship if damaged, and one was lost in the Seine Estuary after D-Day.

In addition there were 4126 landing craft, ranging from the large LSH (Landing Ship Headquarters), Attack Transports, LSTs etc, down to small support vessels like fuelling barges and LCMs.

The greatest technical surprise hatched out of 'Neptune' was the provision of artificial harbours. As Dieppe had shown the problems involved in seizing and holding a harbour, and because the Normandy invasion had grown so enormous, it had been decided to design and construct two artificial harbours. Known as 'Mulberries', these would allow supplies and vehicles to be discharged straight onto the beaches and would allow the assault troops to avoid a costly assault on either Cherbourg or Le Havre. The 'Mulberry' harbours proved to be one of two important factors overlooked by the German Army Command, for they had calculated that the Allies could not keep their expeditionary force adequately supplied with fuel, food and ammunition fast enough to survive the first counter-attacks. As things turned out even one 'Mulberry' was sufficient to maintain an enormous flow of supplies during the first crucial days.

The actual assault was timed for the early hours of June 6, 1944, and despite bad weather the first wave arrived promptly off their allocated sectors. Their navigational fixes were provided by two midget submarines which had been lying submerged off the beaches for three days. It is not possible to give a detailed account of the assault here, but all five beach areas, 'Juno', 'Gold', 'Sword', 'Utah' and 'Omaha' were reached as planned. Losses were comparatively light because the initial German reaction was feeble. The combination of rough seas and the formidable beach obstacles of steel ramps, 'hedgehogs' etc, many of them mined or booby-trapped, produced the greatest number of casualties.

The second miscalculation made by the Germans was about the scale of naval and aerial bombardment. Time and again German armoured formations were hit by 16-inch shells or aircraft rockets as soon as they appeared, and soon it was impossible to make any move against Allied ground troops in daylight. The secret of the naval gunfire support was the provision of Forward Observation Officers (FOOs), naval observers with the ground formations who could control the ships' gunfire by radio-telephone. One cruiser is credited with knocking out a German fortified gun position at about 10 miles' range, and putting two shells through the gun embrasures. This degree of naval co-operation was aided by the total air superiority enjoyed over the beachhead, and it should not be forgotten that the Allied air offensive over Germany had only just begun to erode the numerical strength of the Luftwaffe. Had the tide of battle not swung against the Luftwaffe so decisively (or had the Mustang long-range fighter not made as much impact), it is arguable that the Allies might not have enjoyed such a relatively easy success at Normandy. Be that as it may, 132,715 soldiers went ashore in the first 16 hours of D-Day, with many thousands of tons of vehicles, stores and ammunition. Although 'Overlord' is still popularly known as D-Day, this was merely the Combined Operations style for designating the day of the main assault in all landings, just as H-Hour signified the time.

The German Navy and Air Force did their best to counter-attack, but to little avail. The 'Cordon Sanitaire' thrown around the whole invasion area was successful in protecting the huge mass of shipping lying off the beaches, and on the nights of June 14 and 15 RAF bombers virtually wiped out the German Motor Torpedo Boat base at Le Havre. The U-Boats fared even worse at the hands of aircraft and escorts in the Channel. On the night of June 9 a force of British, Canadian and Polish destroyers caught four destroyers trying to reach Cherbourg. In a confused action at high speed HMCS *Haida* and HMCS *Huron* chased *T.24* and *Z.24*, inflicting heavy damage on the latter, while HMS *Tartar* and HMS *Ashanti* sank the *Z.32* and *ZH.1*. The *ZH.1* was a Dutch destroyer captured incomplete in 1940 and completed for the Kriegsmarine. Her sister *Isaac Sweers* fell into British hands at the same time and had a distinguished career in the Mediterranean, a curious example of twin ships in different navies. This action put an end to the last surface force capable of interfering with the invasion convoys.

The worst crisis of the entire invasion was a gale which blew up on the morning of June 19. Not only did it destroy about 800 craft, but it completely wrecked the American 'Mulberry' harbour at St Laurent. Fortunately the British 'Mulberry' at Arromanches survived, and its artificial breakwater helped to shelter a large num-

Warships Allocated To Neptune	Battleships	Monitors	Cruisers	Gunboats	Destroyers	Sloops	Fleet Sweepers	Small Sweepers	Frigates & DEs	Corvettes	Patrol Craft	A/S Trawlers	Minelayers	MTBs, MGBs, etc	Seaplane Carrier	Midget Subs	Escorts In A/S Groups
British	3 (+1*)	2	17		63	14	89	133 (+40*)	53	63		60	4	360	1	2	58
United States	3		3		34		9	16	6		18			111			
French			2		1				4	3				8			
Polish			1		4												
Dutch				3										13			
Norwegian					3					3				3			
Greek										2							
Total	7		2	23	3	105	14	98	189	63	71	18	60	4	495	1	2	58

*In reserve

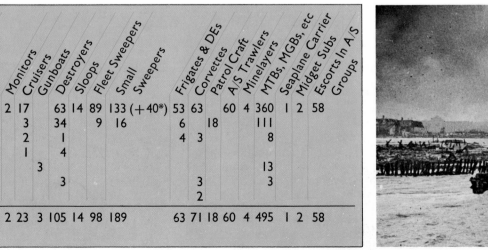

ber of wrecked ships. As much material as possible from the wrecked 'Mulberry' was transferred to help enlarge and repair the one at Arromanches, which landed its first cargo on June 29. The importance of 'Mulberry' to the whole operation can be measured by the fact that even after enormous efforts, the port of Cherbourg was not able to land cargo until July 16.

In retrospect the Normandy landings can be seen as not only the biggest amphibious operation of the war, but also the biggest naval operation in history and arguably the most significant. Its success must not disguise the fundamental difficulties and risks faced, and although the Allies could be accused of being over-lavish in their provisions and precautions, they knew that the invasion of Europe marked the beginning of the end of World War II. With so much at stake who can blame them for being cautious?

THE FAR EAST

The most obvious difference between amphibious operations in the Pacific as against the European theatre was scale. The vast expanse of ocean meant that any attempt to land troops on hostile soil required the transport of every man, every round of ammunition and every gallon of fuel thousands of miles. Ships damaged in action had to effect repairs on the spot or face a long dangerous voyage home. Never before had military strength been deployed so far away from its main bases, and it is that common denominator which affected all the Pacific landings.

The sea battles which were fought in the Pacific were nearly all concerned with landings, either in support of one or opposing one by the enemy. The climate and the geographical conditions made each landing difficult, but for the Americans and their allies the biggest problem was the sheer tenacity of the ordinary Japanese soldier. A feature of the Pacific fighting which was nearly always absent from the European war was the willingness of the Japanese to fight to the last man, no matter how hopeless the situation. Time after time garrisons had to be hunted down like animals, and the recent cases of Japanese soldiers who stayed at large for nearly 30 years after the end of the war only highlight the fanatic zeal inspired by the Japanese military code.

We have already seen how the Battle of the Coral Sea checkmated a Japanese attempt to capture Port Moresby in southern New Guinea, but in July 1942, not long after Midway, they decided to make a second attempt. To guard their left flank they decided to eastablish an air base in the southern Solomon Islands, on the island of Guadalcanal. But almost simultaneously the American Chiefs of Staff decided to occupy the Santa Cruz Islands to the east of the Solomons, and to establish a base near Tulagi just north of Guadalcanal. Thus the Americans were able to act fast when they learned of the Japanese attempt to establish themselves in the Solomons. Their invasion force left New Zealand on July 22 and landed successfully on August 7. The partly completed airstrip was quickly captured and renamed Henderson Field, and although the garrison of Tulagi had fought to the last man, the invaders had reason to be satisfied with the operation.

The Japanese main base was at Rabaul, 550 miles to the north-west. From there Admiral Mikawa led a powerful cruiser force comprising the heavy cruisers *Chokai, Aoba, Kako, Kinugasa* and *Fur-*utaka and the light cruisers *Tenryu* and *Yubari* to attack the invasion transports. Although the Allies were expecting some action on Mikawa's part, and despite an Australian reconnaissance bomber sighting the Japanese cruisers on the morning of August 9, Admiral Turner, the commander of the amphibious force, did not get the message for eight hours. Even then it was garbled, and mentioned only three cruisers, a force that was unlikely to trouble the warships guarding the invasion fleet. The cruisers of the covering force took up their night patrolling stations, unaware of their danger.

The Japanese cruisers rounded the southern end of Savo Island, a small island lying north of Guadalcanal, at about 0130, undetected by an American destroyer on guard-duty. Minutes later the alarm was raised but by now it was too late. The Australian cruiser *Canberra* was overwhelmed by 8-inch shellfire and two torpedo-hits. She did not sink immediately, but she was ablaze with heavy damage, and completely out of action. Mikawa's cruisers turned north to deal with the next group of cruisers, which had heard the gunfire but assumed that it had been at aircraft. The *Quincy, Vincennes* and *Astoria* were caught in a crossfire and suffered the same fate as the *Canberra*. All that was left to stop the Japanese was a scattered force of three cruisers and half a dozen destoyers, but for reasons never fully explained Admiral Mikawa threw away his chance to ruin the landing. Despite specific orders to treat the invasion transports as his prime objective Mikawa took his cruisers on a course for Rabaul, leaving the Allies to deal with the shambles. Only one crumb of comfort remained; the old submarine *S.44* torpedoed the *Kako* on her way home.

The US Marines still held Henderson Field against Japanese counter-attacks, but on August 19 the Japanese tried to rush in 1500 troops as reinforcements. The covering force of three carriers, two battleships, five cruisers and 17 destroyers was engaged by the carriers *Saratoga, Enterprise* and *Wasp*. The US carrier air groups sank the small carrier *Ryujo*, but the *Enterprise* was hit by three bombs. This action, known as the Battle of the Eastern Solomons, was not decisive, but the Americans had the advantage as the Japanese began to withdraw.

The Japanese continued to run high-speed convoys, the 'Tokyo Express', with reinforcements and supplies for the garrison of Guadalcanal under cover of darkness. During the day the Americans controlled the sea, but at night the 'Slot' between the eastern and western Solomons belonged to the Japanese. Their skill at night-fighting and their attention to torpedo-tactics were responsible for this great ascendancy, and it is unquestionable that if the Allied warships had not had the benefit of radar, or conversely if the Japanese had not been forced to rely on eyesight, the Allies might have been more roughly handled.

On August 31 the *Saratoga* was torpedoed by the Japanese submarine *I.26*; although she survived, this valuable ship was out of action at a crucial time. Two weeks later the *Wasp* was hit by three torpedoes. This time the results were disastrous, for the *Wasp* caught fire and had to be abandoned. The battleship *North Carolina* was hit by a torpedo on the same day, September 15, leaving only one battleship, her sister *Washington*, and one carrier to cover the landings. This was the greatest hour of the Japanese submarine arm, but unfortunately it only demonstrated the Japanese talent for wasting their submarines. There were only two submarines in the Solomons, and had there been more the Japanese Navy might have been able to avenge Midway. But the large submarine force was scattered around the Indian and Pacific Oceans in unimportant areas.

OPPOSITE TOP: An LCI(R) fires its 5-inch rockets during the landings in Leyte, October 20, 1944.

OPPOSITE BELOW: LSMs (landing ship, medium) drop their ramps as they approach the beach on Leyte.

LEFT: LCI(G) gun support ships lay smoke screens off the invasion beaches at Leyte.

BELOW: Troops scramble into LCAs from the attack transport USS *McCawley* (APA.4) off the New Guinea coast.

The night battles in the 'Slot' continued to rage, but the next big action was the Battle of the Santa Cruz Islands, fought on October 26. The honours were fairly even, for the Japanese lost the *Zuiho* and the Americans lost the *Hornet*, and each had another carrier damaged. But for the Americans the situation in the Solomons was now close to disaster. The *Enterprise* was the only carrier left, and she had been seriously damaged in the battle. In desperation Admiral King asked the British Admiralty to lend the US Navy one of their carriers until the new construction was ready, and eventually HMS *Victorious* served for a few months under American control.

The night actions around Guadalcanal were by no means confined to light forces. In the First Battle of Guadalcanal on November 12 the Japanese battleship *Hiei* was sunk and two American cruisers were badly damaged. Two nights later came the Second Battle of Guadalcanal, the first time that Japanese and American battleships engaged one another. Off Savo Island the *Hiei*'s sister *Kirishima* was sunk in action with the USS *Washington* and *South Dakota* under Admiral Willis A Lee. The *South Dakota* suffered a peculiar mishap at the start of the action, when an electrical fault robbed her of all power for some minutes. She sustained some

damage, but not enough to cripple her, and the Japanese intention of bombarding Henderson Field was frustrated. These two fierce actions mark the turn of the tide in the fight for the Solomons. Although the Battle of Tassafaronga on the night of November 30 once again resulted in a reverse for American cruisers at the hands of an inferior Japanese force, it was the Japanese Navy which had to admit defeat. By the end of the year the only supplies reaching the defenders of Guadalcanal were being carried by submarines, and early in the New Year the Japanese High Command ordered an evacuation.

One problem which was even more acute in the Pacific was the shortage of landing craft. The lack of protected harbours and the fact that landings were often made in areas with heavy surf and coral reefs meant that a high percentage of landing craft were damaged or wrecked. The problem of distances has already been mentioned, and it must be remembered that even the big bases set up in forward areas were sited on islands which had nothing of military or industrial utility. Maintenance and salvage facilities for ships and landing craft damaged in landings were therefore hampered by the need to bring every single spare part from Australia or the United States.

By February 1943 the ground forces

under General MacArthur had cleared the Japanese from the north coast of New Guinea while Admiral Halsey's naval forces had driven them out of the Solomons. The next step was to breach the so-called 'Bismarck Barrier', the chain of island bases seized by the Japanese early in 1942 as a defensive perimeter to protect their conquests. Although these island bases were in some cases nothing more than a coral airstrip on a small atoll, they conferred such an advantage that they had to be neutralised or captured before the Allies could advance towards Japan. In the Central Pacific, too, Admiral Nimitz was building up a large force of battleships and aircraft carriers for a drive westwards against the Marshall and Caroline Islands. These thrusts were co-ordinated to make the Japanese divide their forces.

In August 1943 a new technique was introduced in amphibious operations, that of 'leap-frogging'. This was the bypassing of powerful garrisons to outflank them and to starve them out. This demanded high mobility, but it had the advantage of allowing weaker objectives to be attacked and so was more economical of lives and equipment. The Americans were steadily improving their techniques of assault, and the Japanese were getting weaker. Apart from the losses of naval pilots at Midway, operations in the South Pacific had frit-

LEFT: Marines hit the beach at Tarawa after a successful landing in November 1943.

BOTTOM: Buffalo amphibious tracked vehicles ferry supplies during the invasion of Noemfoor Island on Dutch New Guinea in July 1944.

tered away more. By November 1943 Admiral Koga at Truk had one aircraft carrier, the *Zuikaku*, but she had no organised air group on board. Nevertheless the Japanese fanaticism made every step a hard one. In the Tarawa landings 5000 defenders inflicted 3000 casualties on the attackers, despite having half their number put out of action by the preliminary bombardment, and only 150 men surrendered.

At the beginning of February 1944 the assault on the Marshall Islands brought the war closer to Japan. Kwajalein was taken after four days of fighting, but the bigger atolls and their garrisons were left to 'wither on the vine'; their garrisons surrendered at the end of the war, greatly reduced by starvation and disease. The small atoll of Majuro was immediately turned into a large anchorage for the Fleet Train, and 10,000 of the troops used to take Kwajalein were sent to capture En-iwetok. This island was only 700 miles from Truk, the main Japanese fleet base in the Caroline Islands, and at long last the US Navy was able to strike at it. But the Americans did not wait for the occupation of Eniwetok. In a brilliant operation under Admiral Spruance the 5th Fleet surprised the defenders of Truk and wiped out over 200 aircraft. Although most of Admiral Koga's Combined Fleet had been withdrawn to Palau, Spruance's carrier aircraft sank 137,000 tons of shipping. In April Admiral Mitscher's carriers attacked Truk again and destroyed its value.

In contrast to the success story in the Central and South Pacific the Allied forces in South-East Asia (SEAC) made poor progress in 1943. Deprived of shipping and landing craft to meet the needs of the European theatre, the ground forces of SEAC had good reason to style themselves the 'Forgotten Army'. A proposed landing on Sumatra had to give way to a more modest reoccupation of the Andaman Islands, 'Operation Buccaneer', but even this plan had to be deferred. Once again Allied strategy was found to depend on the humble landing craft.

Finally it was accepted that the main amphibious effort against Japan would have to be confined to the Pacific, and so throughout 1944 the Americans continued their inexorable progress across the Pacific. Yet despite this progress the campaign in New Guinea under MacArthur did not achieve complete success until August. MacArthur's victory opened the way at last to his main objective, the Philippines. In October the long-awaited invasion of the Philippines precipitated the great Battle of Leyte Gulf.

The last great amphibious operation of the war was the landing on Okinawa in April 1945, in which 1200 warships took part. The greatest one of all never happened, as the dropping of the atomic bombs in August 1945 made a landing on the Japanese homeland unnecessary. With the bitter knowledge of how Japanese soldiers had fought to defend tiny coral atolls the Allied leaders claimed that the invasion of Japan could cost a million casualties. It is hard to counter the claim and even harder to see how the Allies could have avoided choosing the atomic bomb as an alternative.

MIDWAY TO OKINAWA

BELOW: Douglas SBD Dauntless dive bombers in formation over the Pacific.

RIGHT: A destroyer takes off survivors of the crippled USS *Hornet* (CV.8) after the Battle of Santa Cruz, October 26, 1942. The carrier was abandoned and later sunk by Japanese destroyers.

BELOW RIGHT: The battleship USS *Tennessee* was damaged at Pearl Harbor and was completely transformed by reconstruction. Here at Buckner Bay in Okinawa in 1945, she was armed with twelve 14-inch guns and steamed at 21 knots.

The situation in which the US Navy found itself after the Battle of Midway was depressing, despite the tonic effect of the victory. As we have already seen the fighting around Guadalcanal showed up serious weaknesses in training and night-fighting techniques, and the losses were severe. The new construction of the 1940 'Two-Ocean Navy' programme was not yet ready, and the loss of the carriers *Wasp* and *Hornet* in the Solomons reduced American strength to one damaged carrier. It is proof that the Americans showed a truer understanding and grasp of sea-power than the Japanese and that their admirals could rank with any of the great sailors of the past, for at this desperate moment they never surrendered the initiative. By a mixture of luck, skill and bluff the US Navy survived the worst moment and fought back to establish superiority in the Solomons.

The problem of the Japanese 'Long Lance' torpedo could not be countered directly and the only answer was to develop superior tactics to exploit the advantage of radar. American torpedoes were found to have faulty exploders, and some of the disasters in the 'Slot' in 1942 must be partly attributable to torpedoes failing to explode on hitting Japanese ships. It is paradoxical that the two navies credited with having the best weaponry, the German and the American, both entered the war with faulty torpedoes, whereas the Japanese, whose industrial organisation was considerably inferior, had a torpedo which not only outclassed anything else in the world but also had ruggedness and reliability. Some idea of the poor quality of American torpedoes was gained when the *Hornet*, lying crippled, burnt out and abandoned, took nine torpedoes from American destroyers before sinking.

The failure of torpedoes also had the effect of delaying an effective submarine campaign against the Japanese. The Americans were quick to note the vulnerability of the enemy's sea communications. Since Pearl Harbor the Japanese had added some 800,000 tons of shipping to the 6,000,000 tons under their own flag in 1941, but this total was nowhere near sufficient to meet the commitments of the new vastly expanded island empire. The Imperial Japanese Navy regarded the mercantile marine as a bottomless purse from which to draw tonnage for naval use and little or no attempt was made to replace the 1,000,000 tons lost in 1942. Nor did the Japanese pay much attention to commerce protection.

The United States Navy had about 70 submarines in the Pacific, and soon after Pearl Harbor they were unleashed against Japanese shipping. The initial results were disappointing, thanks to the poor performance of torpedoes, but the fault was soon noticed, and an improved exploder was rushed into production. Submarines could be built quickly and the programme was expanded to maximum capacity. The standard hull chosen for mass-production proved a superlative design, large enough to provide the habitability needed for extended cruising in the Pacific and carrying a powerful armament of torpedoes and deck-guns. As US submarines were soon fitted with radar they were able to achieve an ascendancy over Japanese anti-submarine escorts totally unknown in the Battle of the Atlantic. Using radar a submarine could stalk her prey on the surface, fire a torpedo, and then quickly shift position before the escort had time to react. Some daring US submariners even perfected the 'down-the-throat shot', a highly dangerous method of sinking escorts by allowing them to start an attack and then sinking them with a full salvo of six torpedoes at short range.

If the German U-Boats had ever been able to treat Allied escorts with such disdain in the Atlantic or the Mediterranean, the result of World War II would have been quite different. The Americans adopted a modified version of Dönitz' 'wolf-pack' tactics, using hunting groups of three boats, and their success against the Japanese shows just what could have happened to the British had the Battle of the Atlantic gone in favour of the U-Boats. By August 1943 two million tons of shipping was lost, much of it to sub-

BOTTOM: The Australian heavy cruiser HMAS *Canberra* leaving Wellington, New Zealand in July 1942. She was sunk by Japanese cruisers and destroyers in the disastrous Battle of Savo Island, August 9, 1942.

marines, and this figure rose by 855,000 tons by the end of the year.

The basic problem for the Japanese was that their new empire had only the illusion of great strength. It must be remembered that the island bases seized in 1942 lacked facilities, and however useful they might be for operating aircraft, they needed manpower, equipment and weapons to turn them into proper bases. With a mercantile fleet only just adequate for peacetime needs there was not enough shipping to spare for the job of building up these bases. As the islands came more and more within reach of American naval air power, their value deteriorated, and in the long run their most important defensive asset proved to be the indomitable courage of their defenders.

Midway cost the Japanese about 270 carrier aircraft with a large part of their aircrew. Despite the fact that Japanese aircrew losses were less than 45 per cent of the Americans', the Japanese could not train replacement aircrew to anything like the previous standard, whereas the American flying schools were already turning out thousands of skilled pilots. In this as in so many other aspects of naval warfare the Japanese seem to have gambled on a short war, and had made no provision for replacement and training on any scale. This lack of sinew seems to have been endemic in the Japanese war effort, and no amount of technical excellence in men or weaponry could compensate for it.

In November 1943, when Halsey's carriers raided Rabaul, an important lesson was learned. Despite heavy shore-based air attacks the carriers escaped undamaged, and a risk which had previously been unacceptable was shown to be less than expected. This was immediately noted by Admiral Nimitz, who was ready to launch the first carrier attacks in the Central Pacific. The Japanese had repeated a mistake made earlier by Admiral Yamamoto at Tulagi; they sent their precious carrier aircraft ashore and then squandered them in attacking unimportant targets. When the Japanese aircraft returned to their carriers at Truk in mid-November, they had lost 121 out of 173 in twelve days.

By the beginning of November Admiral Nimitz had a formidable fleet at Pearl Harbor. At last the new battleships were coming forward, as well as the powerful *Essex* Class fleet carriers. The ex-light cruiser light fleet and escort carriers were available too, and although neither type carried a large number of aircraft they increased the flexibility. In all Nimitz had

six modern battleships, seven older ships (some of them repaired after Pearl Harbor), six fleet carriers including four *Essex* and the *Saratoga* and *Enterprise*, five light fleet and eight escort carriers, and 15 light and heavy cruisers.

During the Tarawa landings the Japanese submarines tried to intervene against the covering fleet. But this time they achieved only the sinking of an escort carrier in return for the loss of four submarines. The Japanese submariners seem to have shown little initiative, but American anti-submarine training was good, and it is doubtful if any more resolution would have achieved more results. Shore-based aircraft did no better at the hands of the Combat Air Patrol (CAP). Those few aircraft that got past the defending fighters were met by an effective anti-aircraft barrage, and the only success was a light fleet carrier damaged by a torpedo.

Despite the disappointments of the previous 18 months, at the start of 1944 the Japanese still felt confident that their basic defence plan was working. The original island perimeter had been breached, but they had skilfully withdrawn to a smaller perimeter from the Marianas, through Truk and Rabaul down to New Guinea and Timor, and the southern bastion, Rabaul, was still holding its own. In northern New Guinea they were trying to establish airfields to stop the Allied advance, and in Burma they were even planning an ambitious invasion of Assam for the spring. The Navy still thought in terms of bringing on a fleet action on its own terms, ideally with their giant battleships, *Yamato* and *Musashi*. The US Navy also dreamed of a general fleet action, but could afford to wait until the terms were right.

The first big blow to this optimism came in February 1944 with Admiral Mitscher's raid on Truk. The outstanding feature of the raid was the success of the new night-fighting techniques made possible by the AI (Airborne Interception) radar. About one-third of the aircraft destroyed fell to carrier night-fighters, and as a result some carriers were equipped exclusively as 'night carriers' to exploit the advantage. Mitscher's April raid on Truk finished off the destruction of the island, but the earlier raid had achieved its purpose of undermining the strength of Rabaul. This was easily the most strongly fortified base in the Pacific, with 200 aircraft in underground hangars, 400 anti-aircraft guns and a garrison of 50,000 well-trained troops. The Americans had

long since given up the idea of a frontal assault on Rabaul, and instead they subjected it to heavy bombardment. Gradually the defences were worn down as the number of aircraft dwindled, and after Truk had been hit in February there was no way of reinforcing the base. By the end of May Rabaul had been reduced to impotence, and it could be left isolated without a direct assault, a brilliant strategic move made possible by Mitscher's aircraft carriers.

American submarines continued their depredations in 1944, and sank nearly a million tons in the first five months. Japanese submarines never repeated their successes in the Battle of Guadalcanal, and they were suffering at the hands of American anti-submarine measures. In May 1944 the new destroyer escort USS *England*, with little more than ten weeks' training, sank six submarines in twelve days. She stumbled on a submerged patrol line north-east of the Admiralty Islands, and her captain shrewdly guessed that there would be other submarines in the

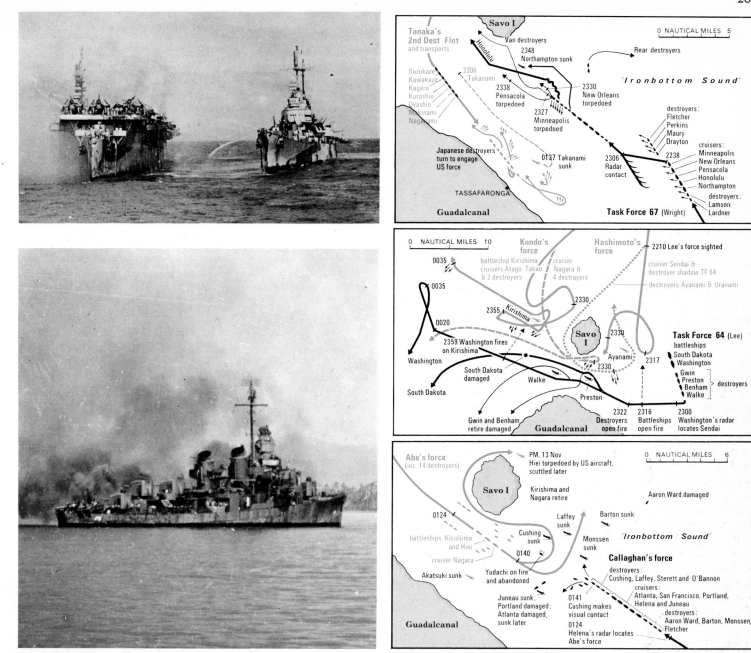

Map 1 (top right):

Savo I

Tanaka's 2nd Dest Flot and transports

0 NAUTICAL MILES 5

Van destroyers
2348 Northampton sunk

Honolulu

Rear destroyers

Suzukaze
Kawakaze
Kagero
Kuroshio
Oyashio
Makinami
Nagami

2306 Takanami

2338 Pensacola torpedoed

2327 Minneapolis torpedoed

2330 New Orleans torpedoed

'Ironbottom Sound'

destroyers:
Fletcher
Perkins
Maury
Drayton

cruisers:
Minneapolis
New Orleans
Pensacola
Honolulu
Northampton

Japanese destroyers turn to engage US force

0137 Takanami sunk

2306 Radar contact

2238

destroyers:
Lamson
Lardner

TASSAFARONGA

Guadalcanal

Task Force 67 (Wright)

Map 2 (middle right):

0 NAUTICAL MILES 10

Kondo's force
battleship Kirishima
cruisers Atago, Takao & 2 destroyers

Hashimoto's force
cruiser Nagara & 4 destroyers

2210 Lee's force sighted

cruiser Sendai & destroyer shadow TF 64

destroyers Ayanami & Uranami

0035

0035

0020

2355 Kirishima

2330

Savo I

2330

Task Force 64 (Lee)
battleships
South Dakota
Washington

2359 Washington fires on Kirishima

Washington

South Dakota damaged

South Dakota

Walke

Ayanami

2330

2317

Gwin
Preston
Benham
Walke

destroyers

Preston

Gwin and Benham retire damaged

2322 Destroyers open fire

2316 Battleships open fire

2300 Washington's radar locates Sendai

Guadalcanal

Map 3 (lower right):

Abe's force
(inc 14 destroyers)

PM, 13 Nov
Hiei torpedoed by US aircraft, scuttled later

0 NAUTICAL MILES 6

Savo I

Kirishima and Nagara retire

Aaron Ward damaged

0124

Laffey sunk

Barton sunk

Cushing sunk

Monssen sunk

'Ironbottom Sound'

battleships Kirishima and Hiei

cruiser Nagara

0140

Yudachi on fire and abandoned

Callaghan's force

destroyers:
Cushing, Laffey, Sterett and O'Bannon

cruisers:
Atlanta, San Francisco, Portland, Helena and Juneau

destroyers:
Aaron Ward, Barton, Monssen, Fletcher

Akatsuki sunk

Juneau sunk;
Portland damaged;
Atlanta damaged, sunk later

0141 Cushing makes visual contact

0124 Helena's radar locates Abe's force

Guadalcanal

BELOW: USS *New Orleans* (CA.32) in a secluded anchorage at Tulagi under camouflage. She lost her bow when torpedoed during the Battle of Tassafaronga on November 30, 1942.

line, so he and his hunter-killer group rolled up the line. Minelaying by aircraft and submarines was also destroying shipping and strangling Japanese seapower.

The British were making strenuous efforts to get ships out of the Far East in accordance with promises made to the Americans to shift shipping from the ETO as soon as possible. Their submarines proved highly successful in the East Indies. They and the Dutch boats were smaller than the American boats, and so could patrol in shallower waters and sink the small coasters and junks which the Japanese were forced to use for

want of bigger ships. Admiral Somerville, formerly the commander of Force 'H', now commanded an Eastern fleet based on Trincomalee in Ceylon. By March 1944 he had the fleet carrier *Illustrious*, two escort carriers, the *Begum* and *Shah*, and the capital ships *Renown*, *Valiant* and *Queen Elizabeth*. Pending the arrival of two more carriers, the *Indomitable* and *Formidable*, the US Navy lent the *Saratoga*, and this enabled Somerville to execute an attack on north-west Sumatra. The target chosen was Sabang, a naval base guarding the entrance to the Malacca Straits. Early on the morning of April 19 the task force

arrived undetected about a hundred miles from Sabang, and proceeded to launch 83 divebombers and fighters. Complete surprise was achieved, and the anti-aircraft guns did not open fire until after the first bombs fell. Extensive damage was done to the oil storage tanks and harbour installations but the anchorage was almost empty. Only one aircraft was lost.

On May 17 the task force raided Soerabaya, and although surprise was again achieved, the results were disappointing because smoke prevented the aircrew from seeing the target. Sabang and Soerabaya were impressive demonstrations of

RIGHT: The destroyer USS *Heermann* (DD.532) lays a smoke screen off Samar, October 25, 1944. The *Fletcher* Class, without doubt the best destroyers of World War II, displaced 2050 tons and were armed with five 5-inch guns and ten 21-inch torpedo tubes.

RIGHT: Fleet Admiral Ernest J. King, Chief of Naval Operations (CNO), conferring with the British First Sea Lord, Admiral Sir Dudley Pound.

BELOW: The destruction of the escort carrier USS *St Lo* (CVE.63) off Leyte in October 1944. She had been shelled and set on fire by the main Japanese battle fleet.

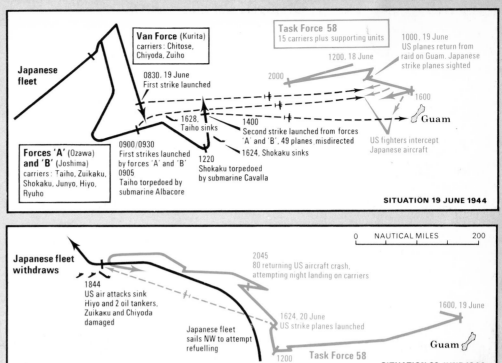

Japanese fleet

Van Force (Kurita)
carriers: Chitose, Chiyoda, Zuiho

0830, 19 June
First strike launched

Forces 'A' (Ozawa) **and 'B'** (Joshima)
carriers: Taiho, Zuikaku, Shokaku, Junyo, Hiyo, Ryuho

0900/0930
First strikes launched by forces 'A' and 'B'
0905
Taiho torpedoed by submarine Albacore

1628, Taiho sinks

1220
Shokaku torpedoed by submarine Cavalla

1624, Shokaku sinks

Task Force 58
15 carriers plus supporting units

1000, 19 June
US planes return from raid on Guam. Japanese strike planes sighted

1200, 18 June

2000

1600

Guam

1400
Second strike launched from forces 'A' and 'B', 49 planes, misdirected

US fighters intercept Japanese aircraft

SITUATION 19 JUNE 1944

0   NAUTICAL MILES   200

Japanese fleet withdraws

2045
80 returning US aircraft crash, attempting night landing on carriers

1844
US air attacks sink Hiyo and 2 oil tankers, Zuikaku and Chiyoda damaged

Japanese fleet sails NW to attempt refuelling

1624, 20 June
US strike planes launched

1600, 19 June

1200   **Task Force 58**

Guam

SITUATION 20 JUNE 1944

FAR LEFT: The USS *Intrepid* (CV.11) survived one torpedoing and two separate *Kamikaze* hits off Luzon and Okinawa.

LEFT: An F6f fighter prepares to take off from the deck of USS *Yorktown* (CV.10), the second carrier to bear that name. The first was sunk at Midway in June 1942.

BELOW: The British carrier HMS *Victorious* was lent to the US Navy in 1943 to replace the carriers lost in the Solomons.

FAR LEFT: The battleship USS *Pennsylvania* (BB.38) fires her forward 14-inch guns during the Leyte landings.

LEFT: The light fleet carrier USS *Belleau Wood* (CVL.24) fights fires after a kamikaze hit on the after end of the flight deck. In the background the USS *Franklin* (CV.13) is also burning after her second *Kamikaze* hit in two weeks: October 30, 1944.

RIGHT: A huge US armada prepares to land forces on Leyte, October 20, 1944.

how fortunes had changed in the East Indies, but the British carriers still needed a lot of practice before they could match the skilful flight-deck handling and launching techniques taken for granted in USN aircraft carriers.

The assault on the Marianas in June 1944 precipitated another great carrier battle, the Battle of the Philippine Sea, otherwise known as the Great Marianas Turkey Shoot. The Japanese dispatched the Mobile Fleet from Borneo, heading north-east to enter the Philippine Sea through the San Bernadino Strait. Admiral Ozawa was sighted twice by American submarines, so that Admiral Spruance and the 5th Fleet had warning of an impending major action. Spruance acted resolutely and cancelled a planned assault on Guam (Saipan had already been invaded three days previously) to allow the transports to be moved to safety. Throughout the remainder of the day Spruance waited for his air searches to give him the location of the Japanese fleet but nothing was discovered until next morning, and the prudent American admiral refused to be decoyed away from the Saipan invasion force, the protection of which he rightly regarded as his first objective.

Admiral Ozawa's flagship, the new carrier *Taiho*, had just flown off her strike aircraft at about 0830 when an American submarine hit her with a single torpedo. The carrier's avgas lines were ruptured by the explosion, and vapour filled every crevice of the ship. Then apparently an electric pump or generator was started, and the spark triggered off a series of terrible explosions which tore the bottom out of the carrier. Some three hours later another submarine torpedoed the carrier *Shokaku* and sank her. The air strikes ran into fierce opposition from the American fighter pilots, who in any case had the advantage of efficient radar control and direction from their carriers. Skilful eavesdropping on a pep-talk to the main Japanese strike enabled the defending fighters to be vectored out to good attacking positions. Just under 300 Japanese carrier aircraft were shot down for an American loss of 30. The Japanese carrier aircrew were poorly trained, and 400 of them died.

Having slaughtered the Japanese air strikes the Americans went on to punish the Mobile Fleet. The carrier *Hiyo* was sunk and the *Zuikaku* (now Ozawa's flagship), *Junyo*, *Ryujo* and *Chiyoda* were damaged, as well as a battleship and a cruiser. Losses among the returning aircraft were heavy, for the pilots were suffering from fatigue and had to find their carriers in darkness. The American reaction to the battle was one of disappointment for they had hoped to destroy Ozawa's fleet. The loss of the *Taiho* was not known at the time, and might have mitigated some of the criticism of Spruance. But with the benefit of hindsight it is hard to support his critics, for his prudence saved the Saipan invasion force and wiped out the Japanese naval air strength. Had he ordered another air search on the night of June 19, he might have been able to punish Ozawa further, but in view of the fatigue affecting the American aircrew after hours of aerial combat, it is doubtful that another strike would have been effective. What was much more important was the effect of the battle on the Japanese. For the first time the possibility of defeat seems to have been considered, and a new note of pessimism could be detected in their planning thereafter.

The Leyte Gulf landings on October 20, 1944, precipitated a similar counter-attack by the Japanese, but this time they threw in every warship that could be spared in a last roll of the dice. The result was the world's greatest sea battle, the

RIGHT: An Elco-type PT boat of the 103–196 Class, armed with four 21-inch torpedo tubes. John F. Kennedy was in a vessel of this class (PT.109) when it was cut in half by a Japanese destroyer.

FAR RIGHT: The mangled remains of USS *Hazlewood* (DD.531) after being hit by *kamikazes* off Okinawa, April 29, 1945. Incredibly the ship was repaired and put back into service.

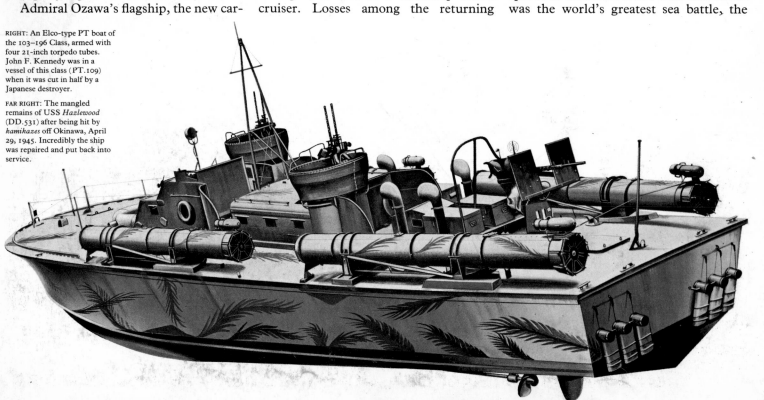

Battle of Leyte Gulf. Perhaps it would be better described as a series of battles, for the actions raged over an enormous area for days. All types of ships were engaged, and battleships, carriers, cruisers and destroyers all played out their designed roles for the last time, fighting their opposite numbers.

The Japanese forces were divided into four groups, and for convenience historians have labelled them as follows:

The Main Body under Admiral Ozawa – the 'Northern Force';

Force 'A' under Admiral Kurita – the 'Centre Force';

Force 'C' under Admiral Nishimura – the 'Van of the Southern Force';

Second Striking Force under Admiral Shima – the 'Rear of the Southern Force'.

The Northern Force had one carrier, the *Zuikaku*, three small carriers, two hybrid carrier-battleships, three light cruisers and eight destroyers. Its purpose was to decoy Halsey's Fast Carrier Task Force away from Leyte Gulf and thereby allow Kurita's Centre Force to destroy the invasion fleet. This force included the *Yamato* and *Musashi* and the *Nagato*, *Kongo* and *Haruna*, twelve cruisers and

fifteen destroyers, and it was to pass through the San Bernadino Strait. The two sections of the Southern Force, consisting of two battleships, a cruiser and four destroyers, and three cruisers and four destroyers respectively, were to reach Leyte Gulf by the Surigao Strait and rejoin the Centre Force off the assault beaches early on October 25. Oddly enough, although Nishimura and Shima had the same objectives, they were responsible to different superiors, hardly the most straightforward arrangement for a battle. It was a formula which helped to destroy the Japanese Fleet.

BELOW: Grumman Hellcats aboard an *Essex* Class carrier are being prepared for take-off while crewmen check their 40-mm. and 20-mm. anti-aircraft guns.

BELOW CENTRE: A British midget submarine of the type which attacked the Japanese at Singapore.

Yet again the magnificent US submariners scored a remarkable success. On October 23 two submarines, the *Darter* and *Dace*, not only spotted part of the Centre Force moving through the Palawan Passage, but managed to sink the cruisers *Atago* and *Maya*, and damage the *Takao*. The *Atago* was Kurita's flagship, and the misfortune boded ill for the Japanese. The sighting reports alerted Admiral Kinkaid, and dispositions were made on the assumption that an attack on the invasion fleet was expected through the Surigao Strait.

When the Centre Force was located in the Sibuyan Sea Admiral Mitscher's aircraft launched a series of attacks, concentrating on the *Yamato* and *Musashi*. Eventually the *Musashi* was sunk by twenty torpedoes and an estimated forty bomb hits. When Kurita temporarily reversed course to avoid further air attacks, Halsey decided that his ships were too badly damaged to be of any consequence. Halsey now mistook Ozawa's decoy force for the main fleet, and took his whole fleet north to attack next day. Through a misunderstanding of a signal Kinkaid thought that part of Halsey's fleet had been left to guard the San Bernadino Strait, whereas in fact this vital route was unguarded. The Japanese scheme was working out exactly as planned.

Still under the delusion that the San Bernadino Strait was guarded by the battleships, Admiral Kinkaid ordered Admiral Oldendorf's squadron of old battleships to guard the Surigao Strait. These six ships were the bombarding force, and their shellrooms were filled mainly with high-explosive rather than armour-piercing shell. Half of that outfit

had already been fired away, and even the destroyers were low on ammunition. As Nishimura's force came nearer its progress was steadily plotted on radar screens. After running the gauntlet of destroyer attacks with gunfire and torpedoes and losing the battleship *Fuso*, the *Yamashiro* and *Mogami* were suddenly blanketed in fire from Oldendorf's battleships and cruisers. Only the *Mogami* and the destroyer *Shigure* escaped this holocaust.

By contrast Kurita's Centre Force passed through the San Bernadino Strait without being detected. A series of inexplicable signalling delays contributed to the danger facing the Americans. At 0412 on October 25 Kinkaid finally asked Halsey if the passage was guarded, but Halsey did not receive the message for two-and-a-half hours. By the time the answer was ready Admiral Sprague's force of escort carriers off Samar was already under fire by the *Yamato*, *Nagato*, *Kongo* and *Haruna* at a range of 17 miles. Sprague's escort carriers and destroyers were desperately vulnerable, but Kurita behaved so circumspectly that it took nearly three hours before shells stopped the carrier *Gambier Bay*. The US destroyers launched forlorn unco-ordinated attacks, and three out of seven were sunk. Even the aircraft, which had no armour-piercing bombs, made dummy attacks on the Japanese ships, until eventually other aircraft arrived and sank the cruisers *Chikuma*, *Chokai* and *Suzuya*. Shortly afterwards Kurita withdrew to the south heading for Leyte Gulf. After all that had been achieved he suddenly seemed to run short of ideas, and after three hours of aimless manoeuvres he made off to the north to 'search for enemy forces'.

RIGHT: The heavy cruiser USS *Indianapolis* in a crazy-quilt camouflage scheme in mid-1944. She carried matériel for the two atomic bombs dropped on Japan to Tinian, and was the last major casualty of World War II.

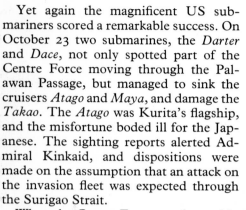

BELOW: Crewmen load a 1000-lb bomb under the belly of a Dauntless dive bomber.

BELOW CENTRE: Vought Corsair fighters are ready to board the flight deck of a British carrier of the Eastern Fleet.

RIGHT: Vice Admiral Jesse B. Oldendorf, victor of the Surigao Straits action.

FAR RIGHT: Admiral Chester W. Nimitz, architect of the US Navy's conquest of the Pacific.

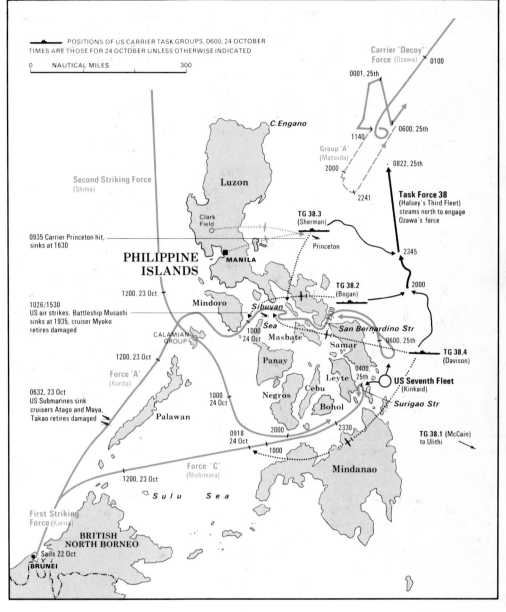

POSITIONS OF US CARRIER TASK GROUPS, 0600, 24 OCTOBER
TIMES ARE THOSE FOR 24 OCTOBER UNLESS OTHERWISE INDICATED

0   NAUTICAL MILES   300

Carrier 'Decoy' Force (Ozawa)

C. Engano

Second Striking Force (Shima)

Luzon

Group 'A' (Matsuda)

Task Force 38 (Halsey's Third Fleet) steams north to engage Ozawa's force

Clark Field

TG 38.3 (Sherman)

0935 Carrier Princeton hit, sinks at 1630

MANILA

Princeton

PHILIPPINE ISLANDS

1200, 23 Oct

Mindoro

TG 38.2 (Bogan)

1026/1530 US air strikes. Battleship Musashi sinks at 1935, cruiser Myoko retires damaged

Sibuyan Sea

San Bernardino Str

CALAMIAN GROUP

Masbate

Samar

TG 38.4 (Davison)

1200, 23 Oct

Panay

Leyte

US Seventh Fleet (Kinkaid)

Force 'A' (Kurita)

Negros

Cebu

Surigao Str

0632, 23 Oct US Submarines sink cruisers Atago and Maya, Takao retires damaged

Palawan

Bohol

TG 38.1 (McCain) to Ulithi

0918 24 Oct

Force 'C' (Nishimura)

Mindanao

1200, 23 Oct

Sulu Sea

First Striking Force (Kurita)

BRITISH NORTH BORNEO

Sails 22 Oct

BRUNEI

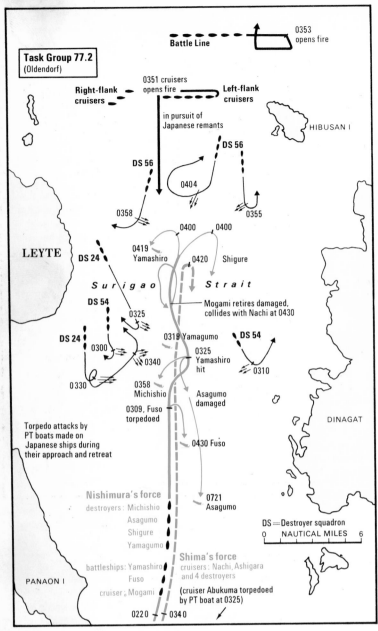

Task Group 77.2
(Oldendorf)

Battle Line

0353 opens fire

0351 cruisers opens fire

Right-flank cruisers   **Left-flank cruisers**

HIBUSAN I

in pursuit of Japanese remnants

DS 56

DS 56

DS 56

0404

0358   0400 0400   0355

LEYTE

DS 24   0419 Yamashiro
                      0420 Shigure

S u r i g a o   S t r a i t

DS 54   0325   Mogami retires damaged,
                                       collides with Nachi at 0430

DS 24   0319 Yamagumo   DS 54
0300   0325
0340   Yamashiro hit   0310

0330   0358
                      Michishio   Asagumo
                                       damaged

0309, Fuso torpedoed

DINAGAT

Torpedo attacks by PT boats made on Japanese ships during their approach and retreat

0430 Fuso

0721 Asagumo

DS = Destroyer squadron

0   NAUTICAL MILES   6

Nishimura's force

destroyers : Michishio
                     Asagumo
                     Shigure
                     Yamagumo

battleships: Yamashiro
                      Fuso

cruiser : Mogami

PANAON I

Shima's force
cruisers : Nachi, Ashigara
and 4 destroyers

(cruiser Abukuma torpedoed by PT boat at 0325)

0220   0340

Sprague's escort carriers had to suffer a further ordeal at the hands of suicide aircraft from Luzon. After the *St Lo* was sunk, the survivors withdrew to the southeast. They had suffered 1500 casualties and lost five ships but their dogged defence had saved the invasion fleet.

In the Battle of Cape Engaño Halsey finally caught up with Ozawa's decoy force. He took a terrible revenge, sinking the carriers *Zuikaku* and *Zuiho* in short order. This was the last of the collection of battles known as Leyte Gulf. They have as much interest for the tacticians and the historian as any battle of World War II, for they have the classic mixture of heroism, drama, stupidity and competence. What makes Leyte different is its vast scale, with huge fleets of battleships and carriers steaming hundreds of miles. It was also the end of the Japanese Navy, which never put to sea again as a fleet.

A new and sinister feature was the *kamikaze* or suicide attacks in the closing stages. At first it was assumed that the attempts by pilots to crash into American ships were merely accidents, but soon it

ABOVE RIGHT: USN Curtiss Helldiver dive bombers ranged on the flight deck of an *Essex* Class carrier. The open hangar appears below.

OPPOSITE ABOVE: USN Douglas Dauntless dive bombers take off for a strike against the Imperial Japanese Navy.

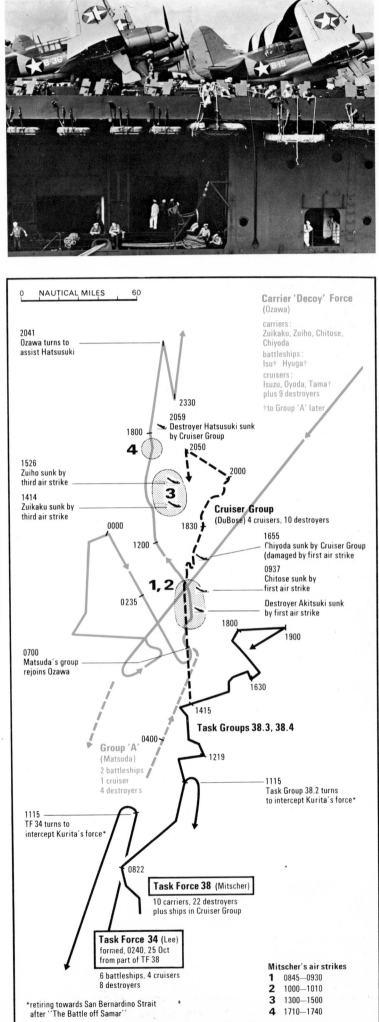

0   NAUTICAL MILES   60

Carrier 'Decoy' Force
(Ozawa)

carriers :
Zuikaku, Zuiho, Chitose, Chiyoda

battleships:
Isu† Hyuga†

cruisers :
Isuzu, Oyoda, Tama†
plus 9 destroyers

†to Group 'A' later

2041 Ozawa turns to assist Hatsusuki

2330

2059 Destroyer Hatsusuki sunk by Cruiser Group

1800   4

2050

2000

1526 Zuiho sunk by third air strike

3

1414 Zuikaku sunk by third air strike

1830

Cruiser Group
(DuBose) 4 cruisers, 10 destroyers

1655 Chiyoda sunk by Cruiser Group (damaged by first air strike

0000   1200

0937 Chitose sunk by first air strike

1, 2

Destroyer Akitsuki sunk by first air strike

0235   1800

1800   1900

0700 Matsuda's group rejoins Ozawa

1630

1415

Task Groups 38.3, 38.4

1115 Task Group 38.2 turns to intercept Kurita's force*

1219

1115 TF 34 turns to intercept Kurita's force*

Group 'A'
(Matsuda)
2 battleships
1 cruiser
4 destroyers

0400

0822

Task Force 38 (Mitscher)
10 carriers, 22 destroyers
plus ships in Cruiser Group

Task Force 34 (Lee)
formed, 0240, 25 Oct
from part of TF 38

6 battleships, 4 cruisers
8 destroyers

*retiring towards San Bernardino Strait after "The Battle off Samar"

Mitscher's air strikes

1 0845–0930
2 1000–1010
3 1300–1500
4 1710–1740

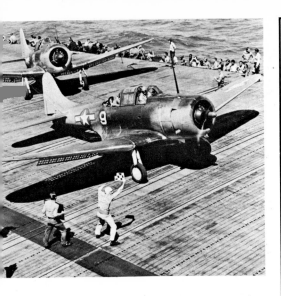

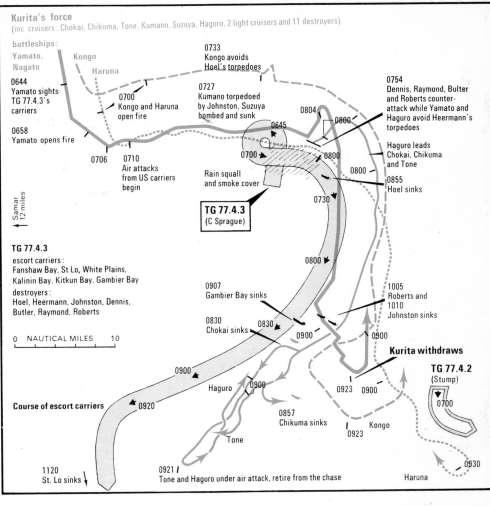

Kurita's force
(inc cruisers : Chokai, Chikuma, Tone, Kumano, Suzuya, Haguro, 2 light cruisers and 11 destroyers)

battleships :
Yamato,
Nagato

Kongo
Haruna

0733
Kongo avoids
Hoel's torpedoes

0754
Dennis, Raymond, Butler
and Roberts counter-
attack while Yamato and
Haguro avoid Heermann's
torpedoes

0644
Yamato sights
TG 77.4.3's
carriers

0700
Kongo and Haruna
open fire

0727
Kumano torpedoed
by Johnston, Suzuya
bombed and sunk

0804
0800

0658
Yamato opens fire

Haguro leads
Chokai, Chikuma
and Tone

0706 **0710**
Air attacks
from US carriers
begin

0645

0700 **0800**

0800

0855
Hoel sinks

Rain squall
and smoke cover

0730

TG 77.4.3
(C Sprague)

0800

1005
Roberts and
1010
Johnston sinks

TG 77.4.3

escort carriers :
Fanshaw Bay, St Lo, White Plains,
Kalinin Bay, Kitkun Bay, Gambier Bay
destroyers :
Hoel, Heermann, Johnston, Dennis,
Butler, Raymond, Roberts

0907
Gambier Bay sinks

0830 **0830**
Chokai sinks

0900

0900

0900

Kurita withdraws

TG 77.4.2
(Stump)

0   NAUTICAL MILES   10

0900

Haguro

0900

0923 **0900**

0700

Course of escort carriers

0920

0857
Chikuma sinks

Kongo

0923

Tone

1120
St. Lo sinks

0921
Tone and Haguro under air attack, retire from the chase

0930

Haruna

Samar
12 miles

was obvious that the Japanese were using them as a battle tactic. If the human brain can be considered a computer, the *kamikaze* aircraft was nothing more or less than a guided missile, with the pilot setting the aircraft on its final course more accurately than any mechanical guidance system could have done. With the fanaticism of the ancient warrior-code of Bushido to inspire them, the Japanese quickly formed special units whose sole task was to knock out carriers and battleships as a last sacrifice for the Emperor and Japan.

In Burma SEAC was finally able to launch an amphibious operation to clear the Japanese out of the Arakan, but as the Japanese were already withdrawing this and other operations were nowhere near as decisive as the Pacific operations, apart from being much smaller. In May 1945 four British destroyers caught one of the last surviving Japanese heavy cruisers, the *Haguro*, off Penang. In a textbook attack the four destroyers came in from four directions and sank the luckless cruiser with torpedoes.

The last big naval operation of the war was the occupation of the Ryukyu Islands 800 miles from Japan. The US Chiefs of Staff wanted to establish a base for bombers and ships for the final assault on Japan. The two island groups were Sakishima Gunto and Okinawa Gunto, and the choice fell on Okinawa. The first plan was to seize the little island of Iwo Jima in the Bonin Islands on the same day as Okinawa, but eventually the decision was made to take Iwo Jima first, on February 19. This tiny volcanic island took over 4000 American lives, a further 17,000 men wounded and 22,000 Japanese casualties before it was subdued.

By comparison the Okinawa landings on April 1 were achieved with relatively fewer casualties, and the main brunt of the Japanese counter-attack fell on the ships covering the invasion. Five days after the landings a mass attack was made by 700 aircraft, of which some 350 were *kamikaze*s. The British carrier *Indefatigable* was hit by a suicide bomber which

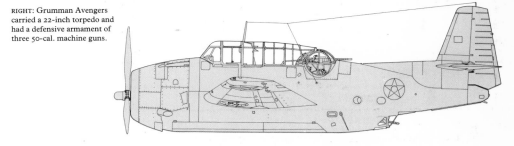

RIGHT: Grumman Avengers carried a 22-inch torpedo and had a defensive armament of three 50-cal. machine guns.

plunged into her flight deck. But as we know, British carriers had heavily armoured flight decks and the *Indefatigable* was back on the line in a very short time. A feature of the Okinawa operation was the 'picket line' of destroyers and destroyer escorts equipped not only with powerful air warning radar sets, but also with fighter direction and control facilities to allow them to direct defending fighters to the appropriate sector. The picket line was able to save the invasion fleet from serious casualties at the hands of the *kamikaze*, but being 50–70 miles from the main fleet they suffered heavy casualties.

The biggest *kamikaze* of them all was the battleship *Yamato*, which was sighted by submarines on the evening of April 6 steaming southwards with the light cruiser *Yahagi* and eight destroyers. The blockade of Japan had become so tight that there was only enough oil fuel for the ships to reach Okinawa, and Admiral Ito's orders hinted that the *Yamato*'s only purpose was to destroy as many enemy ships as possible. Although a very small-scale

action, what followed is known as the Battle of the East China Sea.

While Admiral Spruance stationed a surface force of battleships to cover the north-west approaches to Okinawa, Admiral Mitscher sent out air searches. Finally at 0822 a reconnaissance plane reported the Japanese task force, and an hour-and-a-half later 380 aircraft 'scrambled' from the US carriers. Just after noon they found the *Yamato*, and for two hours they pounded the Japanese giant with bombs and torpedoes. The anti-aircraft fire was heavy and caused some casualties but the attackers had no fighters to contend with. Finally, after taking an incredible total of 20 torpedoes and 17 bombs she capsized, taking most of her 2400 crewmen with her. Although she had the massive total of 146 25-mm anti-aircraft guns, by April 1945 there were insufficient control positions to make them fully effective, and in addition many gun positions were soon put out of action by topside bomb hits and machine-gunning. Even a ship with the

ABOVE: Admiral William F. ('Bull') Halsey (with glasses) goes over a few details with his US Marine Corps staff on Bougainville.

RIGHT: A Corsair on fire.

BELOW: The Grumman Wildcat first saw active service as the Royal Navy's Martlet fleet fighter. It was used throughout the Pacific Theatre to defend the Fleet.

massive protection of the *Yamato* could not take damage indefinitely, and her sinking demonstrated the futility of trying to build an 'unsinkable' battleship.

One of Mitscher's carriers, the recently commissioned *Hancock*, was hit by a *kamikaze* while flying off her strike against the *Yamato*, the first major success scored by the Japanese. On April 11–12 another two carriers were hit, as well as three battleships and many smaller warships. But so far the carriers in particular had shown great resistance, and none had been sunk. The most dangerous part of a *kamikaze* attack was the explosion and avgas fire which usually followed the penetration of the flight deck. Not only was appalling damage done, but even if the carrier survived the explosion, which she usually did, she could not operate her aircraft. A refinement of the *kamikaze* attack was the 'Oka' piloted rocket-bomb. Derisively christened the 'Baka' (stupid), it was released from a parent aircraft near the target, but as the parent aircraft were slow, the 'Oka' was never a serious threat.

One of the most disturbing discoveries of the Okinawa campaign was that both British and American close-range anti-aircraft guns did not have stopping-power against *kamikaze*s. Right up until 1945 ship-to-air gunfire had worked by forcing attacking aircraft to take violent evasive action and to turn away at the last minute. A damaged aircraft would normally break off and limp home, but with *kamikaze*s, once the pilot had entered his final dive he would not pull out or alter course, and so it was necessary to literally shoot the aircraft apart. The standard 40-mm Bofors and 20-mm Oerlikon shells were found to be too light for this, for aircraft by 1944–45 were heavily protected.

On May 1 the British Pacific Fleet, including the carriers *Indomitable*, *Formidable* and *Indefatigable*, the battleships *King George V*, *Howe* and five cruisers left Leyte. Their presence had been urgently requested by Admiral Nimitz as so many

of the US Fast Carrier Task Force had been ·hit by *kamikaze*s. While Admiral Rawlings' battleships were bombarding the nearby island of Miyako on May 4, two of his carriers were hit. But once again the *Formidable*'s flight deck was only temporarily out of action, while *Indomitable*'s attacker bounced off into the sea. On May 9 the *Formidable* was hit again, and so was the *Victorious*. But the tempo of Japanese attacks was slackening. Supplies of the new 'VT' or proximity fuse were rushed out to Okinawa, and this greatly improved the effectiveness of the ships' anti-aircraft fire. Constant bombing of Japanese airfields was also reducing the number of *kamikaze* and normal strikes. By the end of May the stalemate on land had been broken, and as the situation of the ground forces improved, the need to maintain support forces off the beachhead was greatly reduced.

While the Okinawa campaign was drawing to a close, MacArthur's troops were clearing the Japanese from the Philippines. By the beginning of July Borneo had fallen and the troops of South-East Asia Command were making good progress in Burma. In Japan it was clear to thinking people, notably the Emperor Hirohito, that the country was on the verge of collapse. Although Japan had large battleworthy forces on the home islands, in Manchuria and Korea and 5000 combat aircraft, her navy could not put to sea for lack of fuel. There were not enough merchant ships left to import sufficient raw materials and foodstuffs. The Allies did not know the full extent of Japan's economic plight, but they knew only too well that the Japanese would fight to the last man. The knowledge of the terrifying destructive power of the atomic bomb promised a way to avoid what would certainly be the most costly amphibious assault of all, the capture of Japan.

American submarines continued to destroy Japan's mercantile fleet. Between December 1941 and August 1945 the Japanese lost 8,600,000 tons of shipping. During the same period they captured 800,000 tons and built a further 3,200,000 tons. As US submarines had orders to give priority to tankers after aircraft carriers, losses were particularly heavy in this category and accounted for the acute fuel shortage. On July 17 an Anglo-American force of battleships was even able to lie off the Japanese coast 50 miles north of Tokyo, shelling industrial targets around Hitachi. Carrier aircraft rapidly finished off the major units of the Japanese Navy, now lying immobile under camouflage netting in their harbours.

The only blow struck in return was the sinking of the heavy cruiser *Indianapolis* by a submarine on the night of July 29–30. The cruiser had just completed a top-secret mission carrying matériel for the two atomic bombs to Tinian. So complete had the US Navy's mastery in the Pacific become that this valuable ship was allowed to proceed from Tinian via Guam to Leyte without any escort. But this time she crossed the patrol-line of the submarine *I.58*, commanded by one of Japan's top submariners, Lt-Cdr Hashimoto. Hashimoto thought that he had sunk a battleship with his three hits and left the scene. Only two-and-a-half days later a search was organised for the missing cruiser, by which time only 316 of the original complement of 1199 were alive.

The news of the dropping of the first atomic bomb on Hiroshima on August 6 did not immediately affect the naval offensive around the coasts of Japan, and it was not until August 10 that the Japan Government agreed to accept peace terms. Admiral Nimitz ordered all sorties to be cancelled at 0700 on August 15. On September 2 the formal surrender was signed on the quarterdeck of the battleship USS *Missouri* in Tokyo Bay. World War II had come to an end.

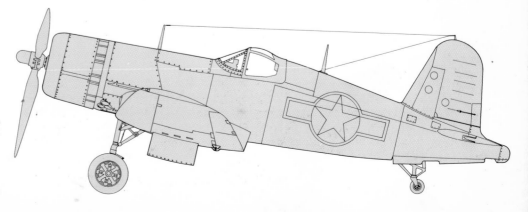

CONCLUSION

The surrender of Japan in September 1945 brought to an end the greatest war in the history of mankind. It represented the final evolution of seapower after centuries of development, and although seapower has never yet decided a war unaided, World War II could not have been decided without it. The collapse of Japan is a vivid example of the consequences of neglecting the principles of seapower. Whereas the German Navy failed in its six-year campaign to beat the British by a war against their commerce, in less than half that time the Japanese were brought to their knees by the very same methods.

Both opponents of the Western democracies went to war very well equipped in certain directions, notably in the air and on the ground, but neither Japan nor Germany had a strong enough base for their seapower. The Japanese were outwardly better off than the Germans because their mercantile marine was larger, but their enormous conquests of 1941–42 suddenly enlarged their shipping requirements. The British and the Americans made many mistakes, and were particularly culpable in neglecting their navies in peacetime. But the basic organisation was sound and the fundamental appreciation of the principles of sea power were never lacking. Unlike World War I, when the British and their Allies followed a mainly continental strategy, in World War II the Allies used maritime power to attack their enemies at points of their own choosing.

World War II saw the renewal of faith in the principles of maritime strategy, particularly the idea of peripheral attacks using amphibious landings. Correspondingly the more extreme claims of airpower were shown to be fallacious. What was eventually proved conclusively was that the three arms acting in concert were vastly more effective than the three operating separately. Ships could not cross waters over which air superiority had been lost, and ultimately armies had to be landed to occupy enemy territory before a decision could be reached. For the British, the shift from a continental strategy back to a maritime one was almost fortuitous: until the Dunkirk evacuation they had intended to repeat their mistakes of World War I by putting a large army into France. With no expeditionary force to involve them in a costly land war, they had no choice but to change to a peripheral strategy, and in the process they rediscovered the principles which had worked so well for them for 300 years. For the Americans the choice of a maritime strategy was easier, cut off as they were from Asia and Europe by vast oceans.

The eclipse of British and Dutch forces in the Far East in 1941–42 can be seen in retrospect as inevitable, given that colonial power was crumbling anyway. Nevertheless the Allies grossly underrated the fighting efficiency of the Japanese in all three arms. Rereading prewar literature on the Japanese armed forces one is struck by the mixture of fact and fiction. Perhaps the worst feature of British and American attitudes was the totally unjustified conviction that the Japanese were merely astute copyists. In fact postwar examination of Japanese records revealed that, if anything, the Japanese were inclined to go too far in their pursuit of novelty.

Although air power as such did not produce the instant successes promised by its propagandists, naval air power made tremendous strides during the war. Virtually every action of any importance involved aircraft, if only in the reconnaissance role. It is often said that air power made the battleship obsolete, but this is not strictly true. In 1945 four British battleships of the *King George V* Class, sisters of the ill-fated *Prince of Wales*, were operating with American battleships off the Japanese mainland. The difference between 1941 and 1945 was that in 1945 they had air cover. The real reason for the disappearance of the battleship after World War II was purely that its chief weapon, the heavy gun with a range of under 25 miles, was outclassed by the dive-bomber or torpedo-bomber which could deliver a greater number of destructive 'projectiles' hundreds of miles away. It was certainly not cost or complexity which downgraded the battleship, for by 1945 aircraft carriers were as complex and carried more men.

The submarine, although already a thoroughly tested weapon in 1939, underwent a major revolution in design in the latter half of the war. After the failure of the U-Boat offensive in the spring of 1943, the Germans pushed ahead with a series of improvements which culminated in the Type XXI U-Boat, a remarkable submarine design which was the basis for all postwar developments by the Allied navies. Unfortunately the effort put into developing the Walther hydrogen peroxide propulsion system diverted scarce resources from the Type XXI programme. Admiral Dönitz promised that the U-Boat would win the war and he came close to proving himself right. But

much of the initial success of the U-Boat campaign can be attributed to the British preoccupation with strategic bombing. If only two more squadrons of bombers had been switched from bombing German cities in 1942, the Battle of the Atlantic might not have been such a close-run affair.

The design of ships changed during the war as much as their equipment. The influence of radar, at first minimal, was paramount by 1945. The Allies never lost their lead in electronics, despite the fact that the Germans had a radar set at sea first. The resistance of ships to damage was improved by such innovations as shockproof mountings for machinery, staggering boilers and turbines, etc. Astonishing feats of salvage and repair saved many a warship and merchantman to fight another day, and by paying greater attention to damage control ships' crews were taught to localise damage and stay afloat. Firefighting standards were also much improved, as bomb-hits were found to be a major cause of fires. By August 1945 some ships were even fitted with gear for jamming guided missiles.

Although the design of guns themselves did not undergo any great improvement fire control improved immeasurably. In 1939 anti-aircraft gunnery was in a primitive state, with close-range weapons relying on eye-shooting, but by 1945 navies were using tri-axially stabilised mountings with built-in fire control. In the Allied navies the Swedish 40-mm Bofors gun and the Swiss 20-mm Oerlikon became universal weapons, largely because the British and Americans had not bothered to develop any equivalent in peacetime.

World War II saw the first homing torpedoes, the German *Zaunkönig* anti-shipping type being introduced at the same time as the American Mk.24 'Fido' for use against submarines. Both weapons were relatively crude by today's standards but they met operational requirements. Magnetic pistols improved the lethal effectiveness of ordinary torpedoes, and the Germans were particularly adept at producing novel pattern-running torpedoes and flying torpedoes. New explosives were introduced for torpedoes and mines, and it was in the field of mine warfare that some of the most unpleasant devices were used. Mines could be primed to lie 'sleeping' until the fifth ship passed overhead, and various acoustic and magnetic systems were devised. The 'Oyster' pressure mine proved the hardest to sweep, but like the other influence mines it had to be laid in shallow water.

It is interesting to speculate on the outcome of the naval war. Could the verdict have been reversed at any time, and was there a point of no return, after which the Axis Powers could not win? The first obvious crisis point was in the summer of 1940, when Germany could hypothetically have negotiated an armistice with Great Britain or invaded her. Under Churchill, who gauged the temper of his people superbly, there was no question of an armistice. In my opinion, the chances of a successful invasion in 1940 were so slim, and the likelihood of a catastrophic failure so great, that it might have been better for 'Operation Sealion' to be launched. But this might have deferred the German attack on Russia and the Japanese attack on Pearl Harbor later in 1941.

Until the invasion of Russia in 1941 the British had little chance of beating Germany, although they could not be beaten themselves, short of a major blunder on their part. But Hitler's large army was left in France with nobody to fight, and it was inevitable that work would be found for it to do, much as Napoleon launched his invasion of Russia in 1812, having been checkmated elsewhere. The titanic struggle against Russia, although it involved a British commitment to supply war matériel to North Russia, put much greater strains on the German war economy, slowing down U-Boat production and diverting men and aircraft.

Pearl Harbor was inevitably the major turning point of the war, for it had an effect on American public opinion much greater than any disaster in the Far East might have done. But even so, most public indignation was at first reserved for the Japanese, until Hitler's declaration of war on the United States. From then on it was truly World War II and not just a European War and a Pacific War, which it might well have been, despite President Roosevelt's intention of fighting Germany. Pearl Harbor was also decisive in the way that Dunkirk was in the strategic sense, in forcing a complete switch away from reliance on the battle fleet. Although naval aviators were influential in the US Navy in the prewar period, it was not until Pearl Harbor that their views on carrier warfare had to be put into practice, if only because there was no battle fleet left.

The Battle of Midway was the last moment at which the Japanese Navy could have administered a big defeat to the US Navy, but it is doubtful if a Japanese victory at Midway would have led to the defeat of the United States. What is certain is that the war would have lasted much longer. The deep sense of anger and revenge which swept the United States after Pearl Harbor would never have allowed any negotiation which left Japan in possession of her conquests.

The battles which followed Midway, important though they were in achieving the final defeat of Japan, were in no way as decisive. Even the dropping of the two atomic bombs, terrifying though they were; did less to bring about the surrender of Japan than the cumulative effect of the Allied blockade. In strictly military terms the final invasion of Japan would have been necessary to obtain physical occupation of the mainland, but the carrier task forces which ringed Japan and the B-29s which rained bombs on her cities had already beaten her.

In the European theatre, the most decisive point of the naval war was unquestionably the crisis of the Battle of the Atlantic in the spring of 1943. We have already seen how close the Allies came to disaster, and there is no doubt that the result was decisive, since immediately thereafter the Allies went completely over to the offensive. Until the Atlantic supply-route was secure there was no possibility of liberating Europe or defeating Germany, and all decisions hinged on it.

The war at sea was a war of great intensity, and after all the facts and figures of ships, weapons and battles have been analysed we must not forget that it was, above all, a war in which millions of men and women played their part. Some were at sea, many more were in shipyards and factories, but the sum total was the clash of rival countries and technologies. The doggedness of civilian seamen was as important a part of the sea war as the determination of any admiral or the men under his command.

In the decade after 1945 the navies of the victors seemed to change little in composition. Enormous numbers of landing craft and escorts were laid up in the

'mothball fleet', with as many of the larger warships as could be dispensed with. Battleships were retained because of their usefulness as fast carrier escorts and shore bombardment ships. The US Navy was by a large margin the world's biggest, but Great Britain and France still retained sizeable fleets.

Despite the apparent calm far-reaching changes were taking place. The *kamikaze* menace led directly to the US Navy's 'Bumblebee' programme to perfect an anti-aircraft guided missile, and the first test firings occurred in 1949. German ideas on surface-to-surface missiles were taken up, and their advanced submarine designs were rapidly copied by every navy. When the Korean War broke out in 1950 none of these new advances were yet in service, but jet aircraft operated from aircraft carriers and played a major role in supporting UN land forces. This outstanding success confirmed the aircraft carrier as the modern capital ship, and the US Navy acknowledged this by arming a new generation of carriers with nuclear bombers to provide a mobile force.

The Russian Navy took longer to learn the lessons of World War II. But in the 1960s it emerged as the only serious challenger to the hegemony of the US Navy on the world's oceans. With their enormous fleet of submarines backed up by a powerful surface fleet, it is quite clear that the Russian Navy does not intend to make the same mistakes that Hitler made in starting the next war with too few.

GENERAL INDEX

Anzio landing 190–191

Battle of Atlantic 72–75,
 165–179, 220
Battle of Calabria 77
Battle of Cape Engaño 212
Battle of Cape Matapan
 82–86
Battle of Cape Spartivento 80
Battle of Coral Sea 15,
 158–159, 196
Battle of Eastern Solomons
 196
Battles of Guadalcanal 158,
 196, 198
Battle of Java Sea 146
Battle of Leyte Gulf 199,
 208–212
Battle of Midway 15,
 160–161, 196, 204, 220
Battle of Philippine Sea 208
Battle of River Plate 28,
 30–32, 63
Battle of Santa Cruz Islands
 197
Battle of Savo Island 196
Battle of Surigao Strait 210

'Channel Dash' 101–105
Crete evacuation 30, 86, 88
Cunningham, Admiral A. 26,
 51, 76–78, 82, 84, 185, 187

Darlan, Admiral F. 52, 71,
 185–186
Dieppe Raid 184–185
Dönitz, Admiral K. 176–177
Doorman, Admiral K. 146
Dunkirk evacuation 69–71

Eisenhower, General D. 191

Fleet Air Arm 24–26
Forbes, Admiral Sir Charles
 62, 68, 74
'Force H' 76, 80, 187
French Navy 12, 14–15,
 17–18, 52–59

German Navy 6, 14, 18–20,
 22, 96–129, 192, 194
Greek Invasion 80–81, 84, 86

Halsey, Admiral W. 198, 202,
 209–210, 212
'Human Torpedoes' 52, 93

Italian Invasion 187–190
Italian Navy 15, 18, 44–52,
 189

Japanese Navy 6, 8, 10–12,
 14–15, 150, 203–215

Kamikaze attacks 212, 215,
 221
Kinkaid, Admiral T. 210
Koga, Admiral 199
Kurita, Admiral 209–210

Lend-Lease Bill 132, 165
'Long Lance' torpedoes 150,
 157, 202
LSTs, Landing Craft etc.
 189–190

MacArthur, General D. 158,
 198–199, 215
Mers-el-Kebir action 76–77
Mitscher, Admiral M. 199,
 204, 210, 215
Mountbatten, Admiral Lord
 Louis 88, 184

Nagumo, Admiral 160
Nimitz, Admiral C. 158, 160,
 198, 204, 215
Nishimura, Admiral 146, 209
Normandy Invasion 187,
 191–195
North African Invasion
 172–174, 185
Norwegian Campaign 32, 182

Okinawa Invasion 199,
 212–215
Oldendorf, Admiral J. 210
Operation 'Avalanche' see
 Italian Invasion
Operation 'Husky' see Sicily
 Invasion
Operation
 'Neptune/Overlord' see
 Normandy Invasion
Operation 'Pedestal' 172
Operation 'Sealion' 72–74
Operation 'Torch' see North
 African Invasion
Ozawa, Admiral 209–210

Pearl Harbor Attack 15, 142,
 165, 220
PQ.17 Convoy 173

Raeder, Admiral E. 96
Ramsey, Admiral B. 69–70,
 191
Royal Navy 6, 8, 12, 14,
 18–20, 22–41, 62–93, 206,
 208, 214–215
Russian (Soviet) Navy 6, 15,
 125, 129

St Nazaire Raid 184
Shima, Admiral 209
Sicily Invasion 187
Singapore 145
Somerville, Admiral J. 76, 78
Sprague, Admiral T. 210
Spruance, Admiral R. 199,
 208, 212

Taranto Attack 27, 78–80
Tarawa Invasion 199, 204
Two-Power Standard 6–8
Type XXI U-Boat 216

United States Navy 6, 8, 10,
 14, 132–147, 202–215

Versailles Treaty 6, 11–12,
 14, 96, 125

Washington Treaty 8, 10–12,
 27, 150
'Wolf-pack' tactics 74

Yamamoto, Admiral I. 160,
 204

'Z-Plan' 96, 98

SHIPS INDEX

AMERICAN

Arizona 142
Astoria 196
Atlanta 139
Boise 188
Brooklyn 139, 188
California 142
England 204
Enterprise 139, 142, 159, 196, 198
Essex 139, 155, 204
Greer 168
Hornet 139, 159, 198, 202
Houston 146
Indianapolis 214
Kearny 168
Langley 135
Lexington 135, 142, 155, 159
Massachusetts 185
Missouri 214
Nevada 142
North Carolina 135, 196
Oklahoma 142
Philadelphia 188
Quincy 196
Reuben James 168
St Lô 210
Saratoga 135, 142, 155, 160, 196, 206
Savannah 187
South Dakota 135, 198
Tennessee 142
Vincennes 196
Washington 135, 196, 198
Wasp 160, 196, 202
West Virginia 142
Yorktown 139, 160

BRITISH

Ajax 28, 32, 88
Ark Royal 26, 76, 82, 90–91, 112
Athenia (SS) 62
Audacity 75
Barham 23, 51, 93
Belfast 27, 62
Courageous 26, 62
Clyde 37, 68
Cossack 66
Dido 28, 88, 139
Eagle 26, 82
Exeter 32, 146
Fiji 28, 30, 88
Formidable 27, 50, 82, 88, 187, 206, 215
Furious 26, 88, 177
Glorious 26, 69, 100
Gloucester 30, 88

Hardy 68
Hermes 26
Hood 10, 20, 76, 107, 112
Howe 188, 215
Illustrious 26–27, 78, 80, 82, 139, 187, 206
Implacable 27
Indefatigable 27, 212, 215
Indomitable 27, 172, 206, 215
Jervis Bay 32
Kelly 82, 122
Kent 28, 30
King George V 22, 39, 100, 114, 188, 215–216
Lion Class 22
Malaya 24, 77
Maori 91
Nelson 20, 23, 39, 62, 187
Orion 88
Penelope 93
Perth (HMAS) 146
Prince of Wales 107, 110–112, 143, 145, 216
Queen Elizabeth 20, 52, 93, 206
Rawalpindi 23, 62–63, 100
Renown 20, 26, 68, 206
Repulse 20, 26, 143, 145
Resolution 59, 76
Revenge 24, 72
Rodney 20, 39, 112, 114, 187
Royal Oak 23, 62
Royal Sovereign 19–20, 77
Sheffield 112
Sikh 91
Southampton 28
Suffolk 107, 112
Sydney (HMAS) 77
Valiant 20, 51–52, 76, 78, 93, 187, 189–190, 206
Vanguard 22, 23
Victorious 112, 177, 198, 215
Warspite 20, 51, 68, 77, 88, 187, 189–190

DUTCH

De Ruyter 146
Isaac Sweers 91, 194
Java 146

FRENCH

Bretagne 53, 76
Duguay Trouin 56, 76
Dunkerque 53, 76
Duquesne 55, 76
Fantasque 56–57
La Galissoniere 71
Jean Bart 54, 71, 185

Latour d'Auvergne (ex-Pluton) 56
Richelieu 54, 71
Rubis 58
Strasbourg 26, 53, 76

GERMAN

Admiral Graf Spee 26, 31–32, 63–64, 66
Admiral Hipper 116, 176
Altmark 66
Bismarck 100, 105, 114
Blücher 67
Deutschland (later Lützow) 11, 54, 62–64, 96, 176
Gneisenau 23, 37, 62, 68–69, 98, 101, 114, 119
Köln 116, 119
Königsberg 26, 67, 116
Prinz Eugen 101, 105, 116, 119
Scharnhorst 23, 26, 62–63, 68–69, 98, 101, 114, 119–120, 177
S-Boats 122, 125
Tirpitz 100, 105, 114, 173, 177, 184
U.47 23, 62

ITALIAN

Andrea Doria 46, 189
Bartolomeo Colleoni 51, 77
Bolzano 50
Caio Duilio 46, 78, 189
Conte di Cavour 46, 78
Fiume 50–51
Giulio Cesare 77
Littorio (later Italia) 46, 48, 78, 189
Pola 50–51, 82
Roma 48, 189
San Giorgio 49
Trento 50
Vittorio Veneto 48, 50, 82, 84, 189
Zara 50–51

JAPANESE

Akagi 155, 160
Aoba 196
Atago 210
Chikuma 156, 210
Chitose 155, 160
Chiyoda 155, 208
Chokai 196, 210
Chuyo 155

Fubuki 157
Furutaka 155, 196
Fuso 152, 210
Haguro 212
Haruna 152, 209–210
Hiei 152, 198
Hiryu 155, 160
Hiyo 208
Hosho 155, 160
Ise 152
Junyo 160, 208
Kaga 155, 160
Kako 196
Kirishima 152, 198
Kinugasa 196
Kongo 150, 152, 209–210
Maya 210
Mogami 28, 139, 156, 210
Musashi 152, 204, 209–210
Mutsu 152
Nagato 152, 209–210
Ryujo 155, 160, 196, 208
Shigure 210
Shinano 152, 155
Shoho 155, 159
Shokaku 155, 159, 208
Soryu 155, 160
Suzuya 210
Taiho 155, 208
Takao 210
Tenryu 196
Yahagi 212
Yamashiro 210
Yamato 152, 160, 204, 209–210, 212–213, 215
Yubari 157–158, 196
Zuiho 155, 160, 198, 212
Zuikaku 155, 199, 208–209, 212

ACKNOWLEDGEMENTS

The author and editor would like to thank the Director and Staff of the National Maritime Museum, Greenwich, for their invaluable assistance in the preparation of the illustrations for this book. They would especially like to thank David Lyon and George Osbon of that institution for their contributions to the technical artist and to the preparation of many of the photographs used here. The author and editor would also like to thank the Director and Staff of the Imperial War Museum, Charles Haberlein of the US Navy and Richard Natkiel of *The Economist*, who prepared the maps for this book, for their contributions to the illustrations in *Navies of World War II*. Last, but by no means least, we would like to thank David Eldred who put all the efforts of the advisors and artists together when he designed this book.

PICTURE CREDITS

Author's collection: 4–5, 6–7, 8–9, 9, 11 (both), 27, 29, 31, 34–35, 37, 38, 38–39, 41 (top), 42–43, 47 (top), 78–79, 88–89, 90–91 (bottom), 93 (bottom), 98–99 (bottom), 100–101 (top and bottom), 104–105 (top and bottom), 106–107 (top, middle and bottom), 164 (bottom), 167 (centre right), 177 (centre), 180–181, 182 (both), 182–183, 183 (both), 185, 186, 186–187, 187 (both), 190 (left), 192 (both), 193, 194, 194–195, 195 (both), 218–219, 220.

Courtesy of John Batchelor: 1, 35 (left and right), 36, 44, 44–45 (bottom), 53, 54–55, 56–57, 63 (both), 68, 72–73, 73, 80–81, 119, 130–131, 136 (both), 136–137, 137 (both), 139, 142 (top and bottom), 148–149, 150–151, 152 (both), 153 (all three), 155 (top and two at bottom), 156, 156–157 (both), 158–159, 159 (both), 160 (both), 167 (top), 168 (top and bottom), 200–201, 210 (top), 211 (top), 212, 213.

Imperial War Museum: 18, 18–19, 21, 30 (left and right), 30–31, 38 (centre), 62, 64–65, 76–77, 82–83, 84, 85, 86–87, 90, 102–103 (bottom), 108, 117 (top and bottom), 118–119 (top), 165 (bottom), 167 (centre left), 166–167, 176, 177 (bottom two).

National Maritime Museum: 2–3, 16–17, 19, 22, 22–23, 23, 24 (left and right), 24–25, 25 (four), 26 (right and below), 35 (centre), 40–41, 41, 46, 46–47 (top), 57, 60–61, 80, 86, 89 (top and bottom), 90–91, 92–93, 93, 122–123 (bottom), 126, 127, 151, 155 (centre), 164 (top), 165 (top), 169 (top), 170 (below left), 170–171, 172 (both), 173 (all three), 174 (both), 184, 188, 188–189, 189 (both), 190–191, 207 (top and bottom), 210 (bottom), 211 (centre), 214 (centre), 215, 216–217 (both), 217, 221.

US Navy: 132–133, 134, 134–135, 138 (both), 140–141, 141, 143, 144–145, 145 (all three), 146–147 (both), 147, 150, 169 (centre and bottom), 170 (two), 171, 190 (right), 191, 196 (both), 197 (both), 203 (both), 202–203, 204, 205 (all three), 206, 206–207, 207 (three centre), 208 (both), 209 (both), 211 (two top), 214 (above), 217.

US Marine Corps: 199

US Army: 198–199.

Naval Photographic Club: 118–119.

Bibliothek für Zeitgeschichte: Dressler Collection: 110.

Conway Picture Library: 64, 65, 66, 67 (left and right), 69, 164–165.

Ministry of Defence: 6–7, 8–9, 9, 26, 94–95, 107, 111, 112, 113 (top and bottom), 114–115, 115 (top and bottom).

William Henry Davis: 10–11, 10.

Charles E. Brown: 20 (centre).

Wright and Logan: 20 (top and bottom).

P. A. Vicary: 37 (right), 50 (centre).

ECPA: 55, 58–59 (top and below), 59.

Cemper and Nicholson: 70–71, 71 (top and centre).

Novosti Press Agency: 120, 121, 122–123, 123, 124, 124–125, 126, 127, 128, 129 (three), 220–221.

RHL/IWM: 20.

Foto Druppel: 12–13, 13, 46 (centre and bottom), 46–47, 47 (centre and bottom), 48 (top and bottom), 49 (all four), 50, 50–51, 51, 52, 96, 98–99 (top and centre), 100, 101 (top and centre), 102, 103, 102–103 (top), 114, 116 (all three), 118 (both).

Bison Picture Library: 82, 97, 142 (centre).